ONE HURRICANE — ONE RAID

One Hurricane
— One Raid

Geoff Rayner

Airlife
England

Dedicated to the memory of
Gerard Hamilton Maffett

First published in the UK in 1990 by
Airlife Publishing Ltd.

British Library Cataloguing in Publication Data
Rayner, G. H.
    One Hurricane one raid.
    1.   Hawker Hurricane aeroplanes, history
    I.   Title
    623.7464
    ISBN 1-85310-199-0

Printed by Livesey Ltd., Shrewsbury

Airlife Publishing Ltd.

101 Longden Road, Shrewsbury, England.

Contents

Author's Note

The following account covers two distinct episodes in the history of one particular aircraft, the remains of which now reside at the Royal Air Force Museum, Hendon. The book has been similarly structured into two distinct sections. These have been reversed from their chronological order of occurrence so as to relate the events as they became known to me: from the first sight of some unrecognizable wreckage, through to the formation of the Hendon exhibit, and then after the aircraft's identification, the revelation of what took place all those years ago.

The first part, spanning a number of years, is very much a personal account of events as I saw them unfold. Some readers may be aware of additional details not recounted herein, but having been personally involved in all aspects from the aircraft's 'initial discovery', through to its display at Hendon, all the salient points have been covered. Notes made at the time together with a comprehensive photographic record, enabled events to be fully reconstructed, even so many years after they took place.

The second part attempts to recreate the sequence of events that led to the aircraft's loss. The story is incomplete as the passing years have erased all trace of some details and others were never destined to be known as they were neither recorded nor witnessed.

The account is based on contemporary records and personal accounts from those who were there at the time, either on the ground or in the air. I am indebted to the large number of local people in Essex and South Cambridgeshire, and former Service personnel from further afield, who allowed themselves to be subjected to my questioning. Some were able to help by verifying incidents recorded in documentation and others were able to add positive details or anecdotes not recorded elsewhere. The latter have helped to bring a more human dimension to the story and a number of accounts are quoted direct. To the former, I am equally indebted as their recollections helped provide confirmation of sometimes rather shaky written evidence in contemporary records, giving confidence to the content where previously there had lain doubt.

In the Fowlmere/Duxford area:
Cecil Adams, William Arber, John Barker, J Dawson, David Ellis, Earnest Fox, Lance Pearce, Peggy Shortley and Harry Wadley.

In the Debden/Saffron Walden area:
James Bayne, Tom Cullen, Winifred Foster, Ruth Hare, Ted Hewett, Fred Mole,

John Ryder, Charles Scruby, Stanley Swan, Janet Tinnion, Dr Michael Weller and John Wiseman.

At High Easter:
Derek Bircher and Martin Hill.

In the Chelmsford/Danbury area:
Bert Bearman, Mrs Bew, Stan Brazier, Gerald Carter, Wilf Chatley, Eric Clark, Ron Joslin, Norah Shipman and Constance Turner.

In the Ovington/Halstead area:
Percy Chinnery, Maxse Gardiner, Dr David Gemmell and Fred Sale.

At Colchester:
Ronald Newcombe.

Brightlingsea to Walton-on-the-Naze:
Sid Bocking, Jo Crook, Alec Cross, Stan Martin and Cyril Studd.

Former aircrew:
No 1 Sqn — Wg Cdr N. P. W. Hancock
No 19 Sqn — Wg Cdr F. N. Brinsden, Air Cdre J. B. Coward, Wg Cdr D. G. S. R. Cox, Wg Cdr B. J. Jennings, Wg Cdr G. C. Unwin.
No 56 Sqn — Wg Cdr F. W. Higginson, M. H. Mounsdon, Wg Cdr I. B. Westmacott.
No 151 Sqn — Air Cdre J. L. W. Ellacombe, Grp Capt I. S. Smith, Wg Cdr R. L. Smith.
No 257 Sqn — Sqn Ldr C. G. Frizell, J. A. M. Henderson, D. W. Hunt.
14/(Z)LG1 — Karl-Joachim Eichhorn.
III/KG2 — Walter Schlüter.
9/JG26 — Heinz Ebeling

Others who although not witnessing the events themselves, led the way to others who did, or gave assistance with other avenues of investigation:
Rev Michael Allen, Rev Michael Baker, Adrian Corder-Birch, Geoffrey Bray, Keith Braybrooke, Derek Drew, Edith Goodchild, Arthur Gowers, Wg Cdr Alick Grant, David Hills, Lt Col Alan Maffett, Martin Sheldrik, Edwin Shuring, Rev John Spread, Jean Stokes and John Weeden.

With the passage of time since the 1939–45 War, many potential witnesses have since passed on, so locating survivors was not an easy task. More difficult was to try and find former Luftwaffe participants and the view from the German side. Here I am most grateful to Chris Goss who, as my enquiries progressed, was able to offer advice on avenues to investigate and also made freely available his own research material covering that period.

Geoff Rayner

Part One — One Hurricane

Chapter One
Early Days, A Curiosity

In 1953 the East Coast floods had done much damage to the lowland coastal areas bordering the southern North Sea. The marshy inlet of Hamford Water, lying mid way between the old port of Harwich and the seaside resort of Walton-on-the-Naze, was no exception. Protective earthen sea walls had been overtopped by the high tide in numerous places and many were breached. In several cases damage was so severe that complete new defence lines had to be drawn up further inland. One such site of man's retreat against the advancing forces of nature lay at the entrance to Hamford Water, on the southern peninsula-like arm known as the Naze; a small spur of land lying immediately to the north of Walton, from which the town has derived its full and more distinctive name. Here, the clay strata forming the high ground around the town gradually descends to the level of the Hamford Water salt marshes. Protecting part of the reclaimed marshland on the seaward side of the Naze was a short, straight length of wall of considerable age, known locally as the Tamarisk Wall. It had suffered irreparable damage in the flooding and a new defence line, in the form of a modern concrete faced dyke, had been rapidly constructed a hundred yards further inland.

Over the next ten years the annual set of winter gales continued to pound away at the remains of the old wall and its immediate foreshore; in doing so, uncovering the results of decades of its use as a firing range. Spent rounds from small calibre Service revolvers, through to 20mm heavy machine gun rounds could be found in abundance and it was this that attracted many a local schoolboy to the area. More prized finds, but less frequently found, were the variety of empty brass cartridge cases and, occasionally, heavy lead rounds from the nineteenth century 'black powder' days of the early breech loading Snider and Martini-Henri rifles. Their large lead content, some three to four times that of the more prolific .303 bullets, invariably meant the melting pot for them, for as well as building collections, there was also money to be made in the production of lead fishing weights.

It was on one such bullet hunting expedition that the 'aeroplane' was first mentioned. Instead of taking the usual shorter route from the town, by bicycle along the coast road and down the cliff edge path to the Tamarisk wall, the group of boys walked along the inland seawall that protected the lowland rear of the town and Naze from flooding. The Tamarisk wall was thus approached from its other end for a change. When almost there the self appointed leader, giving a knowledgeable guided tour of the area, remarked, 'Over there, is the aircraft',

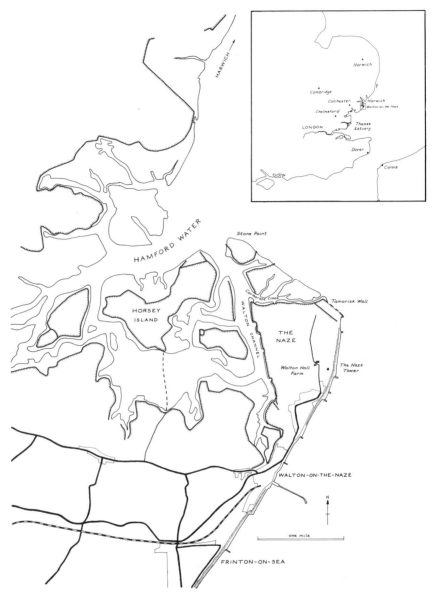

pointing in the general direction of the marsh beyond the Tamarisk wall. German, his brother had told him. He had a piece hanging in the garage at home. Little did I realise that this chance remark would lead to an involvement that was to span, on and off, over twenty-five years.

It was not until sometime later, on another trip, that a visit was actually made to see the wreckage. It was a disappointment to impressionable youngsters: one four-foot length of aluminium spar, projecting out of the marsh grass. So much for the plane! Thoughts of better finds by the Tamarisk wall beach drew the group away. Subsequent occasional visits were made in passing, but the broken and somewhat corroded spar held no real interest. Unlike many boys of that age, none of the group had any particular interest in aircraft anyway.

Interest returned later when the 'leader' announced that of course the remains of a bomber lay in a field further inland, less than a quarter of a mile from the wall. Once again, to explore such remains became an exciting prospect. First there was the challenge of reaching the site undetected by the ever watchful eye of the farm's gamekeeper, whose house on top of the hill overlooked the field where the wreckage lay. Having succeeded in creeping over the fields, sure enough large pieces of aircraft structure could be seen scattered over a wide area. The remains of four massive radial engines, an undercarriage leg, several oxygen bottles, and a variety of spars and fragments of twisted aluminium sheet lay half buried. This certainly created more interest, but as it was risky crossing the fields only a few trips were made, more as a dare than for any other reason.

The main objective in visiting this part of the coast still remained bullet and lead collecting, as well as for a bit of schoolboy adventure away from the confines of the town. Gradually, the so-called aircraft began to be seen as just two more items of wartime debris, so much of which still littered the Naze coast, providing a firm reminder of events some twenty years earlier: pillboxes, anti-aircraft gun platforms and earthworks, and the inevitable bullets, shrapnel and mortar bomb fragments. It was hardly a childrens playground and certainly not an attractive asset for a seaside resort!

As the years passed it was the combination of a growing inquisitiveness in things mechanical and the making of a new school friend, smitten badly with the aviation bug, that began a renewed interest in the Naze 'aircraft'. Trips to the more substantial bomber site became more meaningful, trying to work out what was what. From the powerplant alone, a good guess had been that it was a Handley Page Halifax. The chance find of a wartime book on general aircraft construction, in a second-hand bookshop, helped fuel the interest. The pages were scoured for recognisable diagrams and components. During one visit to the site a rather weighty gearbox was recovered, with the following evenings being spent dismantling, cleaning and re-assembling it. What did it do? Where did it come from?

Such visits were made at dusk to avoid the gamekeeper's gaze but gave little time at the site before darkness really fell; so the honest approach was tried. A letter to the farm owner, requesting permission to cross his fields was more sensible, straightforward and was met with approval. Longer periods during full daylight could now be spent studying the remains and further fragments were subsequently recovered. Unfortunately, the newly acquired reference book did not help very much with the particular Halifax structure, as it concentrated on pre-War types, mainly the Bristol Blenheim, but general systems were shown and there was one large diagram of the Halifax's powerplant, the fourteen-cylinder Hercules radial engine, complete with that auxiliary gearbox.

On one occasion, whilst browsing through the book and pausing at the cut-away diagram of a Hurricane wing, a part was noticed that looked somewhat familiar. The solid front wing spar near the wing root had four circular ports for the Browning machine guns, and looked remarkably similar in size and shape to that lone spar sticking out of the marsh mud by the Tamarisk wall. Perhaps it was part of a Hurricane, or could it be a feature common to other aircraft types? A spark of interest was rekindled in that lone spar.

A little while later the 'Hurricane' identity gained support from a totally different and unexpected quarter. Future historians concerned with the 1939–45 War will no doubt be thankful to the many individuals who kept personal records or diaries during that time. Contemporary official records often, and quite understandably, give just broad narratives of events; there was, after all, a job to be done, not just record keeping.

One such diarist was Mr Lowther Kemp, who had been Chief ARP Warden for the towns of Frinton and Walton. He still lived in neighbouring Frinton and now, with a growing personal interest in local history and in particular the effects of the last war, a visit to see Mr Kemp and his diary became a must. The diary proved a fascinating document, meticulously recording for each day of the war the time of every siren warning, bomb falling, or other ARP incident that took place within the district. Some aircraft crashes were also listed, most with little detail, other than the date, time and a very loose descriptive location. One entry for 29 April 1941 read '1055 — Crashed aircraft, Hurricane, Stone Point'. Only one 'Stone Point' came to mind, the very tip of the Naze peninsula at the entrance to Hamford Water. It was a mile further along the marsh than the Tamarisk wall but it was near enough and some local people often referred to all the marsh beyond the Tamarisk wall as Stone Point. The case for the spar belonging to a Hurricane was beginning to look quite strong and thereafter it was always referred to as the Hurricane.

During one weekend visit to the Naze, an attempt was made to uncover more of the spar. Driftwood was employed to scrape away the mud around its base, hoping to see how deep it went and what possibility there might be of other items lying just under the surface. Most of the group showed no interest in this activity and carried on to the water's edge leaving the two enthusiasts to scrape away with their improvised implements. Such tools proved a poor choice in such difficult conditions. Less than a foot down, a muddy hole full of water, and still nothing new revealed. The spar still held a similar shape at depth and remained solid as a rock. Returning, the other boys were rather amused by this apparently pointless exercise and, after a while, a few well aimed missiles into the pool of water soon brought the futile work to a rather predictable, muddy conclusion.

Undeterred and blaming the failure of any positive result on the choice of implements, a return trip was made a few weeks later, this time properly armed with spades and free from the distractions of the uninterested. A steel pole, found lying nearby from part of the old beach defences, was used to probe around the spar, but although occasional solid contact was made, there was no obvious pattern. A hole, about three feet in diameter, was dug around the spar but by the time a depth of a foot or so had been reached, the naivety of even this attempt quickly became apparent. The sides, small as they were, collapsed letting the mud ooze back in and water filled the hole almost as fast as it could be baled out.

Pausing in the realisation that the fight was lost almost before it had begun, it was noticed that the water had started to take on a colourful sheen — the distinctive effect of petroleum products. There was also a noticeable petroleum smell, mixed with the usual marshland aroma in the vicinity of the hole. Groping around by hand in the slimy water, the spar could be felt going down into the mud as far as could be reached. No new 'cutout' sections though, just the eighteen-inch wide, flat, metal plate. Another piece of metal could be felt lying nearby, almost horizontal and with an outline like a section of scaffolding pipe. Both pieces remained rigid despite the digging effort. Close to the pipe was a rubbery substance. Prodding it resulted in small swirls of rainbow coloured water breaking the surface. Possibly the remains of a fuel tank? But nowhere could be felt the smooth surface of sizeable airframe sections that had been hoped for. Just the solid spar, the 'scaffolding pipe' and, a little further away to the side of the hole, a curious curved piece of aluminium with jagged edges which somehow seemed to belong bent in that particular shape. It was held firmly also and would not budge, although little pressure really could be applied, as it was so flimsy and had sharp jagged edges.

A few fragments did emerge from the hole, most small, totally unrecognisable and certainly nothing to obviously suggest that they once formed part of an aircraft structure. Only one piece looked remotely significant. About a foot long by four inches wide, shaped with one edge slightly curved, and with a stainless steel, spring-tensioned hinge along the opposite edge. Its surface on one side was smooth but the reverse was badly pitted, not right through but enough to halve the thickness of the metal. It could have been the result of corrosion but there were no tell tale signs of powdering or crystallization. It was some years later before the texture was recognised as the effect of fire on aluminium, and the item as part of the retractable undercarriage fairing — hence the hinge.

Another find, which almost did not even make it to the cleaning stage, started out as a solid bar of hard clay material, some six inches long by nearly two inches square. It was almost returned to the hole from whence it had come but was saved by the thought that it certainly was not a naturally occurring piece of marsh and therefore, just possibly, may be related to the aircraft. How could not be imagined, but the by now, well developed beachcombers eye suggested that scraping away at the hardened clay exterior might reveal something.

It certainly did. Back at home, once the outer encrusted surface had been

The lone spar projecting from the marsh. What appear to be bullet holes and shrapnel damage can be seen around the circular gun ports.

broken, a black crumbly powder was revealed. This had been seen before, as one of the ways in which iron objects deteriorate in the harsh foreshore environment. At the heart of the oblong lump was a stunted cross-shaped device, complete with a pivoting lever and ratchet system running across the 'T' arms. It was the feed mechanism from a Browning machine gun, badly corroded but recognisable. After some solid wire brush treatment and a dowsing in acid, the mechanism was free to move again, although not with quite the same smooth action as it was originally designed to have.

Overall though, there was decided disappointment again. Nothing conclusive, no large sections of aircraft waiting just below the surface, and extremely unpleasant working conditions. The Halifax site had far more to offer in a much friendlier environment. Attention switched back to sifting through the bomber's remains.

By this time a firm interest in the local history of the area had been developed, in particular relating to the impact of the last war; probably because its physical impact was still so much in evidence along this section of coast, but why aircraft continued to feature so highly in this interest still remains somewhat of a mystery to me, even now.

At this point, one event took place that could easily have resulted in an entirely different story for the Hurricane. In the spring of 1967 an article appeared in a local Colchester newspaper, describing how two enterprising locals from nearby Brightlingsea had found the remains of a wartime aircraft wreck on the foreshore at St Osyth and were industriously salvaging large pieces of metal for scrap. An accompanying photograph showed one of them proudly posing with three huge propeller blades. Each blade was perfectly straight and, in the photograph, looked in very good condition. Sadly, the root of each one ended in a clean cut stump where it had been laboriously sawn through. The

Items recovered during the 1960s.
A. Part of the spar, showing two of the gun ports and shrapnel damage.
B. Part of the retractable undercarriage fairing with a spring tensioned hinge along the top edge.
C. The 'solid bar of hard clay' which turned out to be the feed mechanism from one of the Browning machine guns.

propeller boss lay at one of the men's feet. What a waste of such an item, but it was something not to be missed.

A flick through the telephone directory, a quick call and a meeting was arranged. They had certainly been busy. Besides the propeller, other recognisable items included several cylinders from a large radial engine, a rather familiar gearbox and some control levers. All were in a remarkable state of preservation as a result of spending some twenty-five years cocooned in the foreshore mud. It seemed a shame that such well preserved objects should be heading for the scrap yard, but time and money were now involved and the latter proved a barrier. An exchange of information did however take place. The location of this apparent treasure trove was divulged and in return the potential of the Naze was described.

Later that same day, a party of three headed along the coast road and down the cliff path to the Tamarisk wall. As it lay on private land, the Halifax was not visited, just the Hurricane spar. They were not very impressed and, without having to say so, it seemed as though they had been expecting more. The Halifax was suggested as something a little more substantial but fortunately there was little outward enthusiasm and it all came to nought. The Hurricane spar and Halifax wreckage remained untouched. A little while later, word came that the newspaper publicity had rebounded on the scrap metal venture. The local Receiver of Wreck had taken an interest in the sideline and the salvage had come to an end.

As time passed attention to the other more normal things in life drew interest from the 'planes'. Further education took its rightful place and, for a few years, the detective work on aircraft wreckage took very much a back seat, almost at times forgotten. Trips to the Naze became less frequent, and when they did occur, attention was focused on the local geology and coastal environment, as studies progressed towards final exams. The aircraft wrecks and other war debris had no place in this.

As the sixties drew to a close, the new decade saw studies complete, a career to be started and fresh challenges sought. Back in the home environment of Walton it was soon found that old interests were hard to erase. A walk along the

By the early seventies, the beach ridge had been rolled back to expose the wreckage on its seaward side. Compare with photo on page 13.

foreshore found the old spar still there, projecting firmly out of the ground, but shorter than it used to be and much more open to view. Others may have guessed its unusual origin and souvenir hunters or beachcombers had been at work, as revealed by the fresh hacksaw marks on the somewhat denuded stump.

By the mid-sixties, the continuous pounding from winter gales had virtually completed the destruction of the old Tamarisk wall. Foreshore sediment had become mobile and erosion of the unprotected salt marsh, directly to the north of the wall, close by the Hurricane, had increased apace. A ridge of sand covering the seaward edge of the salt marsh provided a convenient, dry footpath from the seawall system along the foreshore to the tip of the Naze at Stone Point. Bird watchers, beachcombers, and even the more adventurous holiday makers were all funnelled along this coastal path. For some thirty years the aircraft remains had lain undisturbed in the marsh, twenty to thirty yards inland from the beach and out of the public eye. From the beach ridge, one would only have known where it was by having it pointed out. Steadily, the ridge had been rolled back by the ever advancing sea, so that by the early seventies the spar lay directly in the path of all those who used it. The number of these visitors had grown too, the town's population having increased quite rapidly in the previous decade. The local council had recently purchased the adjacent cliff-top land to create a public amenity and had begun to turn the scrubland into a much more access-ible, grassland, open space. For those seeking solitude, escaping the crowds now meant venturing further along the coast and on to the salt marsh foreshore.

The spar continued to be attacked. By the end of 1970 virtually all the flat plating from its sides had gone, including the section just above ground level containing the last of the four gun port holes. Just by that particular hole had been a further three small, neat, round holes that resembled bullet strikes. Whether made in the air before the crash or later on the ground, when home defence units were looking for target practice, was not known. All that now remained above ground was one edge of the spar a foot high and, attached to it, a small square of plating.

The high tides of the following winter rolled back the beach ridge a little further and in doing so uncovered some of the old marsh surface around the spar. Successive high spring tides were able to eat away at this softer sediment with relative ease as it was periodically exposed then protected by the mobile sand at the front of the beach ridge. By the spring of 1971 this process had begun to reveal the outline of another spar, some six feet from the original one, but lying flat. Thoughts went back to those attempts at digging a few years before. It must have lain only inches beneath the surface. How come it had been missed? Presumably because each time effort was concentrated so close to the other spar.

One day, while pondering over this new feature, the well-known local figure of Bernard 'Nipper' Norman passed by. He was known as something of a local historian, mainly through the displays of photographs he used to show of old Walton. He had inherited a large and unique collection from his father. He was also no stranger to the marshes, having been brought up in Walton and could be found more often than not messing around in boats or wildfowling on the marshes. In characteristic style, he offered a comment in passing. 'It's all down there, boy'. It had an air of overstatement. Did he mean it, or was he just having

Spar section revealed in 1971 as the beach ridge was rolled back over the marshes. The bent section furthest from view was later found to be the torsion box strengthening section, positioned half-way along the aircraft's wing.

fun? He certainly had a reputation as something of a joker and could often be hard to pin down on the reliability of some of his comments. When pressed though, he would merely repeat that 'It was all down there. Left just where it fell'. Could he really know? He was there during the war after all, albeit as a young boy, and, when quizzed, had often related other local wartime incidents which generally had tallied with Lowther Kemp's ARP record. Unfortunately, the detail was often not quite the same the second time of telling. It was an exciting prospect that he might be right, but the scepticism remained. As a boy, surely he would not have been permitted to visit that part of the Naze during the war years? Movement was restricted in coastal areas. Did he say it 'was' all there or 'probably' was all there? The doubt remained, but what of the real evidence?

The new exposure had uncovered a four-foot length of aluminium spar which like the other one years before, was firm and could not obviously be seen to join with any other structure, except perhaps where it disappeared at one end beneath the sand. Consulting the 'reference book' identified the structure as one of the outer wing spars; of composite construction, with braced diagonals between the two edges, top and bottom. Along the upper most edge there were traces of torn or cut aluminium sheeting — possibly the remains of the wing surface — but there were no signs of the large smooth aerodynamic surfaces that give an aircraft its distinctive outline, not here or around the site of the original spar. It all looked rather reminiscent of the fragmented, twisted and broken pieces seen at the Halifax site. It certainly did not look as though a large intact aircraft lay buried, but of course there was always that nagging and ever optimistic hope that there might be.

The sand ridge, confined to the seaward edge of the marsh, was low and narrow. During high spring tides, when the marsh flooded, it was just high enough to stand above the water level but when combined with fresh onshore winds, waves were able to wash right over it, spreading the sand further over the marsh and reducing its height even further. If lowered enough, adjacent to the headwaters of one of the marsh creeks, then come the tidal ebb the falling waters would make for the shortest route direct to the sea, scouring out a channel through the lowered beach ridge. Alongshore movement of sand in the

**Hawker
Hurricane
Mk I Cutaway
Drawing Key**

1 Starboard navigation light
2 Wing tip fairing
3 Fabric covered aileron
4 Aluminium alloy wing skin panelling
5 Aileron hinge control
6 Starboard outer wing panel
7 Inboard torsion box heavy-gauge skin panel
8 Starboard landing lamp
9 Rotol three-bladed propeller
10 Spinner
11 Propeller hub pitch change mechanism
12 Spinner back plate
13 Propeller reduction gearbox
14 Cowling fairing
15 Starboard machine gun muzzles
16 Upper engine cowling
17 Coolant pipes
18 Rolls-Royce Merlin III 12-cylinder liquid-cooled Vee engine
19 Exhaust stubs
20 Engine driven generator
21 Forward engine mounting
22 Ignition control unit
23 Engine bearer struts
24 Lower engine cowlings
25 Starboard mainwheel
26 Manual-type inertia starter
27 Hydraulic pumps
28 Carburettor air intake
29 Cooling air scoop
30 Rear engine mounting
31 Single stage supercharger
32 Port magneto
33 Coolant system header tank
34 External bead sight
35 Coolant filler cap
36 Starboard wing gun bay
37 Ammunition magazines
38 Starboard Browning 0.303-in (7.7-mm) machine guns (four)
39 Fuel filler cap
40 Engine bay canted bulkhead
41 Rear engine mounting struts
42 Pneumatic system air bottle (gun firing)
43 Wing spar centre-section carry-through
44 Lower longeron/wing spar joint
45 Rudder pedals
46 Pilot's foot boards
47 Control column linkage
48 Fuselage (reserve) fuel tank, capacity 28 Imp gal (127 l)
49 Fuel tank bulkhead
50 Control column hand grip

51 Instrument panel
52 Reflector gunsight
53 Starboard split trailing-edge flap
54 Bullet proof windscreen panel
55 Canopy internal handle
56 Rear view mirror
57 Sliding cockpit canopy cover
58 Plexiglass canopy panels
59 Canopy framework
60 Canopy external handle
61 Starboard side "break-out" emergency exit panel
62 Safety harness
63 Seat height adjustment lever
64 Oxygen supply cock
65 Engine throttle lever
66 Elevator trim tab control handwheel
67 Oil pipes to radiator
68 Radiator flap control lever
69 Cockpit section tubular fuselage framework
70 Coolant system piping
71 Pilot's oxygen cylinder
72 Boarding step
73 Seat back armour
74 Pilot's seat
75 Armoured headrest
76 Turn-over crash pylon struts

77 Canopy rear fairing construction
78 Sliding canopy rail
79 Battery
80 TR 9D radio transmitter/receiver
81 Radio shelf
82 Downward identification light
83 Flare launch tube
84 Handgrip
85 Plywood skin panel
86 Dorsal fairing stringers
87 Upper identification light
88 Aerial mast
89 Aerial lead-in
90 Wooden dorsal section formers
91 Fuselage upper longeron
92 Rear fuselage fabric covering
93 Aluminium alloy tailplane leading edge
94 Starboard fabric covered tailplane
95 Fabric covered elevator
96 Aluminium alloy fin leading edge
97 Forward fin mounting post
98 Tailplane spar attachment joint
99 Elevator hinge control
100 Fin rib construction
101 Tailfin fabric covering
102 Diagonal bracing strut
103 Stern post
104 Rudder mass balance weight
105 Aerial cable
106 Rear aerial mast
107 Fabric covered rudder
108 Aluminium alloy rudder framework

109 Tail navigation light
110 Rudder tab
111 Elevator trim tab
112 Port elevator rib construction
113 Elevator horn balance
114 Port tailplane rib construction
115 Diagonal spar bracing strut
116 Rudder control horn
117 Tail control access panel
118 Ventral tailwheel fairing
119 Fixed, castoring tailwheel
120 Dowty shock absorber tailwheel strut
121 Ventral fin framework
122 Lifting bar socket
123 Aluminium alloy lateral formers
124 Tail control cables
125 Rear fuselage tubular framework
126 Diagonal wire bracing
127 Lateral stringers
128 Fuselage lower longeron

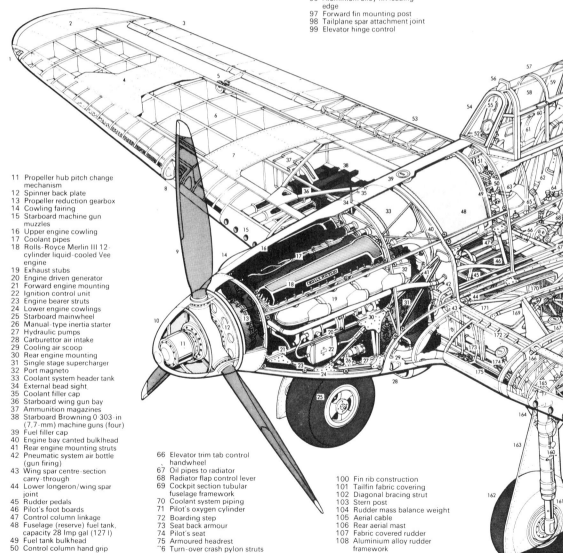

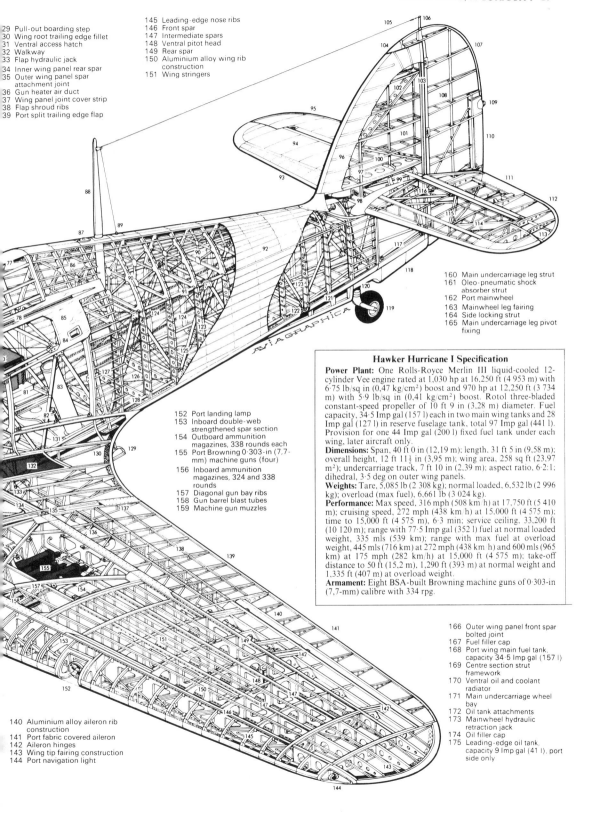

29 Pull-out boarding step
30 Wing root trailing edge fillet
31 Ventral access hatch
32 Walkway
33 Flap hydraulic jack
34 Inner wing panel rear spar
35 Outer wing panel spar attachment joint
36 Gun heater air duct
37 Wing panel joint cover strip
38 Flap shroud ribs
39 Port split trailing edge flap

145 Leading-edge nose ribs
146 Front spar
147 Intermediate spars
148 Ventral pitot head
149 Rear spar
150 Aluminium alloy wing rib construction
151 Wing stringers

152 Port landing lamp
153 Inboard double-web strengthened spar section
154 Outboard ammunition magazines, 338 rounds each
155 Port Browning 0·303-in (7,7-mm) machine guns (four)
156 Inboard ammunition magazines, 324 and 338 rounds
157 Diagonal gun bay ribs
158 Gun barrel blast tubes
159 Machine gun muzzles

160 Main undercarriage leg strut
161 Oleo-pneumatic shock absorber strut
162 Port mainwheel
163 Mainwheel leg fairing
164 Side locking strut
165 Main undercarriage leg pivot fixing

140 Aluminium alloy aileron rib construction
141 Port fabric covered aileron
142 Aileron hinges
143 Wing tip fairing construction
144 Port navigation light

166 Outer wing panel front spar bolted joint
167 Fuel filler cap
168 Port wing main fuel tank, capacity 34·5 Imp gal (157 l)
169 Centre section strut framework
170 Ventral oil and coolant radiator
171 Main undercarriage wheel bay
172 Oil tank attachments
173 Mainwheel hydraulic retraction jack
174 Oil filler cap
175 Leading-edge oil tank, capacity 9 Imp gal (41 l), port side only

Hawker Hurricane I Specification

Power Plant: One Rolls-Royce Merlin III liquid-cooled 12-cylinder Vee engine rated at 1,030 hp at 16,250 ft (4 953 m) with 6·75 lb/sq in (0,47 kg/cm²) boost and 970 hp at 12,250 ft (3 734 m) with 5·9 lb/sq in (0,41 kg/cm²) boost. Rotol three-bladed constant-speed propeller of 10 ft 9 in (3,28 m) diameter. Fuel capacity, 34·5 Imp gal (157 l) each in two main wing tanks and 28 Imp gal (127 l) in reserve fuselage tank, total 97 Imp gal (441 l). Provision for one 44 Imp gal (200 l) fixed fuel tank under each wing, later aircraft only.
Dimensions: Span, 40 ft 0 in (12,19 m); length, 31 ft 5 in (9,58 m); overall height, 12 ft 11½ in (3,95 m); wing area, 258 sq ft (23,97 m²); undercarriage track, 7 ft 10 in (2,39 m); aspect ratio, 6·2:1; dihedral, 3·5 deg on outer wing panels.
Weights: Tare, 5,085 lb (2 308 kg); normal loaded, 6,532 lb (2 996 kg); overload (max fuel), 6,661 lb (3 024 kg).
Performance: Max speed, 316 mph (508 km/h) at 17,750 ft (5 410 m); cruising speed, 272 mph (438 km/h) at 15,000 ft (4 575 m); time to 15,000 ft (4 575 m), 6·3 min; service ceiling, 33,200 ft (10 120 m); range with 77·5 Imp gal (352 l) fuel at normal loaded weight, 335 mls (539 km); range with max fuel at overload weight, 445 mls (716 km) at 272 mph (438 km/h) and 600 mls (965 km) at 175 mph (282 km/h) at 15,000 ft (4 575 m); take-off distance to 50 ft (15,2 m), 1,290 ft (393 m) at normal weight and 1,335 ft (407 m) at overload weight.
Armament: Eight BSA-built Browning machine guns of 0·303-in (7,7-mm) calibre with 334 rpg.

Early 1972. The fully exposed braced aluminium spar gives way to a tubular steel structure as it dips beneath the mud to the left of the photograph.

intervening, more moderate neap tide cycle would attempt to close the gap and so the to and fro of natural forces continually refreshed the landscape of this foreshore zone.

One such area of conflict occurred close to the Hurricane site, so that the newly exposed spar was periodically buried and uncovered as the sands came and went. Throughout 1971, the game of hide and seek continued but gradually, as the sand ridge moved further landward, periods of exposure became longer and the wreckage became a firm feature on the foreshore.

By early 1972, enough of the surrounding mud had been washed away to reveal a little more of the structure and showed how the braced aluminium spar gave way to a tubular steel type of framework. A far more detailed cutaway diagram showing the Hurricane's construction had been obtained by this time — a reproduction of J. H. Clark's dissection of the Hurricane, drawn for a 1940 edition of *The Aeroplane* magazine. Clearly showing the internal detail, it gave much greater confidence that the identification had been correct. From the relationship between the aluminium section and the tubular steel work, it was possible to deduce that the new piece was another wing spar, belonging close to the wing root. The absence of flat plating with gun port holes, where the two sections joined, meant that it was not a front spar and the angle of the bracing pieces meant that it could only be the port wing's rear spar upside down. As the Hurricane was a low-wing monoplane, being upside down meant that there was a good chance some of the fuselage might also be buried further down. Such a possibility gave cause for excitement.

The line of the new spar ran towards the stump of the old one but was slightly offset. Were they connected and, if so, how? Could the vertical 'old' spar be part of the other wing, broken off and sticking up in the air; or was it really the front main spar of the same wing, severely twisted and out of position? Being from the same wing would mean a badly broken up structure. The former explanation looked much more likely and certainly was wished to be so.

On that rather optimistic assumption the layout of the other components could be worked out. The centre section would lie between the two spars with the engine just a few feet landward, (forward) of this. Could 'Nipper's' words really be true and not just guessing or spinning a yarn? It would have been too much to hope that the Rolls-Royce Merlin engine was still there. Surely it would have been taken away soon after the crash, as happened in most cases, and this was just part of the bare framework left behind? A little digging might have provided a few answers, but the memory of earlier attempts came flooding back all too clearly. It was no easy task, as proved before, and this time water to a depth of six inches already surrounded the wreckage, in a natural scour hole, fed by the tidal channel which cut through the beach. It would take long enough just to drain that, let alone start digging before the next tide threatened. It would not be a task entered into lightly, if it was to be meaningful and productive.

Chapter Two
Decisions

The summer of 1972, with the usual influx of tourists, saw fresh nibbling at the wreckage. Who and for what reason, was not clear. The daily trickle of beach walkers had a natural tendency to fiddle with any strange object or piece of flotsam brought in by the tide, or perhaps it was others who recognised the wreckage for what it was. In the last few years there had been a mushrooming interest in a topic dubbed 'aviation archaeology': a strange combination of time frames brought together in one title. Were such people active here? Removal of the final piece of plating from the old spar, leaving a neat saw edge down its side, showed somebody was interested. Passing holiday makers do not just happen to carry hacksaws to such remote places and expend so much energy on the unknown! Souvenir hunters do. All that was left of the old spar now was a mere stump one foot high and three inches square. Bits of the port wing spar had also started to disappear. It seemed a shame that what was left buried should gradually be broken up piece by piece as more became exposed. But how much really was there buried and was it worth trying to save in one piece? Only digging would provide that answer.

Tentative thoughts were given as to how a large structure could be lifted from such a site and transported away? Another question with no obvious or simple answer. Many more were sure to follow. Any digging would best be left until the close of the year as there was no point in attracting the undue attention of wandering tourists. Out of season it was mainly people with a purpose who came that way, suitably dressed for the occasion — bird watchers, beachcombers and the like, and predominantly locals at that. The larger number of casual visitors out for a stroll along the coast were more inclined to turn back once the firm cliff path gave way to the start of the softer marsh near the new Tamarisk wall. At this lower level the scenic view across Hamford Water to Harwich and the Suffolk coast was lost and conditions under foot were not so pleasant. The winter holiday period would provide a suitable time. Best left till then.

During the week before Christmas, while crowds headed for the shops in preparation for the festivities, a lone car pulled into the deserted Naze cliff car park. A solitary figure then set off, spade in hand, down the cliff path towards the marsh. Nobody was passed after leaving the car, and arriving at the site all was quiet. Fortunately the shifting sand patch around the wreckage was deeper than it had been in the summer and although it meant more to dig through, it had the bonus of eliminating the pool of water that normally collected there, so no baling out was necessary.

Only a test hole was planned, to see what might be buried and there was no illusion that all would be revealed thàt day. But where to start? On the optimistic assumption that the remains were to some degree intact, the line of the more substantial port wing spar was used to work out where the fuselage and engine should be. It was just an estimate as no detailed plan with dimensions had been found, and as Clark's sectional diagram was drawn at an oblique angle it was not so helpful for this purpose. To establish the presence of the engine would be a major achievement because being the largest and heaviest single item it would be an important factor in planning any recovery operation. The first strike of the spade aimed for the front fuselage and engine.

The sand was firm and could easily be shifted. A foot down and the old marsh surface reappeared. Now the struggle began. The soft but firm dark grey marsh mud had the consistency of warm butter and each thrust of the spade had not only to overcome the weight of the mud but also tremendous suction. The hole began at just over two feet square, but as it grew deeper the top had to be widened to prevent the steep sides from collapsing. Two feet down the digging became more difficult as the narrowness of the hole restricted proper leverage on the spade. Again the top had to be widened a little more. At intervals, digging was interrupted to remove the excavated mud from the edge of the hole because, unlike the sand, the sticky mud could not be thrown out well clear. Each clod had to be thumped onto the edge of the hole to dislodge the gooey stuff from the blade. The closeness of this growing mound so near to the edge made the hole appear deeper than it really was and effectively made the danger of collapse more apparent.

A little deeper and the spade struck something solid; a definite metallic sound and in the right position. Gentle probing with the spade showed the contact not to be isolated. It extended sideways, mainly in the direction of the exposed wreckage. A boost for morale. A number of sharp edges came into view as the mud was cleared away and most could be felt going deeper beneath the mud. The hope was to recognise a familiar panel shape, but none was obvious. So far there was not even the trace of a smooth continuous surface. The base of the hole was widened and, in the process, a few sections of aluminium tubing came to light. A pile of such finds was begun at the top of the hole. Clearing a little more mud from around the exposed edges a rather badly concertinaed panel came free. Its identity was far from clear. It was some eighteen inches wide and had probably been about the same long, before being folded to little more than a quarter of that. It joined the pile to be investigated later. More solid matter could now be felt at the bottom of the hole and another distinct edge of what felt like a large flat panel. Excavating a little deeper it could be moved and it only appeared to be held at depth by the mud. With a little effort it was slowly worked free and finally surfaced without complaint. It was some two and a half feet square but with an irregular outline that was not immediately recognisable.

Ingress of water had started to become more of a problem and pauses in digging to bale out became more frequent. No proper drainage arrangement had been planned for this test dig, save the provision of a decent-sized bucket. The water was merely flung over the edge of the hole when baling became necessary. With annoying rapidity a large proportion found its way back to its former level as the hole became deeper. Working alone and with limited daylight hours it was far from efficient but appeared the only way.

Just a few inches lower, in what was becoming a rather fluid mud, further contact was made. It felt like another panel, roughly triangular in shape, lying almost flat this time and occupying most of the bottom of the hole. It seemed to extend back towards the main surface wreckage and so the hole was undercut in that direction in search of its edge. When finally cleared, this panel was also found to be quite loose and it gave itself up with minimal struggle. Two and a half feet long by two feet wide, it was flat, appeared undamaged and had a curved extension attached along its longest edge. Wiping the surface by hand a metallic silver gleamed through the muddy veneer.

At a depth approaching some four feet the almost liquid mud at the bottom of the hole had taken on a blackish colour and the air had a distinct petroleum smell. Mixed with the natural marsh mud aroma it did not provide the most ideal of working conditions! Probing with the spade in the space vacated by the triangular panel showed there was nothing substantial directly underneath, except for a large, pipe structure lying diagonally across the hole. It was about an inch and a half in diameter, felt very firm and would not budge at all. Following the line of the pipe towards the surface wreckage end of the hole, it seemed to terminate at an angle against a flat vertical plate, made of what looked like steel — the hypotenuse and base of a triangular structure. Uncovering more of the plate showed it to be almost girder-like in construction and lying parallel to the line of the braced spar section, exposed on the surface some four feet further seaward. It was probably part of the front wing spar. Cleaning the mud away by hand, the sheen of silver paint clearly stood out against the darker background.

The girder feature now formed part of the front, or seaward, wall of the hole, which was being dug facing seaward, towards the exposed structure and hopefully along the line of the fuselage, looking aft. In which direction to extend the hole next? There would not be much time left to start anything major as it was

Test hole dug in the winter of 1972 reveals the solid front spar of the inverted port wing and the bracing strut joining it to the fuselage. Two panels recovered and other fragments lie at the side of the hole.

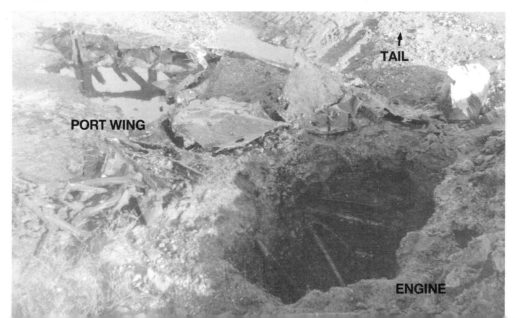

well into the afternoon and the shadows were already lengthening; being so close to the shortest day, daylight hours were very limited. Prodding the floor still revealed nothing either side of the now well exposed pipe, which was probably part of the fuselage bracing, but which part could not be imagined at the time. The cutaway diagram had not been brought along so the interpretation would have to wait until later. A camera had been thought of though, with the intention of providing a permanent record of what might be uncovered and hopefully to give a reliable spatial relationship to the various pieces exposed when checking with the diagram.

To the rear of the hole nothing could be felt and nothing was expected, not at this depth anyway because, being further from the surface wreckage, if anything was there it would be much deeper. To the left, northwards, and away from the Tamarisk wall, there was no further metallic contact, just mud. At the front, the thin edge of another panel lying flat on top of the girder could just be seen, like a lid just ajar. It looked and felt firm and ran the full length of the exposed girder. Any attempt to uncover it would involve removing the three feet of mud directly above it. There would be no time for that.

To the right looked the most promising direction and, groping by hand in the mud, solid objects could be felt, most of which moved a little. That was the way to go. There might just be time to investigate some of them before the light got too bad. After a while a few more small sections of aluminium tubing were pulled clear, then probing further into the side of the hole another reasonably large panel was struck. Like the others it did not appear to be attached to anything else and with some creative hand carving deep into the mud it was eventually freed. It had no distinctive shape and its excessive curvature gave every impression of being different from that intended at manufacture. At one time it would also have been a little longer than its present length, as one edge was jagged and looked rather moth eaten. Despite this it appeared generally well preserved, with the remains of a light coloured paint on one side and a silvery grey on the other.

More pieces could be felt going ever deeper on the right hand side but to tunnel further could easily have started a cave in from above. It was hazardous to risk the collapse of such a large amount of overburden into the remainder of the hole. It was getting late and time to call it a day. Photographs were taken to indicate the extent of the excavation and to attempt to show how different parts of framework related to each other. The camera, wrapped in polythene for protection, even when taking the shots, was the only thing to escape getting wet or covered in mud that day!

It was now time for the final and most soul destroying job — filling in the hole to cover all trace of what had gone on. It took a lot of effort to destroy what had taken the best part of a day to achieve but it had to be done to prevent attracting unwanted attention to the site. Once filled, it was still very obvious that some activity had taken place but the wash of a few high tides would soon mask even that.

The long trek then began back along the cliff path carrying four misshapen panels and a bag of miscellaneous bits. Being aluminium the pieces were not heavy but their size, and being covered in slippery mud, made them an awkward load. By the time the car was reached they could have been made of lead, and a very messy lead at that! Still the camera remained the only item free from mud, everything else was covered in it, as would be the interior of the car also. At the time, it seemed of no consequence as the day had been a success; the hopes had been realised. There was more wreckage buried, probably considerably more and it looked in surprisingly good condition. During the drive home thoughts strayed to planning a return trip but on arrival more immediate requirements came to the fore — the first being a good, hot bath.

The next day a hand brush and hose were employed to scrub the remaining mud from the large panels. The steady trickle of water into the hole during digging had undoubtedly been saline and so the risk of inducing corrosion was great. Despite the proximity of the site to sea water, well-known for its corrosive properties, the aircraft's remains had been cocooned for just over thirty years in the dense marsh mud, almost totally free of the oxygen needed to fuel the corrosion process. A liberal supply of various aviation petroleum products no doubt added to the preserving environment.

The previous day's contact with salt water was probably the first since the war years and its residue had to be removed. The sticky grey mud clung stubbornly to the metal and a good soaking was needed to dilute it sufficiently for the stiff bristle brush to be effective. A thorough rinse in fresh water was followed by careful drying, then storage in the most likely warm place for final drying out of the narrow seams and cracks — the airing cupboard. That was to be just the first of many minor conflicts between the aircraft and home life! The same treatment was given to the bag of small pieces. Although most were not readily recognised at first glance, they might prove significant later; and anyway why neglect items now that had taken so much effort to collect? Cleaning one piece showed it to be made of wood. Laminated and carefully shaped on one edge; it was a fragment of propeller blade.

All the large panels were found to be bent to varying degrees. Identifying three of them was a reasonably simple matter and confirmed without doubt the Hurricane type. The first two pieces to have emerged from the hole, when joined together, formed the port side engine cowling panel; the rear and larger part

The four large panel pieces, propeller fragment and other small items recovered during the first trial dig.

being only slightly out of shape but the front portion being the much folded section recovered first. They were certainly not lying in their correct positions on the aircraft when found and must have been dislodged during impact or moved later before the wreckage became buried. Both showed much evidence of green paint and what appeared to be some brown, as well as a few specks of white along the lower edge of the larger piece. The insides were painted silver-grey and had a blistered appearance. Possibly the result of fire? The large triangular piece was hardly distorted at all and carried traces of white paint. It was the underside of the port wing root fairing, where the leading edge of the wing joined the fuselage. This was consistent with the position of the front wing spar 'girder' at the front of the hole, and the steel 'pipe' diagonally across the hole must have been the bracing strut from the engine mounting to the port wing front spar.

This all confirmed what had been suspected towards the end of digging, that the hole had been dug just a few feet to one side of the aircraft's centreline. Also, the evidence so far suggested that the wreckage was lying upside down, as had been supposed originally. Another hole would really be needed just to one side of the first, a little further south towards the Tamarisk wall.

The fourth large panel was slightly curved and had two damaged edges. One had a torn appearance and the other gradually faded away with what looked like burn marks. The outer surface still had a good coating of white paint, and the inner an even more complete cover of silver grey. As to where on the aircraft it had come from there was no obvious clue, except for the white paint again indicating the undersurface. It was much later before it was finally identified as the lower half of the starboard wing leading edge, immediately next to the fuselage. Impact against the solid wing spar had provided its new shape. It was certainly not found where it should have been and must have been moved sometime after the crash. Perhaps evidence of an early salvage attempt?

The details were recorded. Sketches were drawn to show where different colours of paint had been found and also to locate and list the large number of individual part serial numbers scattered throughout the panels. Each individual piece of metal appeared to have a number along with an occasional quality inspection stamp. It would be interesting to see if a pattern emerged. None was immediately obvious among the various panels but there was some agreement internally within a particular panel.

While searching for these numbers on the rear portion of the engine cowling panel, close to the access hole for the hand starting gear, a different group of numbers showed up. They were in a different style, much shorter and read *P3642*. The other part numbers were much longer than this and looked machine made. These were in a larger format and, having an irregular spacing, looked individually hand punched. Could it be the aircraft's serial number? Could one be so lucky! Being a detachable panel for access to the engine, maybe it had been policy to individually mark such panels with the aircraft's serial number to prevent mix-ups during maintenance work? Although assembly line techniques were used in the construction process, there was still a certain degree of local fit for each aircraft and care had to be taken. A check through the list of aircraft serial numbers in Francis Mason's comprehensive book *Hawker Hurricane* (Macdonald 1962) showed that, yes, a Hurricane had been built with that

An early clue to identification: *P3642* found stamped on the port side engine cowling panel.

particular number; a Mark I from the third production batch built by Hawker Aircraft Ltd with a Rolls-Royce Merlin III engine.

In the book's subsequent breakdown of aircraft by unit, P3642 was listed against No 257 Squadron. In the spring of 1941 No 257 Squadron was based at Coltishall in Norfolk; not very close but certainly in the right part of the country and well within range to be linked with Walton. So, as well as having a date of 29 April 1941, we also had what looked like the identification of not only the individual aircraft, but also the parent squadron. How fortunate could one get at a first attempt! The test dig had certainly been a most fruitful exercise.

The opportunity for a further exploratory dig was eagerly awaited. A few weeks passed with no activity, then the ideal time presented itself — the weekend before New Year when once again all should be quiet as people were occupied with other matters. The time lapse was both helpful and necessary. With the site then regularly covered by spring tides, the fortnightly cycle once again brought the right tidal conditions for that weekend. It was hoped also that it had given time for the infill of the previous hole to consolidate. It had been very tempting to follow up the initial dig with one just days later but as the two areas were adjacent to one another, the danger of collapse from the old hole into the new one was all too obvious. Even a few weeks later might be a little optimistic but it was decided to see how things progressed.

On arrival, the surface sediments were found to have shifted again, a result of the intervening spring tide cycle when the site had been awash at high tide. A small pool had been left very close to the proposed hole and needed draining before any digging could take place. Cutting a narrow channel in the sand diverted its contents to further down the beach. Digging then commenced, a few feet south of the first hole at first, just to be safe. It was then extended slightly further south towards all that remained of the old vertical wing spar, now reduced to a stump little more than six inches above the sand.

It was not long before metal was struck quite near the surface, just by the old stump, and the further north towards the earlier hole, the deeper the contact became. Widening the hole to expose the full extent of the framework now coming to light meant going close to the old workings. Soon water began to trickle in at a steady rate and signs of impending subsidence began to show. Once again the mud turned black, a petroleum smell filled the air and the muddy water began to take on an oily film.

Lying across the hole in almost a north-south direction, parallel with the shoreline, was the edge of a large panel. Clearing the loose mud away from its shallowest end soon uncovered the distinctive outline of an undercarriage leg fairing dipping down from near the stump towards the earlier hole. It was slightly bent but the outline was unmistakable. At the deeper end were signs of another panel adjoining it. Uncovering its edges revealed the start of a triangular shape; most probably the partner of the one already recovered. Unlike the undercarriage fairing, this piece moved a little despite still being largely buried and so might, with a little encouragement, come free. A sloppy mixture of mud and oily water still half-buried the panel and a glance to the left showed that collapse from that direction could come at any moment. Feeling around its edges the panel appeared to be free where exposed and as far down as the arm could reach into the mud and water. Being the middle of winter that was not very far! The steady flow of water was an adequate reminder to keep one eye on the wall to the left. The hole was already three feet deep, allowing for boots being pressed ever deeper by the digging action, that effectively made four. Bending to attend to the panel meant virtually the whole body being below ground level. With no one else around, as it had hopefully been planned that way, the hazards were all too obvious. Wriggling the panel, it appeared to be held right at the bottom. It would pivot slightly against the pressure of the mud but would need more of a sharp twist to finally wrench it free.

Starboard side undercarriage leg fairing lies above an oily pool of water in the hole. A distinct break in the wing spar is directly beneath it.

Second test dig showing triangular wing root fairing and starboard undercarriage fairing.

A realisation then that, inconvenient though it was at that particular moment, the photographic record should not be ignored. At the first dig it had been left until the very end and the panels removed from the hole instead of being photographed in situ. Their relative positions as found not being recorded until the following day and then as best as memory would serve. With cameras and mud not mixing well together another disadvantage of working alone soon became apparent. To get the best shot the black sludge had to be baled out to as low a level as possible, then a rapid exit from the hole, wipe hands clean, set up and 'click', before the water level rose again. It was a simple camera with no flash and the long winter shadows did nothing to improve the result but at least something was on film.

Back into the hole and after a little more manoeuvring the panel came free. No damage except for a bend at the bottom where it had been attached by a couple of rivets to a supporting strut. The edge of the front wing's spar could now be seen more clearly and a distinct break in its line was very obvious, not swept backwards towards the tail as might have been expected, but upwards as if the aircraft had literally fallen on its back and broken a wing.

The Hurricane's construction contained two main parallel spars, nine feet long and four feet apart, which ran through the lower fuselage to form the basic framework of the centre section. Across these the fuselage occupied the middle three and a half feet and the remainder either side provided a solid framework in which the two wing fuel tanks were housed, one on either side of the fuselage. The outer ends of the front spar also accommodated the hinge points for the inward retracting undercarriage. The resulting wide track gave a very stable landing arrangement, useful on rough grass airstrips and provided one feature whereby the Hurricane had a distinct advantage over the Spitfire which had an outward retracting undercarriage and subsequently a much narrower track. The main, or outer part of the Hurricane's wings were then joined to the ends of the two centre section spars by four bolts, two to each spar (top and bottom). It could be seen that the old vertical spar was still attached by one of these bolts but the other of the pair had sheared, thus allowing the stump to pivot through almost ninety degrees into the near vertical. There was consequently no wreckage directly beneath it, it all lay to one side, further north. No wonder the earlier investigations around the old spar had been so disappointing.

The bracing strut from the wing spar to the engine mounting frame could be seen disappearing deep into the mud, a mirror image of that found in the earlier hole. The engine, therefore, lay to the north, underneath that precarious cliff of unstable mud. The precaution of leaving a narrow strip between the two holes for the sake of stability had meant that the second hole was then just that bit too far to one side. It was becoming obvious that there would be no positive proof of the engine's existence that day. Prods with the spade deep into the mud in that direction indicated something was there but varying resistance at different points hinted that it was probably sections of fuselage framework that were being hit. With the light starting to fade, all that could be done was to clear the mud off what had been exposed so far, photograph that, and then call it a day. Clawing at the mud by hand was the best way to achieve this, and with the starboard undercarriage fairing almost fully exposed, a final bale out of water and the photographs were taken.

Once again, with great reluctance the infilling began. Besides undoing all the day's work, it was also not just a simple task of pushing mud to the edge of the hole and leaving gravity to do the rest. Each sticky block had to be lifted and plopped back into the depths from whence it had come. Watching the final lumps just cover the top of the undercarriage fairing near the old spar stump, it could not be helped but reflect on those early half-hearted efforts of some five years earlier. How only that piece would have been detected anywhere near the old spar with the bulk of the remaining wreckage being so much further away, albeit with much of even that now found to be so tantalisingly close to the surface.

Walking back along the new Tamarisk wall towards the cliff path, churning over in the mind were the possibilities of what else might lie buried. But as the sun began to sink beneath the horizon, and the true cold of the early winter's evening began to bite, this soon became blurred with an eagerness for the more immediate requirements of warmth and dry clothes.

The following day it was time for the brush and hose treatment on the pieces recovered. Not so many this time with only one large panel; the triangular wing root fairing, and also a bag of small bits, mostly of small diameter aluminium tubing. Unfortunately there were no more large detachable panels like the port side engine cowling recovered last time, complete with a possible serial number, and so there could be no added confidence in identification. The metal surfaces revealed were similar to those of last time: shiny aluminium with minimal, if any, corrosion. There was also much paint still evident, mostly a dull white colour on the external surface of the fairing piece and a blistered silver again on the inside. If this was the condition of pieces close to the surface and nearest to the hostile marine environment, there was hope that the remainder would be at least as well preserved, if not better. The remarkable lack of serious distortion from impact found so far also raised hopes that the remains had survived structurally intact also. So, what was to be done now?

Chapter Three
Forces Joined

A reasonable assessment could now be made of what lay buried, in what attitude and at what depth. The aircraft lay pointing slightly south of west, away from the sea; was on its back and inclined at a shallow angle, nose down. The propeller hub would be at a depth of some eight feet or so, assuming the intact engine was still there, with the inverted fuselage breaking surface at just over a third of the way along its length. The curved panel, first seen in the mid sixties, just above the surface and a few feet from the lone vertical spar, was now identifiable as part of the bulbous radiator that hung directly beneath the cockpit and which helped give the Hurricane its distinctive outline. The fuselage aft of this should have been lying on the surface, or just above it, so that part was probably missing. The main port wing structure had been traced close to the surface for about half its length but minus most of its surface skinning. The starboard wing had been broken close to the fuselage which should have left the outer section projecting skyward from the marshes. That too had most probably gone, although it was just possible that these other main sections might have been detached and lay buried close by.

In volume it was estimated that a good forty to fifty per cent of the aircraft probably lay buried but this relatively small percentage formed something like seventy per cent of the aircraft's total structural weight. All the major heavy components were in this forward fuselage and wing centre section. The presence of the engine had not yet been proven of course but had to be allowed for in any weight consideration. With the nose down attitude it seemed most unlikely that a wartime recovery team would have dug to the deepest part of the wreckage, removed the engine and then left the remaining airframe section in situ. It must be there.

With time, the encroaching sea would steadily uncover more of the structure leaving it exposed to the effects of weather and the constant pounding of the waves. What was left would no doubt gradually be dismantled by passers by, be they souvenir hunters or just plain beach walkers. Surely here was something worthwhile saving as a whole. The question was how? Digging the two small test holes had certainly revealed the potential of the site but had also emphasised how difficult any excavation would be.

The sheer weight of such a structure would be a problem enough in itself. It was estimated that of the original 6450 lb normal flying weight of the Hurricane Mk I, something like 4500 lb of wreckage lay buried. Hardly a one-man-and-a-shovel job! This figure included 1400 lb just for the Rolls-Royce Merlin engine, the presence of which might therefore prove critical. Added to the estimate for the structure would have to be an allowance for the weight of mud inside the framework.

Wet mud had undoubtedly filtered into every available nook and cranny and there was no guarantee that any of it could be removed from the wreckage on site. The volume of mud was estimated at a good 70 cubic feet. Converting that to weight produced a staggering 6000 lb addition to the total weight calculation. Clearly as much mud as possible must be removed in situ. All these figures were very approximate but gave a general feel for the scale of any proposed recovery operation.

Of all the obstacles to overcome, the actual digging, although a large and messy undertaking, did not head the list. Even if a suitable mechanical system could not be found, enough bodies armed with spades could do the job and some manual effort would be needed anyway to winkle out as much mud as possible from inside the complex structure. The big problem was how to get the weighty remains intact from the marshland site to a place of relative safety above the high water line, where they could be properly attended to and transport would have easy access. A number of possibilities were considered. Of prime importance was the actual feasibility of the method, followed very closely by how much it would cost. At this stage financial considerations were ruled by the simple fact that there was no source of money, nor was there likely to be. Any scheme would have to be cheap or on a voluntary basis. In fact, as it turned out, it was voluntary effort and self-help that was to be a feature of this salvage operation, from start to finish.

No end was in mind for the wreckage at this stage, other than to save it from further gradual destruction and also, after all those years, a personal inquisitiveness to discover just exactly what was there. The RAF's collection of old aircraft, previously scattered throughout the country, had been found a central home at RAF Hendon on the outskirts of London just recently. Intended as the Museum for the RAF, it had been open for just a couple of months. Would it be interested in such an item? The question was thought but not asked — probably too trivial an item for such an organisation. It could be argued that like so many well intentioned projects of this type, much thought can be put into the emotive process of location and recovery but less into the more mundane work of proper preservation and little real thought given to the very long term future. Sometimes, with justification, it can be said that things would have been better left as they were. In this case, despite an uncertain future, the destructive process of coastal erosion would not wait.

The problem of recovery was essentially two-fold: first, lifting the wreckage out of the hole and second transporting it away. Flotation — water power — was one possible solution. At spring tides the site was liable to flood with a depth of water dependant upon the time of year and prevailing weather conditions. Lashing oil drums to the framework and using the force of a rising tide might do it. However, even at the highest tide of the year, a maximum depth of only three to four feet of water could be expected above the site. That would barely float the drums alone, even if lashed on top of the wreckage let alone be able to lift the wreckage clear of the hole. For greater lifting effect the drums would need to be placed under the wreckage but that would involve an enormous digging effort, as at least ten forty-five-gallon oil drums would be needed for the weight involved, and far more if the mud could not be removed from inside the structure. It was possible but could enough drums be strategically placed to provide sufficient lifting force? Probably not.

Once digging had begun, there would be no going back. The remains would be exposed for all to see and corrosion would begin in earnest on all those parts previously protected by the marshland mud for the last thirty years. The lift would have to work and 'floating' it would be hard to guarantee. So many things could go wrong; not least the effects of the fickle British weather. High pressure and a strong offshore wind on the day of the lift could easily lower the predicted high tide level sufficiently to cause failure. It was an uncomplicated solution, required little outside involvement, a lot of hard work but had a risky outcome. There also remained the problem of transport away from the site. If the lift was successful, it would then be asking much of the same tide to also float it completely clear of the marshes, even though the open sea was only a mere fifty yards away.

A method providing a greater certainty of success would be more preferable. 'Sheer legs', consisting of a stout wooden tripod arrangement with block and tackle lifting gear suspended from the apex, would enable a direct lift from above. It was a system reasonably easy to erect and designed to be portable. The local Sea Cadet Corps was known to have a set and enquiries were made. After some discussion on the practicalities of such a system, it looked as though size rather than weight considerations would be the problem this time. Even if the weight could be lifted, it was very doubtful that it could then be raised high enough to clear the hole from which it had emerged. The higher the load got towards the narrow apex of the framework the more restricted the space became. It was not looking so good. Providing a firm base for the three legs might also prove difficult on the soft marsh surface. Even with padding, the vision of many hands hauling at the tackle only to see their energies spent on driving the legs into the mud was all to apparent!

Even with a direct lift, removal from the marsh still remained a problem. The yachting world held one possible solution. To haul boats in and out of the water and to move them around on land, local boat yards used makeshift, heavy-duty trailers, made from modified lorry chassis. Stripped of everything except axles and main chassis longerons these basic structures were custom built for that particular manoeuvreing job. The town of Walton, with its splendid facilities for small craft and ready access to the Thames Estuary, had no shortage of boat yards and so the idea was pursued. The response was a cool one, far from enthusiastic, and with no small element of disbelief. The idea was just not taken seriously, but maybe the proposed project was not put over very well. Once again, a possibility existed but the feeling this time was that it would take an awful lot of persuasion to borrow a trailer and some means of pulling it, or a relatively large sum to hire one.

Transport and lifting capabilities were combined in a mechanical digger. Even if it did not have the power to lift the remains directly, it would certainly be of enormous value in excavating the soft grey mud. It might even be able to drag the wreckage out afterwards. Access to the site was far from straightforward, however. After leaving the nearest track by the new Tamarisk wall, to get to the site one followed the line of the seawall system, an earthen bank some fifteen feet high with narrow, ridge-like crest that would be impossible for a mechanical digger to cross without the assistance of a substantial long low ramp. Constructing such a structure was totally out of the question. To go round meant a seven hundred-yard detour along the sand and muddy foreshore, with the inherent danger of becoming stuck en route or, having made it round, being cut off by the rising tide on the return trip. Would anyone risk their machine on such a venture? Advice was sought in the form of a local digger operator and yes, after some consideration, he thought it would be possible. He knew the route intended and was used to working in such difficult terrain. How then to persuade a company to risk a digger? There would certainly be a high financial penalty with this solution.

Other, more fanciful ideas were considered, but dismissed as just that. Taking the wreckage to pieces in situ would take, even if possible, a very long time, run a very high risk of salt water contamination and attract far too much attention in the process. Was it possible that the area Water Authority would be operating cranes or mechanical diggers nearby in the immediate future? So the ideas came and went.

As it was still the depths of winter, with the new year only just begun, there was still time for planning and further enquiries. Nothing could realistically be done on site until the weather improved and daylight hours became longer, but something had to be planned as another summer was certain to see greatly increased nibbling at the exposed sections.

It was also about time for a little more detective work into the identity of the wreckage. The aircraft type was known, date of incident, serial number and squadron, but what had happened? Attention turned to possible archive sources. Until 1972 the RAF had several small displays of old aircraft spread amongst a number of RAF Stations. In the late sixties it had been proposed that a national RAF Museum be constructed to house a full collection of representative aircraft and to store relevant archive material. The proposed site had been RAF Hendon, using two of the still surviving First World War hangars as the nucleus of the complex. On 15 November 1972 the RAF Museum was officially opened by Her Majesty The Queen. A visit to this new centre seemed a most appropriate starting point and was planned for early in the New Year.

As a public relations exercise, the Museum was operating a scheme of 'your questions answered'. Just fill in a question card with a query and in the fullness of time back would come the answer. Here was a likely first point of contact and so a card was duly completed requesting information on Hurricane P3642. In early February back came the rather deflating reply: the record card for that particular Hurricane no longer existed. The letter continued:

> All that could be learned is that it was built at Brooklands and was allocated to No 257 Squadron on 11 June 1940. It made operational flights with No 257 Squadron until 16 September 1940. On that date, when being flown by Sergeant Hulbert to Hendon, it had to make a forced landing and was placed in Cat 2.

There the official record ended and the Museum had no further information.

What had appeared so hopeful then began to look very doubtful. With no further record after a crash in September 1940, was it likely that the aircraft would be flying again in April 1941? Maybe those numbers did not refer to the aircraft serial number after all. On the panel the 'P' was stamped above the number 3642 rather than in front of it, as is normally found. Alternatively, the panel may have come from P3642 and for some reason may have been put on another machine. If that was the case it would leave the identity wide open. The panel could have been salvaged and gone anywhere as a replacement. Grasping at straws, it was reasoned more likely for any transfer of panels to have taken place before P3642's forced landing. In other words, despite the rationale behind the marking of individual panels to keep them with their parent aircraft, a swap had taken place, for one reason or another. If that was the case, what was the recipient aircraft's identity? It was almost back to square one but with one possible common link remaining: No 257 Squadron.

Close examination of the known facts was needed. The date 'April 1941' was based on the entry in the local ARP records. Even all those years ago, when it had first been seen, there was some doubt about the location's description but it was accepted on the basis that surely two aircraft of the same type do not crash literally within a few hundred yards of one another, with one being recorded and the other totally ignored? The doubt had been temporarily reinforced but ignored a couple of months earlier, just before the test digs, when some of the original County ARP records had been examined at Chelmsford. There, sure enough, had been the entry for the Hurricane at Stone Point on 29 April 1941, but also a reference to waiting for the tide to fall before trying to reach it. Now, scrutinised more closely, it did not seem to fit. Even at high spring tides there was only a short period when the marshes by the Tamarisk wall were covered. The height of the tide should not have been a barrier and certainly would not have been worth mentioning in an ARP message because, even in the worst case, the delay in getting to the wreckage would only have been an hour at the very most.

The doubts now took on a new significance and the notes taken at Chelmsford were sifted through again, for mention of any other aircraft crashing at Walton. When first looked at, mention of all others had been casually ignored, as there had been no real reason to doubt the April 1941 date. Besides the Halifax bomber, actually named by type, there was only one other listed as crashing on land at Walton — on the golf course at 0850 or 0856 (the writing was unclear) on 31 August 1940. No type was given, just that it was British, completely smashed and the pilot dead. Before the war, the land by the highest part of the Naze cliffs had been a golf course but that was just as far from the crash site as was the real 'Stone Point', named in the 1941 crash. Crosschecking with Mr Lowther Kemp's local ARP records, an entry for 31 August 1940 was found but it merely read '0855 British plane crashed', and gave no specific location or type.

The combination of naming 'Stone Point' as a general term for the location and the type 'Hurricane', clearly described, swayed the decision back in favour of the original 1941 date but not without a lingering element of doubt. Tentatively, the identity would remain — Hurricane crashing at 1053 on 29 April 1941, probably from No 257 Squadron, and maybe P3642. Further evidence would really be needed to make it really convincing. No 257 Squadron's records might help, as had been suggested in the RAF Museum's reply. A trip to the Public Record Office in London would be needed, as the RAF's Squadron Operations Records Books had recently been transferred there from the Ministry of Defence,

Air Historical Branch. An appointment would have to be made in the near future, but in the meantime events were developing elsewhere that were to have a significant bearing on the proposed recovery of the aircraft.

In the third week of February 1973 a small article appeared in the local paper announcing that cadets from the Colchester and Clacton Air Training Corps units had come across the remains of a wartime bomber at the Naze and were planning an excavation at the site. It could only be the Halifax. A 'phone call to No 308 Squadron ATC's Commanding Officer, Flt Lt Percy Wheatley, RAFVR, confirmed this and the following Sunday, 25 February, saw a large gathering of cadets and other helpers at the site. The area had changed quite considerably over the past few years. Much of the clumpy uneven surface left as grazing land after the 1953 floods had gone under the plough as new drainage schemes had been put in hand. The remains of the bomber lay in a section still left to gorse and scrub but there was little evidence left above ground of the once mighty machine. Over the years, what had not been taken away or buried by the original RAF recovery effort had been gradually removed by the farmer, as the jagged edges were a hazard to his grazing cattle. The site looked much tidier than it had seven years earlier, with most of the smaller pieces, then lying on the surface, gone. Only the four battered and half-buried Bristol Hercules engines really gave evidence to what had once happened there.

Hand digging commenced in earnest by the army of eager cadets, who concentrated their initial efforts close to three of the engines that lay together. It was not long before finds were being made and it soon became clear that the remains had been purposely buried for they did not lie as they would have on the aircraft's impact. One propeller was buried in such a way that, if complete, it would have had one blade projecting well above the ground. The saw marks on the stump revealed its fate. It had been deliberately cut through and the offending blade then thrown into the hole alongside the rest of the propeller.

As the day wore on, the site began to take on the appearance of a scrap yard as piece after piece was uncovered and stacked into piles. Large though the volume was, all the fragments were small, badly broken and heavily corroded. The influx of salt water during the 1953 floods had no doubt accelerated the corrosion process but, also, the salt subsequently trapped in the soil, when combined with a mobile water table before the installation of proper drainage, had created a vertical band just below the surface where the effects of corrosion were particularly severe. Any aluminium found in that zone was very badly affected and was invariably reduced to just a blue and white crystalline powder. It was such a contrast to the oxygen free environment of the natural salt marsh mud where the Hurricane lay and such an irony that far more damage had been done where man had intervened to keep out the hostile environment than where salt water was free to wash over a site twice monthly!

As the piles of wreckage grew, the expectation of finding large, intact sections diminished. It was looking as though any such pieces had been either taken away, or broken up and placed in shallow holes. Some compensation for this disappointment was provided by the cadets being able to recover the remains of all four engines and propellers, the undercarriage assemblies, and a selection of smaller items of interest. Three blades from one of the propellers now form a Royal Air Force Association memorial in the town of Walton, dedicated to airmen who died in the 1939–45 War, and in particular to the crew of seven Canadians and one Briton of No 432 Squadron, who died when their Halifax, RG475, came to grief on the night of 5/6 March 1945, after returning from a bombing mission to Chemnitz.

The equipment the cadets had been able to muster for their operation was impressive: a breakdown truck for hauling the heavier pieces out of the shallow holes; and an open-backed truck, complete with hydraulic lifting arm, for removing items from the site. Here, perhaps, was a solution to the Hurricane recovery if such equipment could be made available. Certainly there was plenty of enthusiasm for this type of activity but, with a guarded thought, that in itself could be a hazard, especially if so many eager hands descended all at once on such a small compact site as the Hurricane's. Nevertheless, it was worth a tentative enquiry. The Commanding Officer was approached with the mention of a Hurricane lying just over the sea wall. The response was favourable but having just started work on the Halifax site there was much to be done there before anything new could be considered. Also, publicity about the ATC's activities in the local papers had already generated other potential sites for investigation.

The following weekend, as work on the Halifax was being consolidated, a small group came to have a look at the Hurricane site. The initial reaction did not appear very hopeful. Doubt was expressed about the distance of the site being some 150 yards from the nearest track for vehicles, together with the added complication of it being the other side of a tidal waterway. It would also involve a great deal of digging. Perhaps it could be considered when the Halifax job was complete.

Towards the end of March, the Halifax operation naturally began to wind down, with no further significant finds being made. The Hurricane project was mentioned again and, after a second visit to the site, it was agreed that an attempt to remove the remains could and would be made, once their exact extent had been established and the wreckage uncovered. Timing for the operation would be important. Spring tides flooding the area regularly at that time of year would make a prolonged dig most difficult and to spread it over a series of weekends, as at the Halifax site, would hardly be a practical proposition. Another difficulty would be the compact nature of the site, limiting the numbers able to dig at any one time. Nevertheless, a rapid dig would be needed, followed by immediate recovery in between two spring tide cycles.

A broad plan began to take shape. It was decided that a small group of two would dig daily to expose the wreckage, starting immediately the spring cycle began to wane. They would have a week to expose the wreckage so that recovery could take place the following weekend, during the neap tides. Along this part of the coast neap tides coincided with low water during the middle of the day. Just what was needed for the recovery, and the associated lower high tides should reduce the risk of flooding the excavation. Recovery was to be made by pulling the remains with a direct lead from the sea wall, 150 yards away, possibly using pneumatic lifting bags first to raise the structure from the bottom of the hole. The plan was thought feasible. Start date would be Monday 26 March, with recovery the following Sunday, 1 April. An omen? Time would tell, but the project was on.

Chapter Four
Digging

A week's leave from work was rapidly organised. For the other budding 'archaeologist', Tony O'Neil, no such arrangement was needed, he being between jobs at the time. Nine o'clock Monday morning saw an ageing Morris Minor gently wind its way through the streets of Walton, heading for the Naze. There would be no long walk along the cliff edge this time as arrangements had been made with the farmer to use his private track that, passing the distinctive landmark of the Naze Tower and the ruins of Walton Hall, lead almost all the way down to the marshland sea wall and to within just a quarter of a mile walk of the site. As a prerequisite to the dig, the farmer's permission had also been sought to actually go ahead with the project, as it was believed the marshland, even outside the sea wall network, was legally his. The presence of the wreckage was news to him but approval was freely given, (it was suspected), with a mixed feeling of indifference and incomprehension as to why anyone would want to bother, but, 'Yes, by all means, go ahead'.

The day was grey and overcast but looked free from rain. Ideal really, just fine enough to work in but not good enough to attract beach walkers and their undesirable curiosity. A major concern about the week long dig was the potential attraction of outside interference. What could be worse, after exposing the remains ready for recovery, than to find pieces going missing to the casual inquisitiveness of passers by? It would present a rather obvious target. The only real way to discourage such tampering would be by just being there on site. The intention therefore was, that once digging had begun, to arrive each morning before anyone else and to stay until dusk. Outside those times anyone purposely intent on interfering with the site would have the opportunity to succeed and, if so strongly motivated, it had to be assumed, that without an elaborate system of some sort, they would succeed anyway.

The pair left the car and set out over the sea wall towards their objective, armed with no more than a spade apiece and a couple of buckets for dealing with the inevitable drainage problems that would arise. It was hardly a sophisticated approach, but it was all that was available and, as time would show, both spades and buckets would prove ideal for delving into the maze of small crevasses present in such wreckage. The experience of the test digs at the end of the previous year had shown that to be the case. Some form of mechanical digger would have been useful for general excavation around the perimeter, but at the time it was not known for certain if other wreckage lay buried nearby and if struck by the digger's heavy scoop, unnecessary damage could be done. No such device was available anyway so there was little point in dwelling on the possibilities.

The need for protective clothing had been well-learned; in particular for the hands when working close to the jagged metal surfaces where the skin could be sliced open so easily but go unnoticed at the time in the cold murky water. The very fine particles that made up the mud also managed to penetrate every pore and line in the skin, the resulting black stain lingering for days afterwards. Lunch would also be much more appetizing without a blackened hand grasping the sandwiches! Thigh boots covered the lower part of the body but otherwise it was accepted that the mud would get absolutely everywhere and so the remaining clothes were to be considered as expendable by the week's end.

A bag each, containing lunch and an invaluable vacuum flask, completed the load, with last, but not least, a camera to record the activities. So armed, the pair arrived fully equipped at the site, with a somewhat daunting task ahead, as anyone foolish enough to have tried hand digging in such marshland would appreciate, but the feeling was amply tempered by the excitement of impending discovery.

Before digging commenced, the immediate shoreline was scoured for flat pieces of wood; anything that would provide a solid platform on which to stand whilst digging. Extracting one's feet from the mud in the test holes had been a major problem. While applying leverage to remove a shovel full of mud, most of the energy was directed through the shovel but the remainder forced the feet ever deeper into the sticky stuff. After collecting a respectable pile of driftwood, one final photograph was taken of the undisturbed site, from as near as possible the same angle as the first photographic record, taken some six years earlier.

A small pool of water left over from the last spring tide had gathered again by the wreckage. It was drained away with a bucket and by cutting a small drainage channel through the sand. The anticipated extent of the wreckage was marked out and a rough circle drawn beyond it, which would form the line of a protective wall. Its diameter measured about thirty feet; the scale of the operation could be seen clearly. The wall was to have two functions. It would absorb the mud removed from the hole, and also act as protection against the vagaries of the high tide, even though it was not anticipated that flooding would be a problem with the dig taking place during the more moderate neap tides. The timing relied on this, but surges in the tide level are a feature of this southern North Sea coast and given the right meterological conditions, tidal heights significantly different from those predicted are quite commonplace.

Where to start? Most logical was close to the exposed sections. A spade ceremoni-ously struck the sand to signify that the

A final view of the wreckage before full-scale excavation commenced. Taken from the same angle as the first photograph, six years earlier. The foreshore landscape is considerably different from that in the photograph on page 13.

dig had begun. It did not penetrate very far and when levered backwards was barely half-covered. That first mark in the sand looked a pitifully small dent in the marked out circle, and was yet a further reminder of the scale of the task at hand. Digging in earnest began to the seaward side of the exposed port wing spar. The thin surface layer of sand proved relatively easy to move. Once on the spade, all that was required was a swing round and throw in the general direction of the wall, but the marsh mud underneath was a different matter. Being a thick, sticky substance, the momentum of the swing was insufficient to break the mud's suction on the blade. Either one held on, with the disastrous consequence of having boots firmly anchored and ending up spread-eagled in the mud, or to let go of the spade and see it disappear into the wall, along with the mud; a squelchy walk was then needed to retrieve it. The solution was to laboriously move each clod twice, first from the hole to as far as could be reached and still be able to knock it off, then afterwards a second movement to carry it the rest of the way to the wall.

A trench about six feet wide was begun, parallel to the spar, starting furthest from the fuselage. It was not expected that any new extension to the spar framework would be found there, but it was possible that something broken off might be lying nearby. The nearer the digging got to the fuselage end of the spar, the more likely this might be. There was every reason to suspect that the rear fuselage had completely broken free from the rest of the aircraft. Could it still lie buried? It was also felt that the extra width would prove useful when digging got deeper. The overall plan was to try and dig under the wing roots on both sides of the fuselage, as one possible aid to recovery had been the suggestion of inflating lifting bags under the structure to prize it free of the mud.

The full outline of the spar was quite clear when the trench was still less than two feet deep. The wing's top surface skinning (now inverted) was truncated about six inches to a foot away from, and parallel to, the spar. All the signs were that it had been cut methodically and had not just sheered off in the crash. There was little sign of any underside skinning (now uppermost), except directly along the length of the spar itself. So far, nothing had been found in the trench extending any distance away from the spar. The end of the spar itself (and probably the whole wing) was verified by probing the surrounding ground towards the far end of the trench with a spade.

The trench soon became a quagmire, requiring frequent bailing out, and a line of boards was necessary to provide a solid working platform, as work progressed slowly in towards the fuselage. A little closer and some small fragments of wood began to come up with the mud; totally unidentifiable but, as they might form part of the aircraft's wooden structure, each piece was carefully collected for assessment later. Concern arose after a piece of wood had been spotted in the wall during a break from digging. Anxious that small pieces might be discarded inadvertently, each clod of mud was then broken open as it was added to the protective wall while working in this area, in an attempt to miss nothing.

The trench gradually progressed up to, and through the line of the fuselage, confirming the definite break. The traditional braced framework structure that made up the Hurricane fuselage was constructed around four main, steel tube longerons, giving a basic square section, extending from the cockpit to the rudder post. The break, in the upside-down lower two, was obvious from the exposed structure, and as the trench cut into where the fuselage should have been, there was still no sign of airframe sections down to a depth of two feet. Forcing a spade deep into the mud where the two 'upper' longerons should have been buried revealed nothing so, either the rear fuselage had detached and lay elsewhere (perhaps further seaward?), or it had been dismantled after the crash and removed entirely. More small pieces of wood emerged but still nothing that was readily identifiable. Digging progressed around the fuselage at what was estimated to be about the rear of the cockpit, then out towards the starboard wing root.

By that time, the light had begun to fade. It was agreed that a good start had been made but that it was time to call a halt for the day. A trench two to three feet deep and five to six feet wide had been dug about fifteen feet along the seaward edge of the wreckage, exposing the port wing rear spar along its entire length, the truncated rear fuselage and remains of the starboard wing root. Around this, in a wide semi-circle, was the start of the protective mud wall. The rear (seaward) line of the surviving wreckage had been delineated and it was concluded that all the surviving framework must lie landward of that. The progress was photographed, the small pieces gathered and two rather muddy individuals made their way back; stopping occasionally for a stretch, with a feeling of relief that the car was only a few hundred yards the other side of the sea wall — no mile-long walk back along the cliff edge this time. Sleep came very easily that night.

Day two began a little brighter and the forecast looked promising. At the site, things were exactly as they had been left and it was a relief to find that water seepage overnight had been relatively small. Drainage was quickly achieved by cutting a small gully along the previous day's trench, through the various depressions, so that all the water drained to the lowest hole which was then bailed out by bucket.

It was decided to concentrate this day's (Tuesday) effort on extending the trench to expose the full extent of the starboard wing. It was not expected to extend too far out from the fuselage, as the test hole of last year had shown its front spar to be broken and bent upwards, indicating that the remainder of the wing, in all probability, would have projected, originally, vertically up from the marsh and not far along it.

The protective wall half-way round the wreckage after the first day's digging.

A trench (right) is started behind the inverted port wing rear spar, and extends through the line of the fuselage.

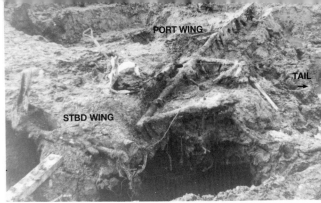

Excavating one of the two holes either side of the truncated starboard wing, second day.

Day three. Timber-lined steps are in place (upper left) as digging progresses around the wreckage to the landward side of the port wing.

From the previous day's work, it was appreciated that some effort could probably be saved by narrowing the overall width of the trench. However, there was a risk of it being too narrow to prevent easy access for any later deep digging that might be required, but it was felt that the previous work was perhaps somewhat excessive, considering the overall time scale for the operation; there would be a need to be more selective if the objective was to be met. Digging started in two places: by the rear of the starboard wing root where the previous day's work had ended, and six feet further landward, where the forward edge of the same wing was expected to lie, and very close to the site of the second test hole. The aim was to meet in the middle, underneath the wing.

It soon became clear that much was missing from this wing and what existed was badly broken. The maze of pieces, some loose but still connected to the framework, made digging more difficult as there was no logical structure pattern to follow. Digging had to go deeper to reach the upper wing surface, and soon the restrictions of the narrowed trench were being felt. Ingress of water was also more rapid, the main source of which could not be found but frequent bailing out soon became necessary. Not that the water made much difference to the actual digging but it certainly felt more comfortable standing in just mud, rather than a sloppy mixture. The petroleum aroma returned and the water developed an oily surface as digging progressed in towards the wing root, close to the fuselage where the wing fuel tank lay. It was there that the very first digging attempt had been made, with similar indications of remnant fuel. No doubt the fuel tank (designed to fit so snugly in between the two solid centre section spars) had disintegrated as the two main spars had fractured. The corresponding section in the other wing was intact and not badly deformed.

The two holes were each dug to a depth of about four feet, with a ridge only two feet deep left in between, at the outer limit of the wing, which was just sufficient to outline the limits of that part of the structure. Probing deeper with the spade suggested that no large framework lay further away from the wreckage out along the line of the starboard wing. It could only be assumed that, sometime soon after the crash, the remaining outer wing must have been removed, leaving just the vertical four-foot stump that, some twenty-five years later, had first attracted the boys' attention.

As the starboard wing section was so short, access to the up-turned fuselage was more immediate on that side, and it was tempting to carry on digging inward to make contact. It could be done relatively easy in the section by the rear spar, where the fuselage approached the surface but the landward hole by the front spar, even at four feet deep, only just reached the 'top' of the fuselage wing root. Effort turned to the vicinity of the starboard rear spar, close to the truncated fuselage section. A few more pieces of wood emerged and also some fragments of broken black bakelite, from what might once have been the battery. Probing in towards the fuselage side, the mud soon began to fall away in lumps, revealing a smooth surface behind — the fuselage panelling, but then great disappointment, as a touch with the spade showed it to be merely paper thin. It almost crumbled to the touch so there would be no hope of saving any of it. It looked as though fire had raged in the hole after impact and had severely burnt this part of the panelling. The nagging worry then was what other damage had the fire done? Certainly it had not affected the whole aircraft, as the test digs had brought up intact panels from the front part of the aircraft, with little sign of any such damage. The hope was that it might just be localised to this starboard side section, maybe a result of the proximity of the damaged starboard wing fuel tank?

The other side of the paper wall showed thick mud packed into what was once the fuselage interior. It would be a pains-taking job to remove it all, especially trying to manoeuvre the spade in between the mass of tubular framework and wiring, now starting to be exposed. A simple garden trowel would have been the ideal tool for such intricate work; a mental note was made to pack one for the next day.

In the meantime, digging continued, going deeper down the outside of the fuselage side until the 'top' main tubular steel longeron, which ran the full length of the fuselage, could be felt. Beyond that, the upper fuselage was entirely constructed of wood, which presumably lay crushed underneath. The corner of another silver coloured panel could just be seen below and, following the outline by hand, it went deeper under the water level, right at the bottom of the excavation. It was smooth, gently curved and appeared to be of a thicker gauge aluminium than that of the panels recovered previously. It was rigid and did not move when touched. It seemed to disappear under the wreckage and gave no obvious clues as to its identity.

The narrow hole was now becoming far too restrictive. It was necessary to almost duck down and under to work on the fuselage side, and there was little room to man-handle the spade. Working in such a position was most uncomfortable and it seemed sensible to stop excavation work and widen the trench at that point. Also, it would allow a little more light on the work and provide a much needed improvement in air flow. The marsh surface rose gently away from the hole so, even a little widening involved the movement of a considerable quantity of mud. It was frustrating to expend so much energy on such an apparently non-productive task, especially so late in the day when the limbs were already starting to tire. In the opposite direction, only a matter of inches away, lay new discoveries but common sense dictated that they must wait. To ease the load, a compromise was reached whereby only half the depth was widened, giving a stepped arrangement. This made access to and from the hole easier and, after laying boards on the steps, it gave the structure a certain professional touch.

As only one could work in the hole at a time, a start was made on the other side of the fuselage also, to fully expose the port wing surface, starting from the exposed rear spar, uncovered the previous day, and working landward. However, there was little time to make much of an impression as it was not long before the light began to fade and the second day of the dig drew to a close. Before the sun finally dipped beneath the horizon the site was cleared again of all the loose fragments uncovered. Wiped clear of excess mud, they were gathered up and packed, ready for removal. Photographs of the site were taken, then it was back over the sea wall to the waiting transport and the short trip home.

The third day (Wednesday) was forecast as another rain-free day; it began and stayed overcast but once more the early spring weather held. An early start again ensured that the wreckage was found just as it had been left the previous night and no tampering had taken place. The water level was quite high in the deeper holes created the previous day by the starboard wing, and some effort was needed to bale them out.

Digging commenced by nibbling away around all the exposed sections but eventually the main effort was concentrated on exposing the full extent of the port wing. Continuing the start made on the first day, progress was made in between the two wing spars, working in a general landward direction across the line of the wing, digging deeper all the time. The lack of any metallic contact was disconcerting, however towards the fuselage, what looked like a main rib could be followed as it gently dipped beneath the mud's surface. Further out from the fuselage there was nothing. Eventually, about three to four feet landward of the rear spar, and a good foot or two lower down, the front wing spar was reached, but the gap in between did not look encouraging; there was no flat skin surface to the wing and much of the internal structure was missing.

As the wing dipped deeper away from the sea so, as luck would have it, the general marsh surface rose slightly, once again increasing the volume of mud to be removed. All effort was directed in that area, in order to lower the general ground surface between the spars and beyond, ready to dig down and outline the full extent of the remaining wing structure. Landward of the front spar, digging would have to be deep, so the work was extended some way back to allow for the extra width. It meant the removal of a large quantity of mud, and was definitely one occasion where a digger would have been useful. Nothing was expected to be found, as it was most unlikely that any other fragments would lie in this forward area of the wreckage. The growing assumption was that the aircraft had sliced its way, nose first, into the marsh, leaving any pieces broken off lying behind, seaward, rather than in front.

While involved in this more mundane activity, one of the few visitors appeared, specifically stopping to chat and enquire as to what was going on. (Some degree of seclusion had been hoped for and being so close to the beach path more interruptions were expected than actually occurred.) The visitor turned out to be none other than the County Archaeologist, down from Chelmsford for the day to look over the general area where, earlier this century, the receding marshland had uncovered evidence of prehistoric remains. Our activities were a little too recent to interest him professionally but at least we were able to offer some help by pointing out where flint fragments and burnt mud patches of some antiquity could be found on the foreshore nearby. In its ceaseless drive landward, the sea had erased much of the earlier evidence he now sought, just as it now threatened the Hurricane wreckage. The interruption came as a welcome interlude; a chance to stretch the legs and have a legitimate excuse to take a break from the mundane digging.

The excavation landward of the front wing spar was soon beginning to take on sizeable proportions. To allow for the anticipated depth required there, digging had commenced a good five to six feet further out and was stepped in towards the wreckage. This gave easier access to the deep hole and also provided a degree of stability. To add a rather luxurious but really functional finish, each step was again lined with driftwood, collected from the beach. It provided a firm footing and prevented the steps from disappearing as clods of mud stuck to the boots of those vacating or entering the hole.

The inner edge of this part of the excavation was marked by the long, straight outline of the front wing spar and, as the general level was lowered, its shape became clearer. Close in to the fuselage, the spar appeared perfectly shaped and, wiping the mud away by hand, a clean but pimpled silver surface was revealed. On closer inspection, the rough texture was found to be blistered silver paint — more evidence of fire. In places where the blistering had broken, the blued steel of the spar itself showed through; still virtually as fresh as the day it had left the assembly line. The effects of corrosion were almost non-existent but, to prevent introducing contamination at this stage, a thin layer of mud was pressed back on to the front of the spar to cover it again. There was no point in exposing such surfaces to the elements until it was absolutely necessary, as it would only make them vulnerable to corrosion after over thirty years of natural protection. There-after, attempts were made to maintain a veneer of mud over the framework as a barrier, except where exposure was necessary for identification.

Working along the line of the front wing spar, the transition from a solid steel sheet structure to a compound aluminium spar could be seen. This transition marked the join between where the wing was an integral part of the fuselage framework and the outer wing, which was made from aluminium and started about three feet out from the fuselage sides. Of the four securing bolts (two on the front spar, two on the rear) which held the outer wing unit to the steel centre section, it looked as though all were intact on the wing; a welcome contrast to the more severely damaged starboard wing.

Moving outward, away from the fuselage, the line of the spar was followed. Nothing could be found of the curved leading edge, not even fragments of its outer skin, impacted against the spar. It was almost as if it had never existed. A little further on, the outline of something protruding from the front of the spar was seen. The remains of a three-inch diameter tube were uncovered. At one time it had obviously projected directly out from the spar but it now lay compressed against it, pointing skyward; it was the blast tube from one of the Hurricane's eight Browning machine guns. A stab at the mud just the other side of the spar, where the gun bay structure should have been, offered nothing, only mud. There was no gun, just the blast tube. Most likely the missing skin structure immediately above the gun bay area was the result of recovery activities during the war, tearing into the wing to remove all ordnance from the wreckage as it lay so close to the surface. Cutting equipment would have had to be used as the only designed access to the gun bay was through the removable panels on the upper wing surface, which now lay buried underneath. One other distorted tube was then uncovered but that was all. There should have been four.

Clearing further along the spar, it was not long before a break was felt, approximately where the outermost gun should have been, and about eight feet from the fuselage. Beyond the four gun ports in the outer wing, the spar changed from a more solid, aluminium, girder style to a lighter, composite, braced structure, like that of the exposed rear spar. The break felt final with nothing further on and, looking up from the hole, this coincided with the extent of the rear spar, now fully exposed and standing proud of the general mud level. Here the wing structure terminated.

Digging began next underneath that front spar; not along its entire length but, initially, close in to the fuselage, in an effort to tunnel right under the wing at that point and create a hollow beneath the more rigid wing root structure. This, it was hoped, would be able to take the strain if inflation bags were used underneath to lift the whole structure clear of the mud's suction. The added depth soon began to tell as it became even harder, not so much to dig, but to remove the mud from the hole. It had to be slung shoulder-high, knocked off the spade on one of the wooden steps then lifted again from there to form the wall. Progress was slow, to say the least.

By the end of the day, although no individual pieces had been recovered and only the front spar of the port wing exposed, quite a large quantity of mud had been shifted, as was reflected in the growth of the wall. It now enclosed three-quarters of the site, from the original starboard wing stub, seaward across the line of the rear fuselage, around the port wing and back to the aircraft's centreline, beneath which should lie the Merlin engine.

That evening, leaving the site and looking back, it no longer appeared something that might attract attention, it was a full-scale structure of considerable size and purpose; more reason to ensure being last on the scene at night and first back in the morning.

Still the weather held. The fourth day (Thursday) started with a clear sky and bright sunlight. Strangely, as the day would show, this type of weather did not provide the best working conditions. It was pleasant enough but the low winter sun cast strong shadows in the hole, producing starkly contrasting areas of light and shade. With one's head in the sunlight it was the difficult to adjust one's vision to the gloom of the area being attacked, with the spade so deep in shadow.

Several areas were earmarked for attention, mainly to consolidate earlier, unfinished sections. Some tidying up was done around the previous day's work by the port wing front spar, and also extended a little further towards where the forward fuselage and engine lay. However, the main effort of the day went into deepening the area behind (seaward) the rear spar of the port wing, where work had first begun on the morning of the first day. Then, it was intended to tunnel close in beside the fuselage, with the aim of meeting up with the previous day's excavations from the other side of the wing.

There were some welcome distractions. In lowering the mud level close in to the fuselage, the outline of a panel corner began to emerge. It was vertical, remained firm, even when quite well exposed, and gave every indication of being a substantial section. A slight curve was evident as it went deeper and a wooden frame lined the rear inside edge. It was undoubtedly one of the main fuselage side panels, intact and strong this time with no evidence of fire damage so far; hopefully, a good sign for that (port) side of the aircraft. Digging gradually exposed more, still in good condition and with no signs of impact damage. Then a hole appeared. Wiping the mud clear by hand its outline could be felt. It had smooth edges and was about six inches square, with its sides at a slight angle to the vertical edge of the panel that had been followed to depth. It proved to be one of the foot steps, used by the pilot to climb into his machine; the last one he would use before gripping the windscreen and opened canopy top, and hauling himself up over into the narrow cockpit.

Another six inches deeper and the smooth firm surface of the panel came to an abrupt end, only mud being felt beneath. It was at a similar depth to that reached on the other side of the fuselage on the second day and virtually confirmed the, not unexpected, total obliteration of the upper fuselage's wooden structure, near the cockpit. The panel began to ease away from its mud seal as the lowest edge was exposed and then began to lean into the hole under its own weight. Behind, was a solid wall of stiff mud, just like on the starboard side. What items lay suspended in the solid mass in between? Again, it was tempting to burrow straight away into it with the trowel and find out, but to be done properly would be an intricate job, very time-consuming and the main objective had to be kept in mind: to uncover the full extent of the wreckage before the weekend.

The panel was still connected to part of the fuselage, somewhere beneath the wing, and it began to get in the way as it hung down into the already cramped hole. It was temporarily tied back with a length of the aircraft's own wiring, while tunnelling began in earnest under the wing, following along the line of the panel. When well underneath and having scraped gently at the mud against the panel it began to spring free again, only this time revealing some jagged edges. Soon the outline of the entire panel became clear and it fell away from the mud. Releasing the securing wire, and giving a gentle tug the panel was pulled clear, to be examined with some excitement. There were three straight edges, one of which was slightly buckled but the fourth and shortest (the furthest under the wing) was far from straight. It was not bent but had a moth-eaten appearance, gradually giving way to an irregular edge. Fire damage, again. The external surface showed signs of green paint as the mud was wiped off, and again, no evidence of corrosion. The inside was lined with strengthening ribs of 'top hat' sections, all intact and still fulfilling their function. The panel, almost three feet long by about two feet deep, was put to one side while digging continued.

Breakthrough under the wing was eventually achieved, after much effort, and the tunnel then gradually enlarged to about three feet square; again the laborious process of removing and disposing of the mud necessitated the double action of dragging spadefuls of mud back out and then lifting them clear of the hole. At the roof of the tunnel should have been the upper wing surface, but no clear, smooth structure could be felt. In places it was buckled but in others — nothing, just soft mud. Obviously, there was some damage to that part of the wing, but what exactly would have to wait until the aircraft was the right way up. The trowel had to be employed to work close in to the wreckage but even using that, tucked up inside the tunnel, proved a difficult task. Enough of a tunnel was produced to take a lifting bag, any trimmings necessary being left to the day of the lift as it was not certain, even at this stage, if such devices would be needed to free the structure from the mud. It all depended on what was finally achieved and eventually found at the end of the week's dig but basic preparations had to be made, just in case. The excavation was not progressed underneath the remaining outer part of the wing, as it was felt that suction would not be a problem there, with effectively only two thin spars forming the wing and no significant structure in between where the gun bay should have been.

Before tunnelling had begun, and in order to give better access, the general area behind the wing root had been cleared. Part of this had now been filled in again with material dragged from the tunnel during excavation. With time getting on, instead of starting afresh in a different area, it was decided to devote the rest of the day's activities to clearing this out again and joining up both sides of the rear fuselage to the same level. That would then leave two clear days to concentrate on the final area above and around the engine.

As the surface was lowered, boards had to be put down to give a firm footing as, by then, the area was awash with sloppy mud, having been trodden over continuously during the day. When back down to the earlier level, the boards were laid as permanent fixtures to form a solid walk-way. Careful nibbling then began at what had been left as a ridge, lying where the line of the fuselage should have been, about four feet behind the cockpit. A gentle approach was made, remembering the wood fragments found in that vicinity on the first day. A heavy thrust with a spade could easily destroy pieces left reasonably intact by the crash. If the aircraft had sliced nose first into the mud then it would be there that any trail of debris from the upper wooden structure should lie.

Fragments of wood did begin to emerge. Some larger chunks, with no obvious shape, could easily have been bits of driftwood thrown into the hole after impact, but all the pieces found were put to one side for cleaning and sorting out later, just in case. Other pieces were flat and looked as though they were made of plywood. Machined edges and holes could be made out, and on some a few pieces of electrical apparatus, wires and bakelite fragments were still attached. Nothing was identifiable at the time but it was hoped that later cleaning might show that some of the pieces joined together. Nearer the surface, pockets of sand were mixed with the mud. Wood found there was badly worn, soft to the touch and oozed water. Deeper, in the pure marsh mud, preservation had been much better, leaving the wood firm and with edges still sharp. Most pieces still retained significant traces of paint. Silver, green and grey colours were all much in evidence, with some of the green blending into a surprisingly bright turquoise shade in places. Most of the fragments were small and all were found localised to this particular area, behind the broken fuselage. After initial inspection, the wood recovered was smeared with mud in the hope of preventing rapid drying and subsequent distortion. How it would adapt to its new environment was not known, but slow drying was thought a sensible precaution.

Working a little further away from the fuselage section, at the outer edge of the hole, a spade struck something solid. Not wood this time but hard and producing a metallic ring. Careful tunnelling with a trowel revealed the outline of a metal frame. There were some straight edges, but overall it had an irregular shape. Then glass fragments appeared. Excavation of the mud from above revealed what could only have been the aircraft's armoured windscreen, shattered but intact. An estimate at the time was that it lay in line with, but about eight feet back from its proper position on the aircraft. That, together with the wood recovered, added weight to earlier speculation that the aircraft had sliced into the mud at a shallow angle, nose first and upside down. Retrieving the windscreen intact presented quite a problem; a gentle nudge at the metal surround showed the whole structure to be very fragile. Any attempt to lift it bodily from the mud meant it would undoubtedly disintegrate into thousands of tiny glass shards. The solution was a compromise, part solved there and then, part left for later inspiration. A large, flat section of plywood was forced into the mud just under the windscreen. The surrounding mud was then cleared from the sides to expose the board, with the windscreen left perched on a thin cushion of mud, supported on the board. With a little persuasion the board was lifted free, leaving the final problem of prizing the glass from its bed of mud until later.

In the hope of other such finds, digging continued further away from the main wreckage, along the line of where the fuselage should have been. It was not long before the character of the mud changed to a firmer variety that looked distinctly undisturbed. The trail had gone cold. Attention returned to nearer the broken rear fuselage framework. Quite close in, where the girder-like rear wing spar passed through the fuselage, sand was in evidence again, near the surface. There, pockets of small, delicate, silver-coloured tubing were picked out with the trowel. Badly broken, twisted and weakened, presumably by fire, they were parts of the tubular, honeycombed structure that once made up the oil cooler (the large bulbous feature that lies slung under the Hurricane's centreline, just behind the undercarriage, which gave the aircraft its distinctive silhouette). Directly above the wing spar was a small, curved sheet of aluminium, about eighteen inches square which was all that remained of that otherwise distinctive feature. In fact, that was one of the two original pieces spotted projecting above the marsh surface in the early sixties; the other being the much larger remains of the front starboard wing spar. The purpose of this otherwise insignificant curved structure was now apparent.

With the major part of the day spent, the remaining time was used scratching away with trowels at the rear stub of the fuselage, made more difficult by the long, heavy shadows cast by the gently sinking sun. Few further loose items were found but some hollowing out of the complex and intricate structure was achieved. It all helped to lighten the load that much more. However, for that area in particular, providing that leaving the mud packing did not create too much of a weight penalty, it was best left in situ and removed in better working conditions, after recovery. Of the small pieces to emerge then were more

The armoured windscreen.

fragments of thick, flat bakelite from the battery, and a packet of lead plates, sandwiched between thin plywood dividers from one of its cells. A couple of the plastic top-up stoppers were also collected, still reasonably intact.

The end of the day's work showed a clear area to the required depth, around three quarters of the wreckage. In that part, only tunnelling beneath and into the wreckage remained outstanding, to help reduce suction and further lighten the load. The circular protecting wall was complete in outline, save one final section which would be the major area of work for the final two days. This was directly above where the engine should lie, and immediately on the aircraft's starboard side where the second test hole had been dug, three months earlier. Packing up took a little longer than usual with a couple of trips to the car carrying the large fuselage panel, fragments of wood and, very carefully, the rather weighty windscreen tray. Darkness had fallen by the time everything had been packed into the back of the old Morris Minor. With headlights piercing the gloom, a passage was carefully woven between the pot-holes of the rough lane leading back to the main road, ever mindful that one sudden jolt could easily be the end of the delicate glass package that hopefully might one day be restored again to something resembling a windscreen.

That evening, closer inspection was made of the selection of wood brought back. Two larger, wedge-shaped pieces drew immediate attention as they both had large fragments of canvas clinging to one face. These, the largest intact pieces of wood recovered, later proved to be from just underneath the cockpit windscreen, on either side of the instrument panel. No effort was made to clean the mud completely from the larger pieces, as previous experience had shown how difficult the stubborn stuff could be; it was best left until partly dry, then levered off in lumps. Trying to wash off the sticky substance would have taken volumes of water and no small amount of scrubbing. The latter would very likely damage the delicate wood surface and the excess of water might unnecessarily soak the wood which, for the most part, appeared surprisingly dry and firm, encased in its cover of marsh mud. Only those parts found in pockets of sand nearer the surface showed any real degree of sponginess, together with the distinctive texture of wet rot in wood.

Inquisitiveness caused a few of the smaller pieces to be selected for a quick wash and careful scrub. A toothbrush proved the ideal instrument and left no marks. Using water sparingly, detail began to show through. Drying was achieved by dabbing with a cloth which, when complete, showed the items to be in a remarkably fine state of preservation. One delicate piece, made of very thin plywood and quarter-inch square blocks, was still completely coated in dark green gloss paint, with splinter breaks in the wood looking as fresh as if they had been made the day before. A check on the structural diagram showed it to be one of the composite junction pieces from the curved ribs, on the top of the rear fuselage. It was one of only two small sections found from that part of the aircraft's intricate carpentry. Not so remarkable, but just as interesting, were a couple of one half by one inch section blocks of wood. Four inches long and beveled at each end they were not broken but each was curiously date-stamped in the same style as found on date stamps in old library books. Still clearly legible were: '16 Feb 1940' and '14 Sep 1939'.

Another temptation was to pick away some of the mud from the windscreen to check on the damage. Around the edges, the glass was still lying perfectly in place but totally shattered. The fractures all pointed in towards the centre where there was no distinct pattern, just a complex mosaic of granulated glass and mud. Any attempt to wash the surface would have disturbed the delicate structure and was not considered at that time, tempting though it was to get a clearer view. It would certainly be a difficult process just to separate glass from mud, even when the mud had dried; but there was the added problem of having to sort out the five different layers, each of varying thickness. However, to make the job easier, it was hoped to find sandwiched between each layer of glass the thin layers of 'plastic' sheet which helped make up the armoured property of the windscreen. Reassembling this item looked a very doubtful proposition, with all five layers being shattered and giving the whole structure a flexibility it was certainly not designed to have. It was most definitely a task that could and would be left to one side until a later date.

The fifth (Friday) morning and back to the mundane digging — pure volume being required again to lower the mud level in the remaining uncleared section, directly above where the Merlin engine was expected to lie. The first three to four feet would be almost a repeat of those done a few months earlier, except that there would be no demoralising infill afterwards. Re-digging the loosely com-pacted material close in to the wreckage proved relatively easy but further away, in the, as yet, undisturbed mud, the going got more difficult. Digging was concentrated, initially, close in to the wing spars where the work was easier and familiar items should come to light first.

As the two diagonal bracing tubes for the engine bearers came into view, about three feet down, the limit of the straightforward work was reached. From then on, digging would be concentrated in and around the various framework members, but first the upper layer had to be expanded out to the full extent of the engine's anticipated position — in all an area about seven feet long, from wing spar to propeller tip, by at least three feet wide. The hope was that the engine had not sheared off during impact and projected itself further into the marsh, as the greater surface area of the wings had retarded the downward drive of the remaining airframe. Certainly something solid had been felt when probing with a spade during the test digs, but there was nothing to confirm that it was the engine. Extending the excavation further 'landward', to leave the required seven feet clear from the wings, was done both from above and from within the hole, following the line of the engine bearer bracing struts. This took the best part of the morning and continued well into the afternoon, working slowly deeper all the time as contact was maintained with the metal framework.

So far, the excavated mud had been piled into the last remaining gap in the encircling wall but it gradually became apparent that the wall, at that point, had been started too close to the projected site of the engine. The further from the wing spar, the deeper the framework lay and with the excavation work only four feet out from the spar, the outer edge was already close to vertical, and almost immediately above it was the base of the wall, looking dangerously steep. It had to be moved further back and progress was halted while the unwelcome task was undertaken. Shifting the mud by hand was difficult enough, to do it twice was really quite frustrating. It was late in the day before attention returned to the base of the, by then, widened hole, although the full seven-foot width had still not been achieved completely.

Earlier, some sections of aluminium had started to show through the base of the hole, they needed to be dealt with next, as they lay where standing room was required for moving back the cliff wall. The solid, tubular steel framework had, at first, been able to provide a useful platform on which to stand, having been relieved of its delicate covering of panels during the test digging, but moving further landward other panelling had come into view which could not be stood on without the risk of damaging it. Unfortunately, it was not simply a case of lifting them clear of the mud, as some went much deeper and would have to be dug free as well.

The first to show had a long curved edge, bent back on itself into a horseshoe shape. This configuration then disappeared deep into the mud, on the starboard side of the engine bearer framework. It took a while to free, not from any other framework, just the gripping suction of the mud. Around the panel's edges were the familiar quick release 'Fairy' fasteners, showing it to be a detachable panel. There was no obvious fire damage but it was badly crumpled. It proved to be the large, starboard side, engine cowling panel, bent double and presumably displaced from the airframe by the impact, just like its counterpart from the port side, recovered the previous December. Clearing the mud away, dark green paint was much in evidence. It had been well-preserved, despite its deformation.

Along one edge ran a length of square section aluminium tube — the remains of part of the supporting framework. In construction, the strength of the Hurricane's fuselage came from the zig-zag pattern of steel and aluminium tubes, set between four main steel longerons and providing an overall square section, which was braced with adjustable stainless steel straps, held in tension. Around this main load bearing structural frame a minor, lightweight frame provided the base for the final, smooth aerodynamic shape. Forward of the cockpit it was of square section aluminium tubing to support aluminium panels, and aft an arrangement of wooden ribs and stringers, over which was stretched a canvas cover. Small sections of the secondary, aluminium structure had been

Digging down to the engine. Some concertinaed panels overlie the inverted engine bearers. Lower centre — the outline of the folded starboard engine cowling panel.

Day five and the engine bearers are exposed. On top of them (lower left) lies the engine cowling 'belly' panel and, upper right, the truncated 'zig-zag' fuselage framework.

recovered during the first test dig, and here was another two-foot length still attached to its panel.

A little further down lay a small triangular shaped piece; flat with a straight base, the other edges curved symmetrically about the apex. It came away quite easily but, once free of the mud and held to the light, it was seen to be riddled with tiny holes. Fire damage again, but at least it was intact. The curves were very distinctive and it was recognised immediately as the small infill section, usually positioned between the two retracted undercarriage wheels, just behind the carburretor intake. It was strange that it should be found lying buried so far forward of where it had fitted on to the aircraft.

When lifted clear, a gentle prod revealed another panel, lying a few inches lower down. Lying flat, it was much larger than the previous one, and disappeared under the, then cliff-like, outer edge of the hole. It would not budge and there was no doubt that it would not do so until the edge of the hole was pushed further back. While one continued cutting back from above, the other continued deepening the hole beside and in between the framework then exposed. Both bracing struts from the wings to the main engine bearers were now clear and, criss-crossing betwen them, the adjustable bracing straps could be felt, no longer under tension, of course. They were a nuisance really, interfering with direct access to where the carburretor should like. Following the two side braces forward of the aircraft, they met at either end of a short crosspiece, which lay parallel to the wing spar, about two-and-a-half feet further forward, towards the nose. Two struts then continued forward from the cross-piece, and disappeared under the large panel, still held firm in the mud (see photo on page 53). Except for the panel, all the engine support structure so far uncovered had been seen before, as individual pieces, and under slightly different circumstances during the test digging. Now it was all laid bare the relationship between each piece could clearly be seen.

Effectively, the hole was now complete all the way round, when viewed from the beach above. The outlines of the wing stubs, truncated rear fuselage, and forward engine area could be made out without difficulty. One more day was left to clear the remaining mud from around the engine area. Before departing mud was smeared over as many parts, uncovered that day, as possible. All the steel tubing had been found to be free of rust and much original paintwork had been seen. For over thirty years the metal had been encapsulated in a totally air-free environment; uncovered, oxidation would begin its destructive work in earnest, unless protective measures were taken.

The trek back to the car was done laden with the spoils of the day's work — large panels and more fragments of tubing that once formed the secondary framework around the nose of the aircraft. Later, at home, a hurried attempt was made at cleaning the port engine panel, in the hope of finding more identifi-cation markings similar to the controversial ones found on the starboard panel. None could be found around the same location, by the starting handle access and, being bent in two, the inner section could not be studied properly. (It was many years later before similar numbers were eventually found on that particu-lar panel, stamped in a different style, on the bottom edge reinforcing rim.)

An early start was made on the sixth day (Saturday). There was full cloud cover but, once again, thankfully no rain. For the time of year, the weather certainly had been at its best. An icy blast from the east, so common on this coast, would have been uncomfortable but bearable, protected by the hollow of the excavation. However, just a couple of days' rain would have put the whole programme in jeopardy. Once started, we were committed as the lift had to take place the following weekend, before the next spring tides. Already the level of the high tides was increasing towards the full spring cycle and, at its peak, the loose mud wall would be the only protection against its flooding the excavation. The wall's effectiveness had not been tested yet, and it was hoped it never would be.

Again, all effort went into the forward fuselage sections around the engine. To begin with the sheer edge to the hole was carefully carved back. It was only about five feet deep, but lay at a dangerously steep angle for that type of material. Being the last full day of digging, there was no time for the relative luxuries of gently sloping or stepped sides and planking. All effort had to go directly into exposing the engine. The first job was to free the large panel exposed the previous day. Its form became clearer as the sheer edge of the hole was eased back to reveal a partially moth-eaten surface yet again — more fire damage, but fortunately not severe enough to have destroyed the internal strength and it was quite rigid when finally dragged free. About three-and-a-half by two-and-a-half feet, it was the engine cowling belly panel. Despite fire damage, a whitish paint was still evident over much of its muddy exterior.

As an increasing amount of the framework supporting the engine was exposed, more panelling began to appear on the aircraft's port side, near the front spar of the port wing. One piece lay hard up against the engine bearers and at right angles to the wing spar, under which it disappeared. It was bent but, again, looked intact. Following it beneath the wing meant squeezing into the tunnel, carved out a couple of days previously. After removing only a few inches of mud from inside the tunnel, the continuation of the panel and another long thin one, could be seen going right under the wing. With a little effort they both fell away quite easily, bringing with them further remains of the secondary tubular framework. Cleared of most of their mud coating, these pieces were in a variety of conditions: strong, intact, twisted, fragile, and burnt. The sections belonged to the wing root fairing and remaining port side fuselage panels. There was still no obvious pattern to the fire damage; it appeared to be scattered throughout various parts of the wreckage, not concentrated in just one area. All that could be hoped, was that perhaps re-assembly, following recovery, would reveal something clearer.

Both spade and trowel were employed to clear away the mud from around and between the complex maze of spars that formed the engine support. In the process, fragments of laminated wood were uncovered, most with violently splintered ends, and some coated with a black, plastic-like material. They were pieces of the three-bladed wooden 'Rotol' propeller, which had obviously shattered as it tried to wind its way into the mud. One small piece, from the tip of a blade, still retained a clear section of yellow banding. Another, much larger piece projected vertically from the mud, was firm and appeared to go deeper.

Clearing out the section between the two substantial side braces and the front wing spar gave the first indication of the engine's presence. Pipes of varying diameter, both solid tube and a flexible corrugated type started to show and then

The engine bearer assembly uncovered. Lower left — blast tubes for the Browning machine guns project through the inverted port wing front spar.

a rather large lump of what could only be a machinery casting of some sort, not framework. As the mud was cleared, the outline of two enormous vacant eyes stared back — the twin, six-inch diameter intakes of the Merlin's 'SU' carburretor. It was a welcome sight, but its presence made the removal of mud from around the framework even more awkward. As its full shape emerged, it brought a disappointment: It could be moved; only a little, but sufficient to imply that the engine beneath was not completely intact.

The first positive sighting of the engine proper came from excavating to one side, rather than directly through the engine bearer framework. That was despite the solid surface of what should have been the oil sump being felt, but not seen, through the maze of supporting framework pieces. To the side, where digging was more straightforward, a curved shape appeared, metallic and having a hollow ring — the exhaust manifold, still in its straight line along the length of the engine. Anxious feeling for its inner edge beneath the mud revealed that there was no clear break but a solid mass of what could only be the cylinder block casing.

With most of the engine bearer framework clear of mud, and with the sump of the inverted Merlin starting to show, the hole was at a depth of about six feet. The height of the parapet around the edge of the almost sheer sided wall accentuated the depth, making it seem almost twice that amount. At that depth, the general character of the mud changed from a thick, sticky grey to a much drier, light brown, more compact clay. Stabbing the spade into the clay produced little direct penetration but caused the clay to flake and crumble. It looked as though most of the engine lay buried under this harder material. Such a change in the mud's consistency had not been anticipated and progress began to suffer.

With time limited, the size of the excavation was narrowed considerably to just the immediate vicinity of the engine and chipping away at the hard mud around the edge of the engine was all that could be attempted in the time remaining.

By the end of the day, all the supporting framework and engine sump were clear, together with the starboard side of the engine casing, down to the exhaust manifold. The same had not been achieved on the engine's port side, as it appeared to lie slightly canted over thus hiding the port side even deeper. The carburretor intakes were now considerably exposed and, although a clear break could not be seen, their free movement was quite pronounced. However, the carburretor was still positioned correctly in the airframe and so far that still looked like the only damage the engine had sustained. Despite earlier fears, the engine did appear to be intact and, in part, was still attached to the airframe. On wiping the smooth sump casing, a solid coating of black paint was clearly visible; it looked well-preserved. At the edge of the hole, a three-foot length of propeller blade had been uncovered. It could not be moved and appeared to be still attached to what, a little deeper in the clay, should be the propeller hub.

The day was drawing to a close and, reflecting on the week's activities, for the time available all that could have been done, had been done. The main objective had been achieved: to expose the full extent of the wreckage. Hopes rose for the next day's big lift.

The engine bearer assembly stripped of its panels, underneath which lay the Rolls-Royce Merlin engine. The break in the starboard wing front spar can be seen top right. The folded undercarriage fairings follow the line of the front spar.

Chapter 5
Recovery

The following morning the weather still held. A light wind was still edged with the chill of winter. Cloud cover was complete but, most importantly, there was no rain and the forecast looked good.

Twenty miles away, in Colchester, an earlier than normal start was made that Sunday morning with preparations for the day's forthcoming activities. Dick Hipkin, a mechanic by trade and with a wealth of experience in the vehicle recovery business, set off to collect the team's breakdown vehicle and its associated recovery gear. He had experienced this rather different type of recovery work a few weeks earlier, retrieving the four Bristol Hercules engines from the nearby crash site of the Halifax bomber, RG475. Sunday morning's job was to be somewhat different. In the Halifax's case, the vehicles were driven over firm ground, right up to the excavation site and, with the loads already at ground level, the task was achieved with little difficulty. In the Hurricane's case, the closest access for vehicles was one hundred and fifty yards away, at the northern end of the new Tamarisk wall, requiring extra wire and joining shackles to ensure that the large distance could be covered. The massive earthen structure of the wall itself also provided another obstacle to be overcome.

Elsewhere, in the surrounding district, many a household was stirring earlier than normal. Packed lunches were prepared, warm clothing, rubber boots, spade, and the inevitable camera were gathered; all was ready. Groups began to arrive at the natural assembly point at the end of Hall Farm Lane. Passing through the town of Walton the road gradually narrowed until by the time it reached Walton Hall Farm it was only a single carriageway. Beyond the private farmyard, the surface changed to a single-lane dirt track, lined with mature and substantial hedgerows. Down a definite slope to the level of the reclaimed marsh and a hundred yards short of the new Tamarisk wall it disappeared into a maze of gullies, gouged out by the comings and goings of farm machinery. This being no place to test the suspension of the average family saloon, the cars were left at the end of the lane and the remaining gap was crossed on foot.

The original pair had reached the marsh early, as they had done for the previous six days. Again, there were no signs of tampering overnight. The lack of publicity had worked well, but that was about to change. Figures began to appear over the top of the sea wall. They paused, scanning the marshes for signs of activity then, spotting the excavation's parapet, they began the short walk along the sea wall to the start of the beach ridge and down onto the marsh. These were the first dozen or so volunteers who were to be actively involved in the final digging and recovery operation. Their common link was the Colchester Air Training Corps, either as adult members, associates or enthusiastic friends. Cadets were also present, as were a few other local aircraft enthusiasts who, having heard what was going on, were drawn like magnets. As the day wore on, a steady stream of sightseers came and went, many being friends and relatives of the group; for most, the site became the objective of the traditional Sunday afternoon stroll.

Very little water had collected in the lower hollows of the excavation overnight and was soon baled out. Soon, half-a-dozen spades were at work, prizing as much mud away from the wreckage as possible to try and lighten the load, while the recovery gear was being manoeuvred into position. The tunnel dug under the port wing was not used for the inflation bags, after all; it was decided, first to attempt a direct pull with the breakdown truck from the landward side of the sea wall. The tunnelling had not been in vain though, as it had eased the effect of suction over a considerable surface area on the fuselage side and wing root. Suction on the remaining outer section of that wing was to be negligible because of the lack of structure present in the gunbay area. Being unaware of the latter, one of the volunteers started clearing out the sand and mud between the outer ends of the two wing spars and, to everyone's surprise, uncovered coils of .303 ammunition less than a foot down. Darkened by the mud, it was still linked firmly together and, apparently, in very good condition. Although the gunbay had been emptied of its armament, something had obviously been overlooked during the wartime recovery efforts. Very early on in the day, the find provided a useful reminder to all assembled of the potential dangers associated with the kind of activity in which they were involved.

Meanwhile, the breakdown lorry was taking up position. Driven along the narrow maintenance track, just behind the wall, it stopped at the closest point to the excavation site, where the new Tamarisk wall joined onto the old sea wall network, still a hundred and fifty yards short of the target. The earthen walls, providing protection against flooding, rose to a considerable height and at the Naze, as with many vulnerable areas along the Essex coast, they had been raised even further and strengthened, following the disastrous floods of 1953. The crest

A reminder of the potential hazards in this type of activity — the unexpected discovery of over 100 rounds of linked .303 ammunition, found near the Hurricane's port wing.

Laying out the wire hawser. A view of the marsh's terrain from the towing position at the crest of the sea wall.

was well above the height of the breakdown lorry's small crane jib and, in order to clear the crest, the lorry had to be backed up the landward slope of the wall, until the top of the jib had an unrestricted line of pull over the top. Positioning the lorry just so was made more difficult by the line of the sea wall not lying directly across the direction of pull; if it had, the lorry could have reversed directly up the slope. Instead, the lorry had to be aligned at an angle, which meant that it leaned to one side on the sea wall slope. If the winch drum, the top of the jib, and the target were not in correct alignment, there was a risk, that when tension came on the wire the load could slip off the jib or, worse, topple the lorry. The positioning had to be just right.

When the lorry was in position, the wire was payed out. Between the hole and the lorry lay one of the marshland's natural water courses, Cormorant Creek, empty of water at the time because the tide was low, but its twenty-yard width was lined with a deep carpet of uninviting, sloppy mud. Paying out the wire across there presented a few difficulties. Not only did the line of pull cut the creek at an angle, increasing the span to be crossed, but it did so at a junction in the creek. The wire was too short to go around the head of the creek, so it had to be man-handled across, volunteers for the job performing a variety of unrehearsed balancing acts on sections of driftwood thrown onto the creek's bed for footholds. At the end of the long wire was a length of chain which was laid diagonally across to the far side of the wreckage and connected around the rear spar of the port wing, which was considered a reasonable strong point for the pull. The aim initially was to roll the wreckage over itself, to where it would lie the right way up against the edge of the hole, half in and half out. A further pull would then slide it up the slope and completely clear of the hole. That was the theory.

When all was secure, personnel were ushered clear of the wreckage and the slack in the wire was taken up. Slowly, the steel hawser slithered into a straight line, catching every now and then on a clump of marsh grass, then whipping free as the wire continued to straighten. As more strain was taken, it began to lift clear of the surface in places. The chain around the spar creaked as the grip tightened, but the framework did not move. The wire went slack as an adjustment was made at the vehicle end, then another try. As the strain was taken up again, there was a slight quiver from the spar — but that was all.

A re-think was needed. The lead was extremely long, but nothing could be done about that. The angle of pull was not ideal but thought the best to give the maximum purchase. Examining the wreckage more closely, the framework appeared still to be connected to the engine and with that still half-buried in the hard, brown clay it was thought that could be acting as an enormous anchor for the whole structure. Also: could the overall weight be further reduced? The hollow interior of the airframe was still largely full of the mud that had, for years, filtered into every nook and cranny. Trying to scrape it away from the intricate internal structure the previous week had proved a very slow and difficult process, and much had been left intact, while effort was concentrated on the more important aspects of exposing the external limits and reducing suction.

A small band, armed with spades and trowels, got to work. Digging further down each side of the engine proved again, very difficult but, eventually, all four engine supports were uncovered. The two furthest from the recovery vehicle, on the inverted engine's port side, were clear of the engine bearers and detached. On the starboard side, they touched and appeared still to be connected. The supporting framework on the starboard side had been broken in a number of places by the force of impact, leaving only a couple of sections connected directly to the rest of the airframe. It was thought there should not be too much resistance in twisting the frame free, but it would leave the engine still in the hole, together with part of the starboard engine bearer. However, it looked as though there was no other way, and that recovery would have to be in two sections.

In the meantime, mud was being coaxed out of every access possible. Two highly productive sources were the wheel well and around the rear part of the fuselage, where access for three or four diggers was possible, even if they could remove only a trowel full each at a time. During the previous week's dig, once the existence of the retracted undercarriage legs had been confirmed, a layer of mud had been left covering them to deter possible identification when the site was unmanned. Work had then been concentrated underneath the aircraft, rather than on top. The true size of the internal space had not been appreciated. It was then attacked with vigour. In the centre, where the two wheels should have almost met, there was only mud. There were no wheels or tyres; in their place was a large amount of white crystalline powder, around each stub axle — the sure sign of corroded magnesium alloy. The wheel drums were non-existent and there was absolutely no sign of tyre rubber. All that lay suspended on the stub axles were the brake drums, shoes and pneumatic air sacks, in a large pocket of corroded magnesium. Whatever had caused the destruction of the magnesium alloy wheel hubs had failed to affect the surrounding structure because the interior floor of the wheel well was still strong and intact. Tunnelling either side of the two substantial shock absorbers brought out a rewarding volume of undesirable weight.

The time had come for another try. Standing back, the remains looked decidedly leaner, so much so that the, by then, cavernous wheel well made the structure appear worryingly fragile. The strain was taken again and there was a sign of movement; the rear spar lifted, a little. A quick moment of concern; it might be breaking off. The remaining structure was scanned. No! There was also movement from the front spar, and the rear fuselage! Slowly, the port wing rose — one foot, then two. The starboard undercarriage and what was left of its associated wing stub hardly moved, highlighting the fragmented nature of the structure there. The port engine bearer was also lifting clear of the engine, but the opposite, starboard one looked firm. The structure was pivoting on the starboard wing root. As the port wing was lifted higher, the fuselage interior could be seen for the first time. The crowd, that had gathered by then, began to move round to get a first glimpse of the cockpit area; some people began to point and speculate also what was what.

With the port wing raised almost vertical, the aircraft lay on its starboard side, nose down, and almost hard up against the side of the hole. Winching stopped while a new lifting point was sought for heaving the frame up and over the side of the hole. The shattered top of the aircraft was exposed for all to see. Crushed, almost beyond recognition, what should have been the upper two feet of wood and canvas around the cockpit did not exist. Everything had been flattened

First view of the fuselage's interior, showing the lack of any upper fuselage structure. The windscreen's supporting arch is swept back over the seat.

The wreckage, pivoted over, is cleared of more internal mud. The port wing points skyward and the pilot's foothold is clearly visible in the fuselage panel, bottom left of the picture.

down to the level of the solid tubular steel framework. The only recognisable shape of the upper works was the arched structure of the windscreen's support frame, neatly folded back into an extreme reclining position.

The wreckage, stable in its new position, was declared safe, meaning that the hole could be entered. There was limited room (two people being a crowd), as much of the internal mud, ejected when the airframe had been lifted, had fallen into the bottom of the hole. The engine had not moved at all; the airframe had pivoted around it, the carburretor intake forming a lone island in the fresh layer of mud. Freed from the framework's mesh, the carburretor intake was lifted clear, coming away, quite cleanly, from the rest of the engine; the break had occurred at the base of the supercharger casing.

While mud and other items were picked out of the newly exposed airframe, the loose material in the hole was sifted for any other wreckage that could have lain buried. It was done very carefully, so that nothing would be missed. Under where the cockpit had been, the outline of two sharp edges could be felt. They were parallel to where the aircraft's sides had been, and curved in towards each other deeper down. Several small holes, about the size of old penny pieces, lined the upper edges and looked familiar. It was the thick, rigid panel, seen, wedged firmly under the fuselage, a few days previously. Inside the hollow formed by the panel were pieces of broken bakelite: solid lumps caked in hard mud; and more wood fragments. Some of the hard lumps were readily identifiable as instruments, each was carefully passed up to waiting hands and kept to one side. All the pieces had been pinned between the airframe and what was soon found to be the upturned curved panel, which covered the Hurricane's fuselage fuel tank, immediately in front of the cockpit. Of the tank itself, nothing could be found and it looked as though, on impact, the large panel had been forced back over the cockpit, enveloping the instrument panel. That, together with the folded-back nature of the windscreen's support arch, again suggested forward movement as the aircraft went into the marsh, nose first.

The glycol header tank was found completely crushed and was removed from the mud as a multiple layer of flattened brass plate. The segment shape of the forward armour plating also was lifted, intact, from the hole, still with the pneumatic system's reservoir bottle attached on its starboard side. Peering into the remains of the cockpit, the shape of the seat could clearly be made out, peeled back and flattened by the impact. In front of it lay the foot rests and, further forward, the rudder pedals and a stump where the control column should have been. The complete control column had been sheared at its base and lay nearby.

Dick Hipkin left his position at the winch to join in the discussion on an improved connection point for the chain to give a more advantageous line of pull. It was difficult to see what could be done because the aircraft was at that time on its side, hard up against the edge of the hole, and had not pivoted completely over to a shallow angle, as had been hoped. What was really needed next was a vertical lift to clear the aircraft over the edge, but that was not possible. In addition to attitude and weight (even without the engine), a section of engine bearer, probably still connected to the engine on the by now partly hidden starboard side, posed a further problem. Having cleaned the mud away, one tube could be seen, bent over but still attached to both the engine and airframe. Given the poor angle of pull, the section was, more than likely, sufficient to provide a good anchor. It would have to be cut, or the airframe would not be recovered that day. Reluctantly, a hacksaw was sought.

It had been hoped to recover all the remains without incurring any further damage but, at that point, there appeared to be no other solution. Consciences, about purposely inflicting damage, were eased somewhat when fate took a hand and the strut broke, unintentionally. In the hope of lightening the load further, the wreckage had been eased back into the hole to remove mud dislodged by the change in position; hauling it up to the side of the hole again, the double movement had done the dirty work and no hacksaw was required. Despite the damage, there was some comfort in the thought that it had not been done deliberately.

Finally, the chain was moved and attached to part of the tubular steel structure, near the engine bearers. Onlookers were moved back to a safe distance and, again the strain was taken. The chain tightened its grip and, as the winch reached full force, the wire began to hum faintly. The framework quivered but did not make any significant movement. Stalemate had been reached. The extended range and difficult angle of pull, combined, were too much for the equipment. The only solution to the problem of easing the load appeared to be a reducing the slope at the edge of the hole — but that would involve removing an enormous amount of mud. It was already late afternoon, and time would not permit such a solution before darkness fell. It looked as though the day would end in failure. No fresh solutions were forthcoming, other than the provision of a more powerful winching system. 'The Scammell would have done it', was the consensus of opinion from the recovery team; but, unfortunately, the Scammell was not there.

It was agreed reluctantly that nothing further could be done that day, and that a second attempt would be made the following weekend. The airframe was gently lowered again, onto its back. Laden with an assortment of small, loose items, mainly from the cockpit area, the disappointed party withdrew from the marsh to the relative comfort of the sea wall. There, the marshland mud was shaken off, the bits and pieces sorted out, and provisional arrangements discussed for the following weekend. Before darkness fell, the column of vehicles had cleared the narrow track and were heading back through the town of

Walton. The marshland returned once more to its natural state of peaceful tranquillity.

The following morning, the excavation area presented a depressing sight. The framework lay, as before, in its hole; much leaner, having been stripped of its excess coat of mud. Water filled the bottom of the hole, and the surrounding protective wall lay in ruins where it had been trampled underfoot and dispersed during the previous day's activity. There had been no worry then as, with the digging complete and recovery looking imminent, it had served its purpose. It was not clear where the water had come from; there were no signs of sea water having swirled around the edge of the hole, but flooding had occurred to a considerable depth and one thing was certain, the flooding would continue to get worse as the height of the high tides increased towards their full spring cycle. To rebuild the flattened wall would have been an enormous undertaking, given the time to hand, and would have been pointless, perhaps, because the damage had already been done — salt water having been in contact with the aircraft's metal framework.

As the days went by, salt water began to fill the hole completely as the high tides washed across the narrow beach ridge (taking the short cut between the headwaters of Cormorant Creek and the open sea). Before long, the last remaining traces of the protective wall had been cleared away. Ironically, this destructive process offered protection of a different kind. Because the wreckage was submerged quickly, it was, therefore out of sight of any casual passers-by, certainly difficult to reach and, as such, should be safe until the following weekend.

Consequently, a much modified landscape presented itself to the recovery party the following Sunday, 8 April. A repeat of the preparations seven days earlier concluded with the cars gathering at the end of the track by mid-morning. Climbing the sea wall gave the first real view of the marshes (the wall was a good visual barrier as well as a protector against the sea). No sign of the earthworks, only a circular pond marking the spot. Gone was the evidence of the previous Sunday's frantic activity, when black mud was everywhere. It was almost like the first time at the site. The hole appeared smaller and had smooth, clean sand ringing its edge and forming the sides. Looking towards the centre, the faint but familiar outline of the port wing's rear spar could be made out, just below the surface.

The first concerns were, how much had the hole been filled with solid material and, would it need much re-digging? Thinking back on the previous week's hard work, the prospect of re-digging was not welcomed. A small portable pump that had been brought along was, before long, in position and working hard. Meanwhile, on probing the depths from the edge of the hole, things did not look too bad at all. The water, towards the centre, was still very deep or, at least, deeper than could be plumbed from the side. The outline of the wreckage could be felt clearly, and many parts seen from certain angles, before the waters were finally stirred into a murky mixture. What had happened to all the material that once formed the wall? All that could be assumed was that it had been washed nearer to the foreshore by the ebbing tide and, for some unknown reason, had not fallen back into the hole in large quantities.

The pump was slowly starting to have some effect but, obviously, it was going to take a very long time to make a significant reduction in the water level; but, if the engine was to stand any chance of being freed, it had to be done. The engine was no longer attached to the airframe; and there was a possibility of hauling the airframe clear when the water level was reduced only part of the way, but the engine lay eight feet further down. If only some wires had been attached to it the previous weekend! It should have been considered before the hole was finally abandoned the previous Sunday, especially as the failure of the wall with the full spring tides and subsequent flooding would hardly come as a surprise. So much for hindsight! It was positive ideas that were needed at that moment.

A few buckets helped the situation but, with the contents having to be carried a good ten yards clear of the hole before being thrown clear, it was a small contribution. Emptied any closer, the contents would have drained back into the hole. As it was, the pump had a gully specially gouged out of the mud, taking its contents to a downward slope, away from the excavation. It was to be a waiting game; the ultimate time limit was not dusk, but the next high tide. The peak spring tides had occurred a couple of days earlier, but the tides were still very full. Anytime from an hour before high water and the sea was liable to come rushing back across the beach ridge, to top up the hole. High water was due at five o'clock.

While the bucket chain and pump were doing their best, there were other matters to be attended to. The winching system had arrived in the form of a massive, six-wheeled heavy breakdown, Scammell vehicle, courtesy of the Colchester-based *Kenning Car Mart*. It looked somewhat aged, but its sheer size gave confidence that there would be no problem with pulling power that day. It was manoeuvred against the back slope of the sea wall, and positioned as its predecessor had been the previous week. Then started the long muddy process of paying out the towing hawser, across the soft bed of Cormorant Creek, made more difficult this time by the heavier gauge wire being used. Again, a length of chain formed the final link with the quarry. Paying out the wire took longer than anticipated but then it did not seem to matter as nothing could be done until the water level had been lowered.

When the wire was in position, there was still less framework exposed above the water level than there had been when digging first started two weeks earlier. At that rate, it would be well into the afternoon before things were ready! Why not have a go at the airframe now, even though it was submerged? The position on the spar used as an attachment point was only just hand-deep beneath the water's surface. Being a good six feet in from the edge did make things awkward, but a balancing act along the narrow bridge, formed by the spar itself, enabled a connection to be made to the more solid centre section of the spar. All was ready. Onlookers moved back and the Scammell rumbled into action. The wire snaked taut and lifted a little from the sand. Very slowly, the port wing's rear spar began to rise from the water: first the aluminium trellis work of the outer wing, then the solid steel section. Like a great arm, it lifted slowly under control, up and through the vertical. Then faster, with its own weight behind it, down again, to rest on the side of the hole. There was a slight pause while the tension in the wire caught up, then the framework slowly continued to rise up the slope, sideways, port wing first, until the whole structure lay right way up on the level sand. Winching was stopped and the wire went slack.

The airframe (port wing vertical) breaks the surface as it is pulled over.

There she was at last, back on *terra firma*, rather than hidden under it. Immediately, the small crowd closed in to inspect the remains; the first time it could really be done with ease. The salt water bath, although detrimental to its long-term preservation, had, in the short term, been beneficial. It had cleaned much of the loose mud from the complex network of structural supports, pipework, control wires and electrical cables, all clearly visible because the outer framework panels had been removed, earlier during the dig. The complexity of the systems built into even this quite old style aircraft design were very noticeable.

The next major problem was moving the airframe the one hundred and fifty yards to the safety of dry land. The intention was that the Scammell would drag the framework directly across the marsh. The soft mud would act as both a cushion and lubricant to reduce frictional damage to a minimum. However, the main worry, beside the wide expanse of Cormorant Creek, was the maze of minor gullies and runnels that made up the distinctive salt marsh surface. From a distance, a mature salt marsh provides a deceptively flat horizon, especially when the vegetation is in full bloom but, hidden beneath, there is a complex drainage pattern, making the reality decidedly different. A rapid inspection of the framework showed there was no simple, quick way of dismantling sections, there and then; the wreckage would definitely have to be towed as a whole. Port wing first again meant that it would be riding with the two wing spars acting like the runners of a sledge. The port undercarriage leg, which still lay retracted in its housing, would trail 'wheel after pivot point' so there would be no danger of it digging in like an anchor.

The move began. The first twenty yards were level, firm sand, easily covered. Then onto the marsh proper and it did not take long to find the first gully. The problem at each gully was to prevent the leading sections or corners from digging in, spinning the frame around or capsizing it into a larger gully before the winch could be stopped. With communication only by strained vocal chords across the one hundred and fifty yards of open marshland, there was, inevitably, a time delay in passing instructions, which did not help matters. It took a considerable time to negotiate the uneven terrain, much longer than anticipated (including one very necessary stop to break the wire where it had been joined, reconnect it and continue). Then, the worse part, traversing the large divide at the headwaters of Cormorant Creek. Because it had such a soft bed, the fear was that as the airframe slid down the bank it would dig itself in at the bottom. However, there was also a further, unexpected problem. Having taken so long to get that far, the incoming tide had already begun to fill the bottom of the creek, making it impossible to guide the framework by hand, once it had started the crossing. It went down and straight away was almost lost from sight but, to great relief, it still kept moving. There were anxious moments, especially when the submerged load approached the opposite bank, where the two smaller headwater creeks joined to form Cormorant Creek proper. It was feared that the load might get stuck because the depth shallowed by the bank, so a couple of volunteers made the long journey round the maze of minor marsh gullies to watch it round the corner. It passed very close, without incident, as it carved its way through the mud and water; how much of each was not quite certain! Then, diagonally across the main width of the creek until, at the deepest point, it was completely lost from sight. Only the strain on the wire and its continued movement indicated that all was well.

By that time the creek was close to full and it would not be long before only the taller, grassy vegetation stood above the spring tide's level. Pumping had stopped at the hole; as it had become obvious that the battle was about to be lost and the tide was about to undo all the good work. It was obvious that the engine

The main airframe (right way up) negotiates the sea wall slope.

The main airframe section after recovery, supported by blocks on the hotel's forecourt. Viewed from the rear, the port wing gun ports are far left and three bullet/shrapnel strikes can be seen, circled. Part of the armour plating can be seen hanging beneath the seat.

would not be recovered that day. The framework broke surface, a few feet from the edge of the creek, a different colour from when it had entered. Before, it had been clean with a freshly washed appearance following a week's soaking in the hole; what emerged from the creek had a good coating of the creek's soft, black gunge.

As it came up the bank, port wing first, the rear wing spar could be seen pointing at a different angle to that of the front spar. It must have dug in the marsh at some point and been wrenched out of position. Having been exposed to the elements since 1971, it must have been weakened by corrosion at its joint with the rest of the framework and finally given way with the extra forces applied. Otherwise, the airframe had survived its underwater experience very well. Up over the bank, then one small gully to negotiate and it would lie at the foot of the sea wall. At the gully, the weakened rear spar finally succumbed and broke free; the remainder carried on up the slope of the sea wall, leaving behind it a black slimy trail. Near the crest of the wall, the Scammell ceased its static winching and began to move forward, towing the airframe down from the crest to the landward side at ground level. There, a sling was attached to the structure and it was hoisted onto the back of a waiting lorry.

At the hole, all the equipment had long since been evacuated. The high tide had begun to swirl across the beach ridge — the creek waters and sea meeting to lay claim to the saltings, as they did every fortnight. Beside the pump and various other ancillary equipment, the other large section of framework (consisting of the starboard oleo leg and attached framework that had broken from the remainder of the airframe during impact) had been dragged clear as well. The engine remained more than six feet below the ground (or water, as it was then!), abandoned for the immediate future. It was a great disappointment but with the high tide, nothing else could be done that day.

At least the complete airframe section was safe. Secured onto the back of a lorry, it led the departing convoy back along the lane, towards Walton. It was only a short haul to the next stop, a local hotel, where the airframe was unloaded onto the forecourt, as a rather unusual long-stay guest. It was to be its temporary home during the initial stripping and cleaning process.

Chapter Six
Discoveries

Completing the recovery is by no means the end of a salvage operation such as this. Often, it heralds the beginning of many more demanding tasks: cleaning, preserving and, if necessary, displaying the articles recovered. Less exciting, such work does not necessarily capture the imagination as easily as the sense of impending discovery and excavation, but it is just as vital. Without proper preservation, the remains could rapidly deteriorate while adapting to their new environment. The enthusiasm of the work force usually remains high immediately after recovery as the items are inspected for the first time but then, as the objects become familiar, so the enthusiasm can fade. In particular, it is most likely to happen after the initial preservation steps have been taken and the enormity of the task ahead becomes stark reality. With the amateur enthusiast, that is when both the dedication and commitment are put to the test as the difficult and, very often, mundane tasks tend to drag on.

For the most part, the Hurricane's remains were found to be very well preserved, but from then on the effects of salt water corrosion were to present an ever increasing problem: just containing it would be work enough in itself. At the hotel, the airframe's remains had been placed at a workable height, supported on concrete blocks, and covered by a heavy duty polythene sheet. Much of the thick, sticky mud that had filled the intricate structure, after its emergence from the hole, had been washed clear by the haul through the flooded creek. However, it had been replaced by the soft, black mud from the creek's bed. As its surface hardened, the top layers could be flaked off but the bulk underneath, still damp and soft, proved difficult to remove; but it had to go. The first, and most important, task was to wash everything in fresh water in order to dilute and wash off the salt contamination, as much as possible. The large collection of smaller fragments could be cleaned off more easily in a fresh water bath, then dried, before being stored under cover; but the main framework and larger sections, such as the weighty starboard undercarriage leg and port wing rear spar, were a different proposition. A good, strong hose down was the best that could be done. It freed some of the mud but getting the lumps out of the complex framework often proved difficult, the jet of water merely chasing them around the maze of pipes, struts and wires. Even with the airframe stripped of all its external panelling, easy access to the interior was hardly improved. Electric wiring, control cables, and fitments that had remained intact, hung from the various supports, and with most of the cable runs split, the whole of the central structure was covered in a spaghetti-like complex of wiring and junction boxes. Various instruments and controls dangled from the ends of some of the wires: two quite recognisable being the throttle lever and propeller pitch control. The very complexity of the structure showed how technology had made a quantum leap in the short span of twenty years between the two world wars. But even then, the Hurricane's design could be seen as a peak of yesterday's technology whereas in its main rival, the Spitfire, could be seen the beginning of tomorrow's.

After a thorough soaking the main airframe section was allowed to dry, before being draped in a polythene cover; the aim then would be to keep the structure dry. All the loose items, including the unwieldy undercarriage leg and rear spar could be accommodated under more substantial cover, but the sizeable main airframe section would have to lie only partially protected. The next job was to strip, systematically, the airframe of as much as possible, permitting easier access to carry out preservation work on the basic framework, and enabling more to be stored under solid cover while awaiting proper treatment.

As the veneer of mud receded, the extent of structural damage became more apparent. The fuselage's tubular steel framework was mostly intact and retained its overall shape. So had the girder work of the wing's centre section, except where completely truncated at the starboard wing root. Considering the force of impact, which was presumably from some considerable height, the preservation of the Hurricane's shape was quite remarkable and a tribute to its robust construction. The main damage to the fuselage's tubular steel work was found at its upper limit (half way up the actual fuselage), where a number of pieces showed signs of compression and fracture. The Hurricane having landed upside down, that particular part would have taken the full force of the crash.

The top half of the fuselage structure, containing the fuel and glycol coolant tanks, and the cockpit access, was nonexistent and must have been crushed as the aircraft hit the ground, flattening everything down to the level of the basic steel framework. The seat, complete with leather harness strap attached, lay swept back, almost horizontal. Strangely, rather than wrapping itself around the one-inch diameter spar immediately behind, the spar had apparently bent to accommodate the shape of the much more flimsy seat. The most probable explanation was, that the armoured windscreen had been wrenched backwards also, together with its supporting arch, causing the hardened glass to land on the

The cockpit area viewed from the port wing, seat and windscreen supporting arch swept backwards almost to the horizontal.

Shattered, but intact, the armoured wind-screen, still resting on its wooden support.

upper part of the seat; and that it was that force which had bent the spar, the seat being sandwiched in between. (The position of the windscreen supporting arch and the broken armoured glass, impacted horizontally across its width, would seem to support this theory.)

Two holes, at the top of the seat were intriguing, showing obvious signs of penetration from behind. The questions which came immediately to mind were: how could they have been made? and, were they significant? It was easy to start speculating about the causes of the aircraft's demise, but so much could have happened to the remains after impact, lying, as they had done, so close to the surface, that it was difficult to be certain how they had got there. It could have been by a previous recovery effort, using it for target practice, or straight-forward vandalism at some time. A simple thrust from above with a sharp, heavy object could probably have produced a similar effect. As with the holes seen in the starboard wing spar six years earlier (see photograph on page 13), there was doubt as to whether or not such damage occurred before or after the crash. Later tampering looked more likely as there, hanging from the next cross-section down, was a totally intact section of armour plating which had fitted behind the seat. Misidentification of that piece was to have significance some years later.

Running either side of the fuselage were variously sized brass pipes which had carried oil and glycol coolant to and from the radiator situated under the wing's centre section. The pipes were intact but had suffered varying degrees of damage. The largest one, on the starboard side, that had carried the glycol coolant, was very thin and badly weakened by fire damage. It was on the same side that only the outline of paper thin fuselage panels had been seen during the excavation. On the port side, the two smaller gauge, oil pipes were largely intact, straight and, although blackened by what looked like fire, remained strong. The effects of fire could be seen in many other areas, but there was still no clear pattern to the damage. It was common to find that in a single area some parts had almost disintegrated, but those immediately adjacent had survived, virtually intact. Where the aluminium sheeting had been close to fire, it had either completely disappeared or appeared very weak and 'moth-eaten'. In many cases, panels were heavily pitted on one side, caused through burning, but presented a perfectly intact and well-preserved surface on the other. These effects were not confined to either the internal or external surfaces, so did not help in identifying the source of the fire. Indeed, the lack of any clear pattern appeared to be indicative of a blaze after the crash, rather than one while the aircraft had been in the air.

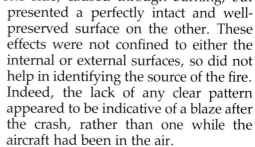

STBD WING

PORT WING

WHEEL WELL

Panels from the front fuselage's undersurface. A mixture of fire-damaged and intact sections.

Relieved of their soft mud coating, the sections of the main tubular structure revealed their remarkable state of preservation, first seen during the excavation work. Despite being made of steel, there was very little sign of rust, except towards the rear of the structure which, being closer to the surface, had been more susceptible to the effects of the elements. On many parts, patches of grey, silver and light green paint could still be seen clearly. The blistering of silver paint on the port wing's front spar was quite evident. Some mud still clung stubbornly to the structure. It was hard, almost cement-like, light brown in colour and appeared to be almost baked onto the metal. Using a wire brush it came away very slowly as a powder; it was removed best by being shattered with a sharp blow from a small hammer — although it still took considerable effort to remove completely. On many sections it was left, as it provided a good protection against the elements while other, more vulnerable sections were dealt with.

During the initial inspection, attention was drawn continually to smaller details which, invariably, offered something new: the numerous, intact electrical fitments, suspended from the ruptured wiring loom; the throttle cable run; hydraulic selection gear stick; and other controls, gauges and dials, located in the lower part of the cockpit. Instruments from the main panel higher up had all been found loose and collected from the base of the hole, when the airframe had first been hauled upright, and awaited detailed examination. Many were partly intact; others were burnt and obviously unrecogniseable at first, but the larger, more robust, metal-cased direction indicator, turn and bank indicator, and oxygen supply instruments were immediately identifiable. Of the number of

A selection of the cockpit instruments before cleaning. Note the intact bulb in its holder.

Cockpit instruments and manufacturer's plate, identifying P3175.

The reflector gunsight.

individual items it looked as though the instrumentation was virtually complete. Thoughts turned to the possibility of finding readings on some of the dials, bearing in mind that the force of impact could have easily affected many of them.

While searching the central area of the cockpit, the manufacturer's plate was found; a small brass tag, two by one-and-a-quarter inches, it was secured by two bolts through a main diagonal bracing strut that ran from the port side, near the instrument panel, down and under the seat. Had the instrument panel been in place, it would have lain immediately beneath it, on the far left-hand side. After chipping the baked mud away, the words 'GLOSTER AIRCRAFT COMPANY LIMITED' could be read clearly. Beneath, was a long serial number and a drawing number. At the bottom, in a section reserved for the date, was the inscription 'P3175' — hardly a date, more likely a military airframe serial number!

The question of the aircraft's identification arose again, the original serial, 'P3642' seeming most unlikely. Francis Mason's book on the Hurricane was sought and therein, sure enough, was P3175! It had been one of a production batch of five hundred, Gloster-built Hurricane Mk Is, numbered from P2535 to P3264; built 1939–40, incorporating Rolls-Royce Merlin III engines and de Havilland or Rotol propellers but that was all. In the subsequent list of squadron allocations and fate of individual aircraft, P3175 was not mentioned.

The next step was to contact the RAF Museum. Apart from announcing the successful recovery, three particular points were raised for consideration. First, that P3175 now appeared to be the aircraft's serial number; could existing records verify that? Second, could any assistance be offered in the form of aircraft drawings, manuals etc? Third, would the Museum be interested in the remains for display, along similar lines to those of the portion of Gladiator N5628, recovered from a Norwegian lake?

The reply was encouraging. The history card for P3175, held at the Air Historical Branch of the Ministry of Defence, was incomplete but showed the aircraft to have been taken on charge by No 10 Maintenance Unit on 29 June 1940. It was then allocated to No 257 Squadron on 9 August 1940 but, after that, nothng else was recorded; no indication of disposal or loss, but the link with No 257 Squadron, and therefore P3642, was there. Supplying drawings was a possibility and although the Museum's library was not yet fully functional, a search would be made to see what could be found. The only disappointment was that the Museum felt it unlikely that it could do anything constructive with the aircraft's remains at that time. It had only been open to the public for just a few months and much still remained to be done in consolidating the existing exhibits and documents. Both 'P3175' and No 257 Squadron had been confirmed, but not the date 'April 1941'.

The next step was to consult the Squadron records. This stage had been reached before but had been deferred when events at Walton rapidly overtook the necessary trip to London. (Squadron diaries, or Operations Record Books [ORBs], are bound volumes of RAF Forms 540 and 541, giving the day-by-day record of individual flights and general activities undertaken by each squadron.) In 1973, they had just been released from the Air Historical Branch of the Ministry of Defence, and transferred to the Public Records Office in London's Chancery Lane. (They are now housed in a large, new complex at Kew.) Access was, therefore, relatively easy.

Forms 540 give a brief summary of a particular squadron's daily activities; 541s a breakdown of each flight made — listing pilot, aircraft, time of flight and for what purpose. No 257 Squadron's 540 page for 29 April 1941 revealed no losses recorded for that day; the corresponding 541 page confirmed it. Then what? The other possibility was 31 August 1940, but again there was nothing relating to P3175. Two aircraft were recorded as having crashed that particular morning, at about the right time to agree with the ARP records, but neither of them was P3175. The pages were flipped back to the first known date, 9 August 1940, when the aircraft was issued to the squadron. With that as a starting point, it was hoped that something on P3175 would emerge soon afterwards.

Then, there it was! 18 August 1940: Flown by Plt Off Maffett on a convoy patrol from Martlesham Heath 12.10 to 13.15 hr.; followed by a scramble, by the same pilot, between 17.00 and 18.00 hr. Form 540 revealed that a combat had taken place over the Thames Estuary when, at 17.50 hrs, No 257 Squadron had intercepted a formation of fifty mixed bombers, Plt Off Maffett claiming one Dornier 215 as 'damaged'. Subsequent pages were scanned for P3175's last entry. This appeared to be some eleven days later, on 29 August, when, once again, it was flown by Plt Off Maffett, as it had been on the previous four days, but the aircraft was recorded as having landed safely. There were no combats recorded for that day, and no losses. There was no further mention of P3175 after that, through to April 1941 and beyond. If nothing else, at least one thing was consistent: as with the Aircraft's Record Card, it left P3175's fate open-ended.

On 30 August, a hurriedly written entry did not list the aircraft by their fuselage serial numbers, as was usual, but by their individual identification letters; Plt Off Maffett flew aircraft 'S'. Looking through the 541 entries for other

Aircraft Type and No.	Crew.	Duty.	Time Up.	Time Down.	Details of Sortie or Flight.	References.
U706	P/O M. Toirs	OP	08.25	09.05		
R4093	P/O MAFFETT				CRASHED	
P3620	P/O CAPON					
P3179	P/O GUNDRY				SCRAMBLE	
P3708	P/O HENDERSON				CRASHED	
P3205	Plt BERGSTROM					
P3776	SGT FRASER					
P3175	P/O HUNT					
P3109	P/O COCHRANE					
V7296	P/O FRIDELL	NON OP	08.00	8.20	TO DEBDEN.	
R4093	P/O SOLOGUBRIN					
1729?	P/O FRASER				TO MARTLESHAM.	
	P/O BORSEIGNEUR		10.40	11.00		
4707	P/O MITCHELL	OP.	13.30	14.15		
P3642	P/O CAPON.					
V7296	P/O FRIDELL					
P3179	PILT BERGSTROM				SCRAMBLE	
P3205	P/O GUNDRY					
V7268	SGT ROBINSON					
P3776	SGT FRASER					
P3708	P/O COCHRANE					

days, it seemed that a particular pilot did not always fly one specific aircraft, except over quite short periods, therefore it could not be assumed that P3175 was aircraft 'S'. On 31 August, Plt Off Maffett was one of two pilots recorded as having crashed, but his aircraft was listed as R4093 (the other pilot being Plt Off Henderson in P3708). Could there have been a clerical error? Certainly the entries for that day were hurriedly written. Then, surprisingly, half-way down the page, R4903 was mentioned again, taking off half-an-hour earlier than noted in the previous entry as part of a pair on a routine flight from Martlesham Heath to Debden. The general area was certainly correct, Walton lying some fourteen miles south-west of Martlesham Heath. The two pilots involved made the return flight from Debden later the same morning, but only one aircraft's serial number was listed. There appeared to be some uncertainty, on the part of the ORB compiler, as to which aircraft were actually involved. This could have easily arisen in the hectic environment of a temporary forward base, during those final days in August, when the pressure on Fighter Command's airfields was reaching its peak. Having been moved from Northolt to Debden on 15 August, and after only four days at the new base, No 257 Squadron had subsequently been split — its aircraft and pilots going to Martlesham Heath, and the administrative and servicing elements remaining at Debden. Repetition of entries, and others being out of chronological order as the month of August progressed, clearly reflected this administratively disruptive condition.

Returning to the 540 page for 31 August, the details of the morning's combat and losses were recorded:

> . . . *In the Clacton area at about 18,000 feet* [the Squadron] *attacked a formation of about 50 ME 110's . . . . P.O. HENDERSON brought two ME 110's down and himself baled out of his aircraft in flames . . . and was taken to BRIGHTLINGSEA NAVAL HOSPITAL. P.O. MAFFETT was killed after baling out of his aircraft which was shot down.*

Everything was beginning to point in favour of Plt Off Maffett being killed after baling out of P3175, as he had flown it up to at least two days before the crash, and perhaps the day before the crash, if the aircraft proved to be 'S'. However, given the inaccuracies in the Forms 541, it was also possible that Plt Off Henderson could have been flying P3175 and not P3708, as recorded. Both pilots had left vacant aircraft to fall earthward. Brightlingsea being some ten miles from P3175's crash site, it was perhaps stretching a point, but it was still quite possible that P3175 could have been Henderson's aircraft; no location had been given for the crash site of Plt Off Maffett's

ARP telephonist's message form announcing the crash of a British aircraft at Walton-on-the-Naze. The handwriting leaves it uncertain whether the time is 0850 or 0856, however, the subsequent message from 'Essex County Control' to 'Regional Control Cambridge' can be clearly read as 0850.

aircraft. Concern arose about the entry of P3708 against P/O Henderson for 31 August because, on looking further through the dates, P3708 was listed as flying on 1, 3 and 4 September! Further back in the ORB, P3708 was also recorded as having crashed, pilotless, on 18 August 1940 (two weeks previously), when Sgt Girdwood baled out of it over Foulness Island. P3708 was a truly remarkable machine!

There was no doubt about the Walton Hurricane being P3175, but who had been its pilot? The answer was provided by Essex County ARP records. Apart from linking Plt Off Henderson with a Hurricane crashing close to Brightlingsea, in the River Colne, a message concerning the Walton crash clearly stated that *the British pilot was killed*. It must have been Plt Off Maffett because the entry in the ORB for 31 August stated that Henderson had been taken to Brightlingsea Hospital. As for R4903, that serial number was later found to belong to a Tiger Moth! The closest to it of No 257 Squadron's Hurricanes was R4094, also coded 'S' and lost in combat on 8 August 1940 — the day before P3175 was allocated to the squadron as a replacement. As with P3708, the Operations Record Book continued to record R4094 as having flown after 8 August; until 18 August, when P3175 was first mentioned. Coincidentally, no further mention was made of R4094 after 17 August. It all appeared to fit.

Much later, having the opportunity to compare some surviving pilots' log book entries with those in No 257 Squadron's Operations Record Book, the riddle of the 'multi-life' P3708 was solved. It was one of the initial batch of Hurricanes, allocated to the squadron in June 1940, three weeks after the squadron's formation. It was designated aircraft 'E' and was, undoubtedly, lost on 18 August. Its replacement was apparently V6601, although no mention of such a serial number appeared in the Squadron's Operations Record Book. However, one of the Aircraft Movement Record Cards, held by Air Historical Branch, recorded its very brief life span: to No 5 Maintenance Unit on 22 August; issued to No 257 Squadron, four days later; struck off charge (FBO 3) on 31 August. In his log book, Plt Off Henderson listed the aircraft he was flying that morning only as 'E' — it could have only been V6601.

A few months after the recovery of P3175, an attempt was made to recover parts of what was thought to be Plt Off Henderson's aircraft from the River Colne, near Brightlingsea. The personnel involved in the operation, and its results, is not known (although it has been reported that there were some substantial pieces), but should the recovered items still exist they may prove the V6601 link conclusively.*

As for the entries in the Operations Record Book, it was easy to see that, for each flight, the far more visible, individual aircraft identity letters had been recorded, later to be translated into fuselage serials and entered on the Forms 541. Given, at that time, the pressure on the airfields, the split administration, and heavy flying schedules, it was understandable that the change of aircraft, as losses occurred, had not always been noted.

---

* Small sections of this aircraft were recovered by the Essex Aviation Group in 1980 but in the spring of 1990 a concerted effort by the Warplane Wreck Investigation Group recovered the remaining wreckage, including the engine, and provided positive proof of the V6601 identity.

Chapter Seven
Back To The Mud

It was some weeks after the airframe's recovery before conditions allowed another attempt at recovering the engine. At least, by that time the fickle April weather had given way to the more stable one of May, and working conditions were guaranteed to be a little more pleasant. Again, it was a fine Sunday morning when the cars gathered at the bottom of the lane. The small groups consisted, predominantly, of ATC cadets from the Clacton and Colchester units, under the watchful eye, again of their Commanding Officer, Flt Lt Percy Wheatley. The enthusiastic Dick Hipkin was, again, at the wheel of the powerful, Scammell recovery vehicle. The sky was bright and clear (a good sign, it was hoped) as the party set off along the sea wall, towards the site.

The foreshore's landscape was different again, the mobile beach ridge having shifted many times since the last visit. There were no obvious signs of the old workings, and no wreckage lay above the surface to act as a marker. Searching the thin veneer of sand, a patch, softer than elsewhere, was thought to be the most likely spot. Its circular boundary defined, digging commenced, at a point within it which was furthest from the sea and beneath which it was hoped the engine would lie. Water seepage was an immediate and continuous problem because the sediments were only loosely compacted, as a result of the previous digging operation, and contained a large quantity of water. Periodically, digging was stopped and a bucket chain formed to drain the workings. It was not intended to re-dig the entire hole, as there would not have been time, only the ground over the engine; but the loose material kept caving in, making the hole ever wider. To confine the activity to one specific area and in an attempt to hold back the fluid mass of unstable mud and sand, driftwood was employed to form makeshift shuttering.

It was early afternoon before contact was made with solid metal, and the engine's location was definitely proven; confidently digging was concentrated then into one narrow area. The confined area permitted limited numbers only to work in the immediate vicinity at one time, which was just as well because the previous few hours' digging in that awful, sticky marsh mud had started to take its toll on the workforce. A rota was organised, giving a continuous supply of fresh labour. By mid-afternoon the high tide had been and gone; fortunately, it was not as high as the spring tide of a few weeks earlier, and there was no interference with the excavation. Eventually, the smooth sump of the inverted engine was clearly exposed. By the time the tide had turned, all the soft mud had been removed from around the sump and along the sides of the crankcase; on the starboard side, that was as far down as the exhaust manifold but, on the port side it was not as far, as the engine lay slightly tilted over to that side.

Standing in the hole beside the engine, the severe contrast between the soft, black, infill sediment and the firm, much lighter, uncut, brown clay was very evident. An attempt was made to chip away the hard but flaky clay, close to the engine, where working conditions gave access; but the afternoon was slipping away and the pressure was on for an attempt to pull what looked like an intact Merlin engine free from its muddy resting place. The Scammell had been in position since mid-morning, and the wire had been laid out; both were ready.

The engine, lying flat, was aligned — roughly north-east/south-west virtually, along the line of pull; nose away from the sea, pointing towards the Scammell. A wire strop was placed around the supercharger casing, at the rear of the engine, and connected to the main wire hawser. The intention was to prize the engine free from the mud by pivoting it on the propeller boss, and rotating it, end over end; then it could be recovered in the same manner as the airframe had been.

While the work force stood well clear, the mighty Scammell took the strain and the wire became taut. Groans came from the hole as the strop tightened its grip, but the engine did not budge. The strain was eased. A digging party re-entered the hole and spades chipped away again at the hard brown clay which held the two large cylinder banks. It was slow work, made all the more difficult by the confines of the improvised shuttering inside the cramped hole. Watery, black mud oozed in, at no small rate, from the crude wooden lining, helping to fill the bottom of the hole almost as fast as the clay chippings were removed; constant baling out was required. After a reasonably brief spell at this work, it did not take much to persuade everyone to agree on another attempt at pulling.

Again the area was cleared, the strain was taken by the wire, and the strop tightened. The wire vibrated gently, but otherwise showed no movement. Then, the ground shuddered as suddenly the clay seal was broken. The wire started to move forward and the engine was hauled slowly into a vertical position, resting on the propeller's boss. The Scammell proceeded to drag the engine, almost vertically, up the side of the hole and onto the surrounding sand. On the way up, some of the shuttering became dislodged and the sides of the hole partially collapsed. While one group started to remove the thicker layers of mud from the engine, the remaining diggers completed the infilling of the hole in order to return the area to a safe and environmentally acceptable state, as there would be no further high tide to do the job that day.

It had been a long day, but worth it. The Merlin was found to be intact, complete with the propeller boss and the stubs of three wooden propeller blades. The only damage appeared to be a large dent along the starboard rocker cover, as well as the severed carburettor (recovered earlier). All that remained for complete success was to haul the prize along the same path as the airframe had taken to the sea wall. It was evening and tiredness was beginning to make its mark; however, the sight of the intact engine on the surface spurred the team on. The winching of the engine across the marsh went smoothly, the load, being a more concentrated weight than the airframe, tending to plough straight through the small rills and gullies. Then down into the soft mud of the creek, gouging out a large scar in its bed, and up the other side, draped in the familiar veil of black mud. Over the wall and the job was complete.

It was a weary group that dispersed from the marshes that night, yet deeply satisfied in the knowledge that all the objectives had at last been met. The engine was taken to Kennings Garage at Marks Tey, near Colchester, which was to be its home for what would be many long hours of painstaking stripping down and cleaning.

Close inspection of the engine, the following day, revealed its remarkable state of preservation. A high pressure hose-down had soon transformed the muddy lump into the recognisable form of a twin-banked, 'V', inline, twelve-cylinder Rolls-Royce, aero engine, complete with propeller assembly. Impact damage was confirmed as minimal, the loss of the carburettor being the main and most obvious damage. The starboard side rocker cover had, in fact, split just over half way down its length, where the dent had been observed, and the exhaust stubs had taken on a new, streamlined appearance, squeezed thin by their passage through the mud. On crashing, the tremendous heat from the engine had baked on some of the mud it had come into contact with and, like the airframe section, it was a particularly stubborn substance to remove. Possible fire damage was evident in small patches, mid-way along the top of both cylinder blocks.

Elsewhere, the array of accessories and auxiliary fitments appeared to be remarkably intact and undamaged. The spark plugs appeared to be in a good condition and a couple were taken to a test bench and a charge applied. They fired! Still wet from the hose-down, the gleam from the almost complete coat of black paint gave the engine a freshness that belied its previous thirty-three-year, resting place. The brass manufacturer's data plates were riveted to the port side of the crankcase. Standing out quite boldly were the words 'ROLLS-ROYCE LTD ENGLAND. MERLIN III No 22637'.

The engine had a good home for its restoration because the garage handled commercial vehicles and its personnel were accustomed to dealing with large capacity engines. Dick Hipkin was in charge of restoring the engine; a man with two useful

Percy Wheatley (left) and Dick Hipkin inspect the engine. (*Essex County Newspapers*)

The engine, after cleaning and re-assembly.

attributes for this kind of work, being both a skilled mechanic and a hard working enthusiast. Gradually, over the summer months, the engine was stripped entirely, including the supercharger, cylinder heads and even the cylinder liners, until only the bare crankcase remained. Some components and sub-sections, such as the rocker assemblies, were sent elsewhere for individual attention, to spread the load.

In preparation for reassembly, a display stand was constructed, and the subsequent rebuild was planned to take place around the main block of the crankcase, supported again on its four mounting points. The detached carburettor was to be reunited with the engine by suspending it in its true position, low down at the rear, beneath the great whorls of the supercharger casing; unfortunately, sufficient small fragments of the casing were missing to prevent its being attached directly to the engine, however its presence would help to complete the familiar silhouette of the Merlin. With the engine almost intact again, the massive, Rotol variable pitch propeller hub was finally repositioned, only with the blade stubs having been rotated into a slightly different position from that when found.

In the hole, the longest, remaining blade had pointed skyward from the inverted engine; however, with the engine the right way up, it was longer than the stand was high, so it had to be rotated in order for it to clear the ground and to give a better appearance when on display.

By the end of August, after work had continued to many a late hour in the long, summer evenings, the rebuild was complete. The ATC's intention was, then, to use the engine as a mobile display, primarily at venues with an RAF flavour. The first opportunity came during that year's 'Battle of Britain' open day at RAF Coltishall, where it featured in a section devoted to aero engines of the past. The following December, it was in the foyer of the Classic Cinema at Clacton, as the centrepiece of an RAF display during the week-long showing of Harry Saltzman's epic film *The Battle of Britain*. In between such displays it was on view in the showroom window of Kenning Motors, at Colchester.

Meanwhile, at the Walton Hotel, work continued on stripping and cleaning the airframe section. By the summer's end, the main unit had been lightened enough to be almost portable. Removal of the one still attached undercarriage leg, which weighed over a hundredweight, had made an enormous difference; as had the removal of the port wing fuel tank and the port side engine bearer. Before being removed, the remains of the complicated wiring loom were gathered at various points, tied, labelled and the whole array photographed *in situ*, to assist identification and relocation, at a later date. The basic framework began to appear both bare and a far less awesome task.

At the same time, the boxes containing other fragments were gradually sifted, for recognisable pieces, once freed of their mud coating. During the search, further confirmation of the aircraft's identity came to light. 'P3175' was painted in one-inch high, stencilled figures, on the inside of the port wing to fuselage fairing. An aluminium blanking plate, set in the top of a tube on the fuselage's framework, was also stamped with the aircraft's serial number. The plate had apparently been placed there for the sole purpose of bearing the serial number, as no other section of structural tube was found to have been blanked off in such a manner.

Despite automated production line techniques there was still an element of local fit about parts of the Hurricane's structure. This was most evident in the forward fuselage's detachable panels, which could prove problematical if panels were exchanged between machines and so the practice of marking each panel with the airframe serial number became commonplace. Finding 'P3642' on the engine's port cowling panel had shown that transfers could be and were made, hence the danger of identifying aircraft based on finding only one of these numbers on a particular panel! As most of the detachable panels were placed around the topside forward fuselage and because, in this particular case, most had suffered some form of fire damage, there was no guarantee that many of these local markings had survived, and cursory searches found nothing. It was only gradually, over the years, that some were eventually discovered — on the more intact engine's belly and starboard side cowling panels; both being P3175.

A considerable amount of green paint was found on the external surfaces of the panels from the fuselage sides and the upper wing surface. It far exceeded the amount of brown paint found, probably because green usually formed the base coat in the painting process, the brown camouflage patches being sprayed on top. The limited amount of brown that was found led to the conclusion that the paint scheme used on P3175 was the standard, upper surface camouflage Scheme A. The surviving underside panel work, which was mainly from the wheel-well area and forward fuselage, was an off-white colour but much of it had been stained badly, so identifying the precise colour was not so easy.

At that stage, the discovery of the aircraft's individual code letter, on the surviving paint work, was most significant. The engine belly panel, although largely intact, had suffered fire damage and had, what was by then, the familiar moth-eaten appearance. Washing off the mud, it was surprising to find that, despite the tremendous heat that must have been generated to burn through the metal, the surviving parts still retained a good covering of paint. Silver grey coloured the inside and, generally, the remains of a discoloured white covered much of the exterior. A darker coloured, horizontal bar could be clearly seen near the top, or propeller, end and, viewed from a reasonable distance, it could be interpreted as the bottom bar of a 'square' style letter. Above and to the left, a further right-angled corner could be just made out, but the remainder was obscured by fire damage. Only the letter 'S' could fit the pattern and it was aircraft 'S' that Plt Off Maffett had been recorded as flying on 30 August 1940; the theory still held good that P3175 was 'S'.

Two other, remarkable and surprising finds were a couple of cartridge case ejector tubes, extremely well-preserved and each carrying the aircraft's serial number, written in pencil, together with the number of the gun to which each one belonged — all legible still after thirty-three years. Pencil writing was clear also on some of the wood pieces. On one piece, which came from the wooden ledge at the base of the cockpit's 'break out' panel, the craftsman's notes, made sometime during manufacture, could be still read. More pencilled notes were discovered on the two largest pieces of wood found: two wedge-shaped, plywood panels that belonged either side of the cockpit's windscreen; one still covered with an external layer of green-painted canvas. Inside both pieces could be found the outline of where other fitments and instruments had once been attached. One wire still hung loose from the port side panel, on the end was a

A selection of wood fragments recovered together with two setions of the 'sutton harness' and a canvas pouch inside which was found the protective cover for the gunsight — clearly labelled 'GUNS LOADED'.

bakelite lamp holder, still containing the remains of a broken glass bulb.

A number of instruments were immediately recognisable: The magnetic compass was fragile and fire-damaged but still in one piece. Attached to one of its supports and angled down, pointing at the remains of the compass card, was a second bakelite lamp holder, with the lamp still intact! The reflector gun site was in three pieces, and its main reflector glass was missing. Fire had been active on its middle section, where the settings were adjusted, leaving it badly pitted. The upper part still retained its smooth, dark brown gloss finish, and the bakelite lamp holder was hardly scratched. When held to the light and looking through its vertical axis, the gunsight's cross and centre circle could be still seen clearly. The turn indicator and direction indicator, having more robust cases, survived intact and both had the remains of their shattered glass faces impressed around their dials' rim. The lighter, bakelite casings of the other large instruments had not survived so well and a pile of bakelite fragments awaited 'jigsaw' action. The smaller, more compact pressure gauges and bourden tube temperature gauges had fared better; so much so that, during cleaning, two of the temperature gauges' indicators rotated when the bourden tubes were flexed.

The brass-cased clock was an interesting survivor. Unfortunately, the position of the hands was not quite discernable but, of course, there was no guarantee that the time had been right or that the clock had been working at the time of the crash — therefore little information was really lost. Fire had destroyed virtually all the instrument's faces, in fact, dashing hopes of drawing any conclusions. Because of their intricate nature, a disproportionate amount of time was spent in preserving those pieces, compared with the far greater bulk of the remaining airframe. No significant part of the instrument panel's aluminium frame survived but, with at least a representative part of each instrument surviving, a false panel of clear perspex was constructed, on to which the instruments were mounted for final display. (That is how they are exhibited today, mounted in the airframe, in the RAF Museum, at Hendon.)

Although the Museum's display halls were already open to the public, the library and research facilities, intended to be an integral part of the final complex, were still being organised. Despite this, access to the library was given, enabling the identification of some of the smaller, broken, and often distorted pieces of aluminium, wood and bakelite from P3175. Many items were taken off the 'unknown' list, as a result. Even more valuable than sifting through various manuals and instruction documents, access was given, outside normal visiting hours, to the Museum's own Hurricane, P2617 (by coincidence, a Mk I from the same Gloster production batch as P3175). It proved of immense value, in particular it helped to identify the cockpit's various components and structure. (The layout of the mock instrument panel was drawn up after one such visit.) A perplexing curved piece of timber, still with green painted canvas attached, was easily identified then as the front section of the cockpit's starboard side 'break out' panel, complete with one of its release catches; obviously, it had not been used when the pilot had vacated the aircraft.

Some of the companies involved in the manufacture of components for the Hurricane were known to be still in business and a few were contacted concerning their pertinent recovered items. Hawker Siddeley Aviation Ltd (later, British Aerospace) provided enlarged photographs, showing the entire interior of the cockpit of Hurricane PZ865, *The Last of the Many*, which provided an excellent medium when transferring what had been seen at Hendon to the working site at Walton. Also, Hawker Siddeley were able to provide a few other, general arrangement diagrams, showing the overall layout of the framework, although not much assistance was required because the bulk of P3175's basic framework had been recovered intact. S.U. Carburettors, then a division of British Leyland, were approached for advice for stripping the carburettor assembly. Although the company had ceased to manufacture aircraft carburettors in the late 1940s, and had finally severed all connection with aircraft products about 1960, some of the old, aircraft carburettor team remained and they managed to find some old drawings of the early series Merlin engines. (Dick Hipkin, using his mechanical expertise only, completed the Merlin's strip and clean without recourse to such assistance!)

One of the instruments recovered completely intact, except for its glass face and dial card, was the turn indicator. Its manufacturer's brass plate could be read clearly at the centre of the dial: 'Turning Indicator Mark IA A.M. No.3479/38 Reid and Sigrist Ltd'. In 1973/4 Reid and Sigrist were part of the large Decca Group; thinking that they may be interested in the rather unusual survival of one of their products they were contacted. They responded enthusiastically and a visit to the factory in Leicester was arranged. The instrument was taken and advice for its dismantling was given by two experienced instrument fitters, still employed by the company, who had, at one time, worked on the old Mk IA instrument.

Chapter Eight
Coming Home

By the summer of 1974, the airframe had been stripped as far as had been intended. Cleaning and preservation were progressing steadily, although no re-assembly had taken place. Occasional 'touch-up' maintenance was all that was required on the engine, then on display for a second season with the Colchester ATC.

Following the RAF Museum's initial inability to deal with the remains, a secure permanent home was still being sought. It seemed that a small, private museum might be the answer. With the interest in aircraft recovery snowballing during the early 1970s, a number of small, private museum collections had been set up, centred around the various groups engaged in the recovery work, but they were early days and their permanency was uncertain. A number of organisations had fallen by the wayside or changed direction radically, for one reason or another; the signs were not good. In the short term, things would probably be all right, but in the long term? That was the real concern.

The motivation and enthusiasm of the 'wreck hunter' are not necessarily the same as those of the museum curator and administrator. What would happen when all the major wreck sites had been investigated? That time would surely arrive and, probably, was not too far away, given that there was a limit to the amount of material available. What would happen then to the initial flush of enthusiasm that was the driving force in seeking out the aircraft? Would it persist through to the aims of long-term preservation? If not, what would then happen to the recovered items? As the fortunes of groups came and went and some recovered items were neglected or disposed of, the activity laid itself open to attack by critics whose view was that the wrecks should be left alone, unless they could be dealt with properly and in a reasonable manner. How would future historians and archaeologists view some of those activities? With hindsight, it could be said that some of the criticism was justified; items have been lost and some sites dug badly, as a result destroying what could have been important historical evidence. The more dedicated organizations have survived both the test of time and the criticism by sound organization at all levels of activity, and by providing a firm investment in the future of preservation and public displays. However, even then the effects of outside influences, and just pure unavoidable circumstances can still lie as pitfalls, as is the case with any other venture. A few steps along some uncertain paths were also taken during the search for a permanent home for the wreckage of P3175.

Early links were made with what was to become the new aviation centre at the former US airbase of Andrew's Field, west of Braintree in Essex. The project was very much in its infancy and the brainchild of Clive Harvey, whose family farmed the land once occupied by the old wartime airbase. He had a growing interest in aviation and, in the early 1970s, had formulated long-term plans to construct a proper grass landing strip, control tower, and hangar on the site. It was ironic that his father, not many years before, had gone to great lengths to remove the wartime concrete runways! A museum was planned, based around the many items found locally, but it would be some time before it would actually exist. Thirteen years later, under the curatorship of Stan Brett, the fully fledged Rebel Air Museum (as it became known) at Andrew's Field had grown sufficiently in stature and reputation to be awarded a trophy for its contribution to aviation preservation, in a competition run by a national aviation magazine. However, at the time of P3175s recovery it ws too early for the Andrew's Field project.

The next significant development came towards the end of 1974 through contacts at the RAF Museum. Although still unable to deal with the remains themselves, they suggested that the longer-established aircraft collection at RAF Colerne in Wiltshire might be interested. It was one of a decreasing number of small aircraft collections still maintained by the Services. There was a degree of reluctance to move P3175 too far outside the immediate area of the south-east of England, where the aircraft had been based in 1940 and the bulk of that summer's air fighting had taken place, but it was worth a try, if a secure home and proper display facilities were available. An approach was made to the Officer in Charge of the Museum and a follow up visit arranged. The subsequent response was not over-enthusiastic, mainly due to the fact that P3175 was not at a display standard at that time. The virtually intact engine was an immediate attraction, but a series of black and white photographs of a 'do-it-yourself' section of airframe did not command the same kind of interest. The full potential of the exhibit was not readily apparent, but before any firm decisions were made one of those 'outside influences' took a hand: In its latest round of defence cuts, the Ministry of Defence announced the closure of RAF Colerne — so that was that!

It was not until the autumn of 1975, while making a general enquiry to the RAF Museum on another topic, that the subject of P3175's display was introduced again. The response was encouraging. The Keeper of Aircraft wanted the Museum Designer to see the remains in order to assess them for suitability and the possibility of exhibiting them in some way, as it was hoped for favourable developments in the Museum itself that would make acquisition of the remains extremely relevant and possible — but it was still only a possibility. Again, a batch of photographs was despatched, showing the extent of the remains. A further photograph was included, showing the airframe's structure, with as much panelling as possible having been replaced to give the effect of how the final exhibit might look.

The news came in 1976 that the 'favourable development' was in fact to be the formation of some kind of Battle of Britain Museum, probably to be established at Biggin Hill, or some other relevant site. However, it was still very early days and the rather ambitious project had yet to receive official blessing. Most certainly, the engine could be incorporated and, providing that the airframe and engine could be joined together, as suggested, displaying the remaining section of the airframe would also be a distinct possibility, creating a most pertinent and historic exhibit for the projected museum development. Although finally exhibiting the aircraft was still a long way off, the news signalled the start of a move in the right direction and, at last, there was a specific, long-term objective to work towards.

Two of the main considerations were, how the remains were to be presented for display, and how the variety of materials were to be preserved. Guidance was offered by the RAF Museum's own restoration unit at RAF Cardington. There, the workshops carried out all the necessary preparation work for the Hendon exhibits and, although nobody there had ever dealt with such a job, various options were explored.

In discussion with the design team at Hendon, it became apparent that a change in anti-corrosion treatment would be needed, if the full structure was to be presented for display on a long-term basis. Up to that time, every effort had been made to retain the surviving paintwork and maintain corrosion-free surfaces merely by treating any corrosion locally, as it occurred, in the hope of arresting its further spread. It had been a temporary solution, until a final, more permanent solution was found, which would be determined largely by the final method of display. When it came, it was hard to accept, but very necessary. The possibility of corrosion gradually breaking out in the ensuing years could not be risked, therefore all traces of existing corrosion had to be completely removed. The corrosion was patchy, of varying degrees and was not confined to one particular area, therefore producing a consistent appearance required that the whole structure to be taken back to bare metal; a soft blasting process would be required. The plan for the layout of the display was more straightforward.

Although the aircraft had crashed upside down, little would be gained by displaying it in such a posture. It would be more easily recognisable if displayed the right way up, re-assembled as much as possible, but in a nose-down crashed attitude. As the actual formation of the new Battle of Britain Museum was still a long way off, the earlier form of preserving the airframe was continued, until definite dates and arrangements were known.

During that waiting period, some interest of a different kind was shown in the aircraft's remains. Tony Harold, a designer on the Hendon Museum's staff, had learned that a private attempt was to be made to build a Hurricane from scratch, and the construction team were interested in borrowing the remains of P3175, using them, as a blueprint, to build it. It was an interesting development but, unfortunately, an accident to one of the key engineers on the project put an end to the scheme before it ever got properly underway.

Finally, in February 1977, plans to establish the Battle of Britain Museum at Hendon, in a separately constructed building, alongside the main museum's complex, went ahead. Also, it transpired that the list of genuine Battle of Britain-vintage exhibits was very short, therefore the display of P3175 had taken on a new significance. Further discussions began as to its refurbishment, display, design and transport to Hendon. In April, two of the Museum's staff, Ken Hunter and Tony Harold, visited Walton to assess the transport requirements and to familiarize themselves with the task to hand.

The entire wreckage would have to be blasted clean and, with that course of

Not much like an aircraft. P3175 loaded onto the lorry and ready to be transported to Hendon.

At Hendon ready for blasting work to begin. The 'closed circuit' Vacu-Blast machine can be seen, bottom right.

action in mind, no re-assembly had taken place. Blasting machines normally took the form of sealed cabinets, the objects to be cleaned being done so in a totally enclosed space. Given the dimensions of the main airframe, that would be totally prohibitive and a closed circuit free moving air gun type was required. It had to use the same blasting medium of fine glass beads, which removed very effectively all the corrosion products but would not mark the undamaged surfaces significantly. The blasting medium was expensive and designed to be recycled, hence the enclosed cabinet concept. A system not necessarily requiring a cabinet but having a recycling capability by using a closed circuit gun was found to be produced by Vacu-Blast of Slough, not too many miles from Hendon. The Museum's approach to the company resulted in the free use of a 'closed circuit' type machine for work on P3175. The machine was available that August, consequently arrangements were made to transport the airframe's sections to Hendon, shortly before that.

On the morning of Sunday, 31 July a three-ton RAF truck arrived at Walton and manoeuvred into position, ready to receive its load. Dismantling had progressed to the point whereby the largest section, consisting of the wing centre section and associated fuselage framework, could be lifted by four people with relative ease. Pushed to the back of the lorry, it was followed by box upon box of other components which occupied more than double the space taken up by the large section. Peering into the back of the truck, P3175 had never before looked so unlike an aircraft. Loaded right back to the tail board, the truck then began the eighty-mile return trip to Hendon. The actual destination was one of the wooden lock-up garages to the rear of the Museum (now occupied by the Bomber Command extension). It was out of sight from the general public, secure and with sufficient storage space and an adequate working area.

The Hendon complex houses archives material and maintains exhibits, prepared elsewhere. It was never intended to be a place where major work would be undertaken to prepare exhibits for display; therefore work on P3175 was largely a part-time activity. In charge and undertaking the lion's share of the work at the Museum was Research Assistant, Ken Hunter, who soon became 'operator first class' of the Vacu-Blast machine and its associated power source — a full-sized, mobile generator! During the ensuing weeks, other helpers came and went, including members of the Friends of the Museum who, previously, had been looking for a project in which to become involved. Work progressed, when other commitments permitted, but there was a also deadline to meet

— the official opening of the new Battle of Britain Museum had been set for 28 November the following year. It seemed a long time away but working on a part time basis it was to prove a tight schedule.

By the summer of 1978, the main airframe structure had been blast cleaned and was ready to be moved to the new building which had been erected by then. P3175's remains were to be assembled, on site, in the display hall, the crucial job being the installation of the heaviest single item: the Merlin engine.

In June, Ken Hunter and the three-ton truck headed along the A12 again, towards the Essex coast. The destination this time was the garrison town of Colchester, home of No 308 Squadron, ATC. Their headquarters occupied part of the Colchester Army barracks complex and there, in a courtyard, ready for collection, lay the Merlin, still mounted on its display stand and resting on the trailer used to transport it to its various venues. Three of the four massive Bristol Hercules radial engines, salvaged five years earlier from the Halifax crash site, lay to one side. The splendid condition of the Rolls-Royce Merlin was quite a contrast to the badly corroded and broken Hercules engines. The Merlin had been repainted black, giving it a very fresh appearance but not one that looked out of place. It was a shame to think that it would all have to come off, if the engine was to blend in with the rest of the display at Hendon, but it was in the interests of the complete exhibit's long-term preservation. A fork life truck loaded the Merlin on to the three-ton vehicle. It proved to be a much simpler operation than that to collect the airframe. Having been loaded, the truck set off on its return journey to Hendon.

At Hendon, little needed to be done to the engine to bring it up to the required display standard. Having lost its coat of black paint, it was moved into the new building and positioned to form the centrepiece of the Hurricane exhibit. How it was set would determine the final attitude of the rest of the display. It was gently lowered onto supports, a couple of feet or so above the concrete floor, in a slight head-down position and tilted gently to starboard. The base of the actual display was then built up around it, thus raising the whole display nearer to eye level. The port engine bearer and main wing/fuselage centre section were placed on steel supports of differing lengths, thereby lining them up with the angle of the engine. It was certainly not a temporary arrangement; once erected, it was there to stay.

With the general attitude of the display fixed and a false floor built up around it (later to be turned into a beach scene), the whole structure was ready for the addition of the panel pieces, wiring loom, pipes and mass of other small components that would together recreate the sense of complex machinery that was once an aircraft. Ken Hunter had been allocated the assistance of two volunteer airmen from the adjoining RAF station; extra help was also given by some of the 'Friends'. Positioning the pieces during the re-build turned out to be easier than had been anticipated, helped no doubt, by the team's growing familiarity with the aircraft's structure. The presence of the Museum's other Mk I Hurricane,

Rolls-Royce Merlin III engine No 22637 awaits collection at Colchester.

P2617, was an added benefit; already inside the new building, just fifty yards away, it was used as and when rapid reference was required. The Vacu-Blasting work continued on demand, sections being transferred from the garage workshop to the display area at a steady flow.

When the aircraft had crashed inverted, all its upper fuselage had been crushed but, fortunately, sufficient individual items had remained intact and been salvaged to be able to represent its form. The display would have been so much the poorer without the large panel that covered the fuselage fuel tank, and the smaller, windscreen arch sections. In fact, much of the final display has been made up of numerous, small individual pieces which, on their own, could have appeared to be nothing special, and could so easily have been discarded during digging while the main components were sought. Had that been done, the final exhibit might not have been as imposing and significant as it appears today. Small pieces can be just as important as the more attractive and immediately recognisable large items.

The area allocated for the display held one disappointment: the space was limited. To permit adequate public access, the stand was not large enough to display all of the remains. Consequently, the remaining structure around the starboard wing which then existed in skeletal form out to as far as the undercarriage leg — (despite being broken on impact) was omitted. Therefore, the starboard wing terminated level with the fuselage's side. The same applied to the rear spar of the outer port wing and that had to be left off. Nevertheless, approximately fifty per cent of the complete aircraft's volume and approximately seventy per cent of its weight have been incorporated in the final display.

The remains of Hurricane P3175 displayed at the RAF Museum, Hendon in the Battle of Britain Hall.

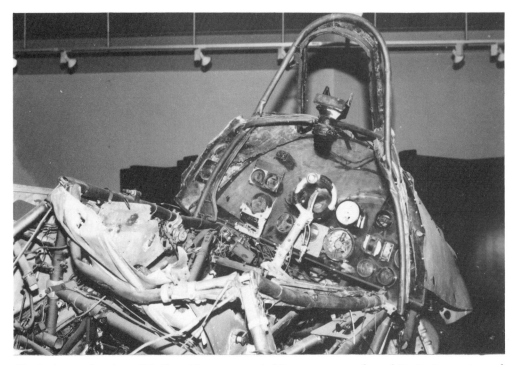

The instruments returned to the airframe, mounted in a perspex replica of the instrument panel. The gun button on the control column is switched to 'fire'.

On Tuesday, 28 November 1978 Her Majesty Queen Elizabeth The Queen Mother officially opened the new Battle of Britain Museum; the remains of Hurricane P3175 were positioned just inside the main entrance. It was one of only a very few aircraft on display that actually participated in the Battle, and forms a memorial to those aircrew who took part in it and became casualties, as a result. Stretching a point, it could be said almost that P3175 had finally returned home. No 257 Squadron was formed at Hendon during the dark days of Dunkirk in May 1940.

Initially, the Squadron operated from Hendon before moving, via a short spell at Northolt, to Debden in mid-August. It was while based there, but temporarily operating from Martlesham Heath, that P3175 crashed, just before 9 o'clock on Saturday, 31 August, 1940.

Part Two — One Raid

Note: Readers may find the Explanatory Notes (page 152) useful before reading this section of the book.

Chapter Nine
Introduction

The following account attempts to piece together what happened during the early morning raid of Saturday 31 August 1940 when Hurricane P3175 crashed. It is based on known incidents, drawn from a wide variety of both official and personal contemporary records, together with recollections of many people who were there at the time, either in the air or on the ground. After nearly fifty years many of those people who were involved with or witnessed the events are no longer alive, therefore it is biased towards being a survivors' account. As such, it must be understood that any emphasis on a particular incident does not necessarily reflect its relative importance in the day's activities, only that it was recorded or remembered by a particular person. Some aspects of the aerial conflict are believed to have been unclear, even at the time when they occurred and it is likely that the true overall picture was never pieced together as a whole. For many who had taken part, and subsequently survived the war, or had watched from the ground, there was nothing to differentiate that particular day from any other of the many similar days that summer, therefore many potential contributions have been lost. For some people, the day's events were to affect their lives dramatically, with things never being quite the same again. Consequently, their recollections are often vivid and, seemingly, affected little by the passing years. Also, the memory is fallible and, after such a lapse of time, some aspects remain clear and accurate, while others have been coloured unknowingly by events and/or accounts read or heard about afterwards. Where possible, cross-checks have been done, in an effort to present a true and accurate account but understandably, it may still contain some factual errors. They are most likely to occur where only one source has been used but, as was found, agreement between two sources does not guarantee any degree of accuracy, unless it can be demonstrated that the accounts originated from completely independent sources.

To unravel what happened, an obvious starting point would have been German archives, to establish which of the Luftwaffe units went where, when and why. The Essex area came under *Luftflotte 2*'s umbrella of operations but, unfortunately, under High Command's orders, their records were destroyed before the end of the war. Luftwaffe casualty lists *have* survived and from them it has been possible to identify some of the units. However, because Luftwaffe casualties were particularly light that morning, a far from complete picture can be drawn from that source. Consequently and contrary to original intention, it has not been possible to narrate events completely from the raiders' points of view. Instead the account has been presented in the form of a chronological sequence of events, based on the surviving evidence of how the defenders perceived things to have developed.

Surviving official British records are quite comprehensive and most are readily available at various local and national archive centres. The Air Historical Branch (of what is now the Ministry of Defence) has a narrative which covers the period. Compiled just after the war, it gives a daily account of events and RAF Squadron activities, but it does not give a complete picture and, in places, it contradicts other contemporary records. During the research for this book therefore, it was considered essential to start from scratch and seek out original source material.

Squadron and RAF Station Operations Record Books provide a prime source of material, together with individual pilots' Combat Reports — all contain detailed data. However, the former vary in quality and depth of detail, and the latter are incomplete. Interpreting these valuable records is made more difficult by clerical errors, such as typing and transcription. A similar situation exists in the records of the ground defences. There, very often, over-generalization, frequent ambiguous wording and incorrect map references all serve to cast doubt on the reliability of some of the information. Such errors cause an amount of cross-checking in order to confirm details, then a check has to be made to try and ensure that they did not have the same origin! But at least a wide selection of records still exists. (To be fair, in many cases such records are being subjected to far more scrutiny than their originators could ever have envisaged when they were being compiled.)

It was more frustrating to find that individual documents from a sequence had disappeared. Such was the case with the Observer Corps' logs for Area No 18, which covered most of Essex, where the majority of the activity took place on the morning of 31 August 1940. The log covering that day is missing. It alone could have provided that all important time base to link incidents recorded in other sources. As it is, individual actions have been linked together by other means where possible (where doubt exists it has been identified as such in Appendix B: the intention being to avoid inventing history).

For similar reasons and because they could not be placed in the chronological order of events with any degree of confidence, a number of known facts have been omitted. It is hoped, however, that more facts and source data will come to light in the future. Should you, the reader, be aware of any, I would be pleased to hear from you. They might be only small and their significance may not appear to be great in isolation. but their true potential often can be realised only when they are combined with other facts. It is hoped that in due course a still more complete picture of the events that morning can be presented.

Chapter Ten
Build Up

31 August 1940, Cambrai, Northern France. Just after 0700 hr, British Summer Time, the engines of III Gruppe KG2's Dornier 17s burst into life, ready for another deep penetration raid, at Gruppe strength, against one of the RAF's inland airfields, north of the Thames. Walter Schlüter, a radio operator on the Gruppe's staff later recorded in his log: '0705,' Take off for *'Angriff auf Debden'* (attack against Debden).

In the air and clear of the airfield, the aircraft manoeuvred into the well-rehearsed and familiar 'Kette' defensive sub-units of three aircraft in arrowhead formation. Walter Schlüter's pilot tucked U5+BD in behind, and to the right, of the Gruppen Kommander's aircraft, to form part of the Gruppe's Staff Flight which made up the second Kette in the formation. The rest of the Gruppe's aircraft, consisting of 7, 8 and 9 Staffeln were strung out to either side and behind. Climbing slowly, the large formation headed north-west over the French countryside, to rendezvous with their fighter escort. A little earlier,[1] another group of Dorniers, from II/KG2, had taken off from Arras eighteen miles to the west. They were some minutes ahead of III/KG2's aircraft, on a similar track, and preparing to attack the RAF airfield at Duxford, just to the south of Cambridge.

The sun had risen in a cloudless sky and there was a light westerly wind. It was going to be a fine day and the crews settled down for the long flight. Visibility would be good, so there should be no problem in locating the targets; but with no cloud cover, the RAF fighters would easily see them. The massive fighter escort gave some degree of comfort, but the long flight over enemy territory in broad daylight would surely not be made without incident for, although the RAF's fighter force had been pressed hard during the previous few weeks, raids were still meeting considerable opposition. Only a few days previously, Luftwaffe fighters had been withdrawn en masse from the Normandy area of France and concentrated in the Pas de Calais to provide extra support to the daylight bombing effort of Luftflotte 2. The raids did not appear to be getting any easier and losses were steadily mounting.

The reality of Fighter Command's perilous position was not particularly evident, in spite of the numerous Luftwaffe victories claimed. RAF losses were high, but of greater concern to Fighter Command was the loss of its pilots. Aircraft could be and were being replaced, but it took time to train new pilots and time was running short. Most pilots were tired after continuous periods of flying three, four or more sorties a day; and the days were long, with pilots at readiness from first light, through until dusk. Enemy raids were expected and occurred any time during the fifteen hours of daylight. Without the early warning advantage, provided by the coastal radar network, continuous patrols would have been necessary. Given the many weeks of prolonged activity, the pilots of Fighter Command would have been under an impossible strain.

General location map

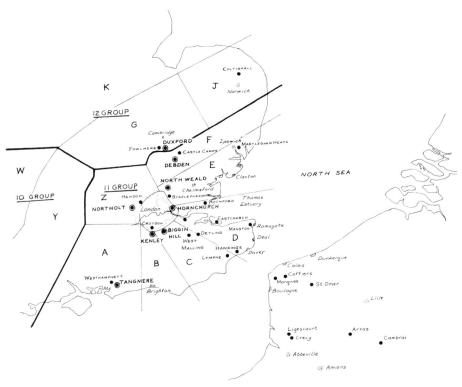

However, for the Dornier crews that Saturday, danger still lay ahead and there remained the likelihood that some of them would not return. The previous Monday afternoon, many of the same crews from III/KG2 had set out on a similar mission to the RAF airfield at Debden. The target had been reached and much damage done but not without cost: three aircraft and their crews had not returned and fighter opposition had been particularly fierce. That Saturday, however, the long-range escort of twin-engined Me 110s had been supplemented with Me 109s from JG26. The RAF airfields of Debden and Duxford were close to the limit of the 109s' operating range, leaving little time for combat before lack of fuel forced them to retire, but their performance made them a severe test for the Hurricanes and Spitfires. The Me 110s however were proving to be no real match for the single-engined, British fighters.

By 0730 hr the Me 110s of V(Z)/LG1 had taken off from Crecy and Ligescourt and were heading northward along the French coast, to rendezvous with their bomber formation over Boulogne. At about the same time the Me 110s of III/ZG26 had taken off from St Omer, linking up with their bombers as they passed St Omer on their way to the French north coast.[2] Ten minutes later, the Me 109s of JG26 took off from their bases at Caffiers and Marquise in the Pas de

Calais. Airfields for the Me 109s had been located as near the coast as possible, to gain maximum flying time over England. The Me 109s[3] took up their position with the combined formation of Dorniers and Me 110s as they crossed the coast.

The build-up was being monitored by the radar stations along the south-east coast of England and two fighter squadrons were scrambled. Nine Hurricanes of No 1 Squadron left Northolt at 0740 hr to patrol Chelmsford, just inland from the Essex coast. Five minutes later, eight Hurricanes of No 151 Squadron were airborne from North Weald's satellite airfield, Stapleford Tawney, and heading south-east, towards the Kent coast. By 0750 hr, radar information estimated that four German formations were on the move between Cap Gris Nez and Dunkirk, comprising some sixty aircraft in all. The KG2 formations, together with their escort, had indeed crossed the French coast and were heading for the outer Thames Estuary. At the same time, a separate formation was detected, crossing the Dover Straits and heading towards Deal and Dover. No 151 Squadron was directed to intercept.

The Squadron had been based at North Weald for most of that summer's fighting, but much damage had been done to the airfield during a bombing raid a week earlier and many of the pilots had lost their belongings. Consequently, the Squadron had been dispersed to the more spartan facilities of the satellite airfield at Stapleford Tawney, six miles to the south. By the end of August, the Squadron was badly depleted of both pilots and aircraft. In the previous two weeks two Squadron Commanders had been lost: Sqn Ldr Gordon lay in

Pilots of No 151 Squadron waiting at their dispersal at Rochford, mid-August 1940. Left to right (sitting), Plt Off Irving Smith, Plt Off John Ellacombe, unknown Sgt Plt; (reclining), Sqn Ldr J. A. 'Pete' Gordon, Flt Lt Dick Smith, unknown. *(Gp Capt I. S. Smith)*

hospital at Rochford after having baled out of his Hurricane on 18 August; his replacement, Sqn Ldr King, had been killed when his aircraft was shot down over Rochester on 30 August.

31 August was to be the Squadron's last full day of action in the south-east, for a while; although some members of the Squadron took part in a couple of scrambles the following morning. The depleted squadron was eventually to move north to RAF Digby, during the afternoon of 1 September, for a rest, having been relieved by the Hurricanes of No 46 Squadron.

For that first scramble of the morning of 31 August, the Squadron had managed to get eight aircraft airborne, and were led by the 'B' Flight Commander (and acting Commanding Officer), Flt Lt Dick Smith. He was flying what was effectively an experimental cannon-armed Hurricane, the remainder of the Squadron flying Hurricanes containing the standard eight machine guns.

In the Ramsgate area, the Squadron met a force of about thirty Me 109s at 14,000 ft. A dogfight ensued in which the Squadron was split up, individual actions then moving south towards the Dover area. Flt Lt 'John Willie' Blair, of Yellow Section, got on the tail of one Me 109 which had half-rolled and gone into a very steep dive. He followed it down but at 5,000 ft, being unable to get his sights to bear, he began to pull out of the dive. At 500 ft, he succeeded, just in time, but as the 109 had shown no sign of doing likewise he considered it highly probable that its pilot had failed to regain control and had dived straight into the ground. A 'probable' was claimed.

Plt Off John Ellacombe also claimed a 'probable' after closing behind a 109 and giving it a five-second burst at 150 yd. He saw the underwing radiator blow off and smoke pour from under the wings. Closing in, a further burst caused smoke to pour out of the engine, and the aircraft went into a spin. Close to the ground, the 109 recovered and headed out to sea. Plt Off Ellacombe dived down to finish it off, but the 109 had entered a low bank of sea fog, about three miles from the coast. He waited for it to emerge from the other side, but nothing appeared.

Flt Lt Smith became separated from the rest of his squadron in the initial engagement. So, he flew first to the west, then to the south and, finally, to the east, trying to position himself up sun of the enemy's anticipated position. The manoeuvre had caused him to arrive at Dover where he spotted three 109s, 1,000 ft below and heading out to sea. He attacked one, but did not wait to see the result because the other two had turned towards him.

The engagement between the two fighter units followed what had become a familiar pattern: a short, sharp, initial engagement, causing the aircraft to scatter and leaving many apparently alone in the sky. No 151 Squadron had come through that first encounter of the day unscathed, and the eight Hurricanes returned to Stapleford to re-arm, refuel and await the next call. On the way back, Flt Lt Smith was sure he had heard German being spoken on the radio. He noted it in his Combat Report, describing how the German words were clearer than those of the members of his own squadron, and he warned of the danger of compromising place-name codes, if the German aircraft were using the same frequency.

No 151 Squadron was in action three more times that day and lost two aircraft, both pilots managing to parachute to safety. Plt Off Ellacombe was one of them, baling out after crossfire from some Ju88s he was attacking caused his fuselage fuel tank to blow up. Later that day, Plt Off Irving Smith had a lucky escape. In the afternoon, he took off for his third sortie of the day, leading a section of three aircraft. He climbed up to 18,000 ft in order to attack a large bomber formation:

I approached from the port beam and below in a near vertical climb, levelling out at close range on a bomber's tail. I fired my whole ammunition load in one continuous burst. A large piece of flap came off the Dornier, went through my propeller and hit my fuselage just behind the cockpit, stripping off the fabric and damaging the wooden formers. Also, while I was shooting I could feel my aircraft being hit by crossfire from other aircraft in the formation. They were in vics of five and we could only engage three of them. Having exhausted my ammunition, I rolled away, in a continuous tight diving spiral (I was over Stapleford) and landed. The whole sortie only took about eighteen minutes. While my aircraft was being refuelled and re-armed, and the holes in the fuselage were being patched, I was standing a few yards away with our Engineer Officer when suddenly he said, 'That looks peculiar.' He walked over to the aircraft, had all the doped patches taken off and found that three of the four fuselage longerons had been shot through. With the extra weight of fuel etc, and the men swarming all over it, the aircraft was bending slowly in the middle just behind the cockpit.

Essex and the Thames Estuary at 0815–0915 Saturday, 31 August.

It needed little imagination to picture an attempted take off in that condition! It also meant that, effectively, the Squadron lost three aircraft that day.

No 151 Squadron's first encounter of the day had achieved the desired German aim of drawing the RAF fighters into action. Consequently, there would be one squadron less to engage the main bomber formations.

Having crossed the French coast, II/KG2 maintained a more northerly course,[4] away from the Kent coast, to avoid the land-based defences for as long as possible.

At 0757 hr, when No 151 Squadron was preparing to go into action over the Ramsgate area, the Sector Operations Room at Debden plotted Raid 29 as being 30+ aircraft at 18,000 ft, some twenty miles further east, over the outer Thames Estuary, and travelling north. An attack on the airfields north of the Thames appeared to be very likely. An Air Raid Warning Yellow was passed to the Essex coastal strip, and the anti-aircraft defences were alerted.

Just after 0800 hr, the Dorniers turned to port, on a more westerly heading, aiming for the coast between the Rivers Crouch and Blackwater. Raid 29 was now updated to 50+ aircraft, at 18,000 ft. No 1 Squadron had already been directed to the Chelmsford area, thus protecting the approach to the RAF Sector Stations of North Weald and Hornchurch. Then, orders went out for No 111 Squadron to scramble and provide cover for RAF Debden, No 11 Group's other Sector Station, north of the Thames.

Like No 151 Squadron, No 111 had been heavily involved in the earlier battles of that summer, mainly while operating further south, from Croydon. On 19 August, the Squadron had been moved further back from the main assault area to the supposedly quieter sector, covered by Debden, but the main thrust of the Luftwaffe's attack was moving also, and No 111's pilots found little respite.

At 0805 hr, air raid sirens began their familiar wail along the full length of the Essex coast, from Southend to Harwich, alerting the public to the impending danger. At the same time, Debden's Operations Room was again updating Raid 29 as being 30 aircraft, at 18,000 ft.

Five minutes later nine Hurricanes of No 111 Squadron took off from Debden's satellite airstrip at Castle Camps and started to climb into position to patrol Debden. At the same time, men of the 9th Battalion Cameronians, dug-in along the coastal strip between Clacton and St Osyth, as part of the anti-invasion forces, looked seaward to see aircraft, at a great height, approaching from the east, then paralleling their part of the coast.

At 0815 hr, Raid 29 was reported to have crossed the coast, just south of the River Blackwater, Debden further updating it as 30+ aircraft at 15,000 ft, heading west. No 11 Group asked No 12 Group, whose area was immediately to the north, to provide additional fighter cover and, subsequently, eleven Spitfires from No 19 Squadron took off from Fowlmere with orders to patrol Debden and Duxford at 20,000 ft. Seemingly, the confrontation was beginning to take shape.

Just after 0820 hr, Raid 29 was reported to be just north-east of Chelmsford, and varying between fifteen and twenty hostile aircraft which were approaching from the east and heading north-west at 20,000 ft. There, an Air Raid Warning Red had preceded the sighting by only five minutes. Soldiers from the light anti-aircraft defences, protecting the industrial centres in Chelmsford, watched the first enemy aircraft approach and pass them, heading towards the north-west. Two minutes later, they reported seeing a second formation of thirty hostile aircraft, approaching from the east which then headed towards the south-west.[5]

At that point the picture became less clear. The surviving records are fragmented and some are even contradictory. Whether that was so at the time, or whether there was just a gap in the records is unclear. It is tempting to conclude that poor quality information during the early stages of the enemy's approach, when updated with positive ground sightings led to the confusion.

Whatever the cause, information about events which occurred in the ensuing vital fifteen minutes remains uncertain. The Observer Corps' records could have eliminated the uncertainty, had they still existed.

In the air, No 1 Squadron was the first to discover the true strength of the leading enemy formation. As the raiders streamed passed Chelmsford, the Squadron was poised to attack. Sqn Ldr Pemberton was leading the nine Hurricanes when the enemy aircraft were sighted travelling north-west, at approximately 15,000 ft and in much greater strength than had been predicted. His Combat Report for the encounter continues:

> . . . they were in formations of ten, stepped up to about 20,000 ft, about one hundred of them.[6] They were protected by fighters. I tried to bring [the] Squadron in on a head on attack (we were both southwest of the enemy formation). As I drew alongside I saw another enemy formation above us, composed of fighters and bombers, and the Squadron had to break away to engage fighters which came down. After a general mill round of the fighters I found myself alone . . .

The bombers' escort had proved its worth, preventing the Hurricanes' attack, but No 1 Squadron was to have another chance later on.

Fifteen miles west of Chelmsford, at RAF North Weald, the possibility of an attack had been realised. It had two resident fighter squadrons: No 151 was in action over East Kent, but No 56 Squadron's aircraft were still on the ground, the pilots having been stood down after flying for most of the previous day. No 56 Squadron was called urgently to 'readiness' followed by immediate take-off.

The leading German bomber formation continued its way north-west, towards Dunmow; the Sector Operations Room at Debden then designating it Raid 29A.[7] A subsidiary raid, Raid 29B, was reported simultaneously as being further west, in the vicinity of Harlow, also heading north-west. RAF Debden's Operations Record Book later recorded the second group as dropping bombs over Harlow.

No 334 Searchlight Battery confirmed that in their War Diary by reporting a message they had received from SLO Debden, at 0823 hr, in which a map reference, plotting Raid 29B to the north of Harlow, was given. The source was the same (the Sector Operations Room at Debden), but there is no other evidence to prove that the area was bombed[8] or that enemy aircraft were in the vicinity. Besides those two, no other references to Raid 29B have been found and it is tempting to conclude that it was a spurious plot. However, it is conceivable that it could have been the second group of aircraft (which had been seen approaching Chelmsford, then reported to be heading south-west), which had perhaps merely skirted round the south of Chelmsford and turned north-west again, thus causing the remark in No 56 Squadron's Operations Record Book about enemy aircraft approaching the aerodrome. The surviving evidence being far from conclusive, the Harlow incident should be treated with caution.

With Raid 29A apparently heading directly towards Debden, Sector Operations scrambled the station's remaining fighter squadron, No 601. As at North Weald, and in the attempt to reduce the effect of bombing on the main airfields, Debden's normal contingent of three fighter squadrons had been dispersed. By late August, No 111 Squadron was operating from Castle Camps, seven miles north-east of Debden, and No 257 had been moved to Martlesham Heath for an unspecified period. Only No 601 Squadron remained at Debden.

No 111 Squadron was already airborne and had been tasked to cover Debden, and the Spitfires of No 19 Squadron (12 Group) were covering the ground between Debden and Duxford. At 0827 hr, eleven Hurricanes of No 601 Squadron took off from Debden. Shortly afterwards, and forty-five miles further east, the Hurricanes of No 257 Squadron also started to climb.

A couple of miles north-west of RAF Debden lay the town of Saffron Walden. There, as in most places, the routine of war duties combined with normal work had become a familiar pattern, after almost a year since the declaration of war.

Janet Farnham had spent Friday night on ambulance duty at ARP head-quarters in Audley Road. At seven-thirty she came off duty and walked home, for an early breakfast, before setting off for Colchester and a day's work with the local auctioneers, Woodward and Priday.

About quarter past eight, a car load of six people, including herself, set off on the Thaxted road, which ran alongside the north-east boundary of RAF Debden. She recalled that it was a glorious, summer's day, the sun was shining brightly but there was a slight haze;

> *I was in the back and so couldn't see out so well. As the car approached the airfield, Mr Page, the Auctioneer, sitting in the front, suddenly made us all sit up by shouting to the driver to step on it, as he thought there looked like trouble. We could see airmen running for their fighter planes and others disappearing into bunkers. We sped past the aerodrome landing ground and down the small dip in the road by the aerodrome buildings. We had just reached the turning that doubles back around the airfield at Elder Street, when Mr Page called 'My goodness! Can you see them [enemy aircraft] all coming towards us in the distance? We'd better get off the road'. Half way up the other side of the dip, just past the turning and no more than a quarter of a mile from the airfield we pulled over, got into a field and went and lay down beside the hedge Looking up, we watched a group of aircraft go almost overhead*

Fifteen or twenty, she thought, passing in an orderly fashion, together with 'little' fighter planes. The minute they had passed over, the party got up, piled back into the car and sped on their way. Despite being close to the airfield, Janet Farnham did not recall hearing any bombs. In fact, the enemy formation had passed just west of the airfield, but had held its destructive load, which was destined elsewhere. No 601 Squadron was only just leaving the ground and neither No 111 nor No 19 Squadrons had been in a position to prevent this apparent near miss.

The bombers continued, unhindered, towards the north-west. Another ten miles and they would be over the No 12 Group Sector airfield of Duxford. This was to be II/KG2's target.

Chapter Eleven
Duxford

Eleven Spitfires of No 19 Squadron had taken off from Duxford's satellite airfield of Fowlmere, at between 0810 and 0815 hr. Sgt David Cox remembers it as having been a real panic take-off. He had been asleep at the time of the alert and he had time only to put an Irvine jacket over his pyjamas. 'B' Flight's aircraft were dispersed on the far side of the airfield and the pilots had to leap onto a lorry, which then careered across the airfield to reach their machines. 'A' Flight, led by Fg Off Frank Brinsden, took off first, but only managed to get five aircraft airborne — the sixth was left behind. Arriving at his aircraft, Flt Sgt George Unwin was surprised to find no ground crew to assist with the start-up and take-off procedures; he soon found out that it was because his aircraft had been placed 'unserviceable'. (Later, he took the flight sergeant in charge of servicing to task when he found it had been done only because a minor inspection was due!)

Within five minutes, six aircraft of 'B' Flight (led by their Flight Commander, Flt Lt Wilf Clouston) had followed. In the absence of the Squadron's commander, Flt Lt Clouston was in overall command of the two flights, which climbed hard to gain altitude as quickly as possible. Initially, the two flights acted independently because a thick haze prevented them from joining up. Fg Off Brinsden remembered breaking through the haze into a clear, blue sky and a blinding sun, as they headed in an easterly direction to the patrol line.

Climbing through 15,000 ft, 'A' Flight lost another aircraft, reducing it to four machines, when Sgt Bernard Jennings peeled off with oxygen problems. At that height, the oxygen had to be turned 'on'. Although he had made the switch on the instrument panel, he soon began to feel light-headed and happily drunk. He recognised the symptoms, as, only a few weeks earlier he had been through a decompression test which demonstrated the effects of reduced oxygen. He checked the oxygen indicator — there was no reading. He rolled the aircraft onto its back, dived for the deck and headed back to Fowlmere on a reciprocal course.

On his approach, he saw what he thought were little piles of smoking ashes on the landing site. He came straight in, over the Royston-Fowlmere road, to land and taxied over to dispersal. Having arrived, he saw the rest of the personnel in the slit-trenches. He swung the aircraft's nose round, parallel with the trenches as his fitter and rigger dashed out. 'Oxygen!' he shouted, and pointed to the tail. Reaching the aircraft, his rigger opened the flap above the tail wheel and turned the oxygen on. From the safety of a trench, Flt Lt Brian Lane, 'A' Flight's commander, yelled to him to get in the trench. No fear! Jennings thought. Too dangerous there. He saw the bubble on the oxygen indicator move, swung the aircraft's nose round a little more, opened the throttle and took off again, over the Royston road, and climbed towards the south-east.

The lack of oxygen was explained when it was discovered that during the daily inspection, his rigger had checked the oxygen by turning it on in the cockpit, then off again. Then, for some unknown reason, he had turned it off at the tail also, leaving the line from the tail to the cockpit fully charged. It was that which must have moved the indicator ball when Sgt Jennings checked it before take-off.

No 19 Squadron had been fortunate in two respects. The piles of ashes Sgt Jennings had seen were the results of incendiary bombs. In the time it had taken him to get airborne, reach 15,000 ft and return, the airfield had received a visit from a formation of enemy bombers. The Squadron had been lucky, for not only had it cleared the airfield, but also the run of bombs had only clipped the northern part of the landing field and no damage was done to affect airfield operations.

Flt Sgt Unwin's aircraft had escaped unscathed and he had taken cover in a nearby slit trench along with his Alsatian dog, Flash. The bombing was to have a lasting effect on Flash. He had been reared from a pup at Duxford and was accustomed completely to aircraft. The bombing terrified him to such an extent that he broke away from his master and disappeared, at full speed, across the landing field. From that day, whenever he heard a multi-engined aircraft, he was off. Squadrons of Hurricanes or Spitfires could fly overhead and he took no notice, but one Blenheim or Wellington and he went into a blind panic!

A clear account of the bombing was given in an official booklet, produced, just after the war, by Cambridge County Council. Entitled 'An Historical Account of Air Raid Precautions, 1935–1945', it was a record of the civil defence organisations' contributions to the war effort.

> . . . [At about 0830 hours] *between 120 and 150 High Explosive Bombs were dropped in . . . two more or less continuous lines at fairly regular intervals of about 50 yards; the distance between the two lines varied from coincidence to about 100 yards. They started on Manor Farm, Fowlmere,* [19 Squadron's HQ] *close to the farm buildings (to which no appreciable damage was done). About 50 were dropped in a clover field in a north-westerly line. The soil is largely clunch, and in most cases the effect of the bomb was to disturb the earth in a rough circle of, perhaps, 12 or 15 feet radius, and leave it piled up without a central crater of any depth or regularity. In the softer ground at the bottom of the field the craters were more defined. This applies to the effect of the bombs throughout. At the bottom of the clover field is a shed in which men working on water-cress beds were having breakfast. Several bombs fell quite close, and a glass window in the shed was broken, and the galvanised iron roof was slightly damaged. The men were not hurt at all. The line of bombs then went through stubble, orchard, and grass land, until it reached the Cambridge-Royston road (Route A.10). One bomb fell on the western grass verge about 100 yards south of the Fowlmere turn. The side of the road was damaged, but one-way traffic was always practicable. The road was reopened fully by Saturday evening. There was a house within 50 yards of the point where the bomb fell, which suffered no damage. The line of bombs continued across stubble to the Hitchin-Cambridge railway, close to the Cam Blue Lias Cement Works, about half way between Meldreth and Shepreth stations. One bomb fell on each side of the railway within a few yards, but no damage was done. The line of bombs continued over a*

grass field, and through an orchard to the Meldreth-Shepreth road, one bomb fell in the middle of the road close to a small bridge which carried the road over the stream dividing Meldreth and Shepreth parishes. The road was rendered impassable, but the bridge was not damaged. The blast appeared to work backwards. A lump of concrete was thrown a considerable distance southwards, but a cottage which was within 50 yards obliquely north suffered no damage. The road was reopened to traffic on Saturday evening. The line then continued close to the same stream until it entered the river, and there were a few bombs north of the river in Barrington parish. A number of Incendiary Bombs were dropped at the same time, but these fell not so regularly, and more to the east. Some fell in Fowlmere, others in various parts of Shepreth, and some on Barrington Green. The exact number is not known. A few of the High Explosive bombs did not explode on landing.

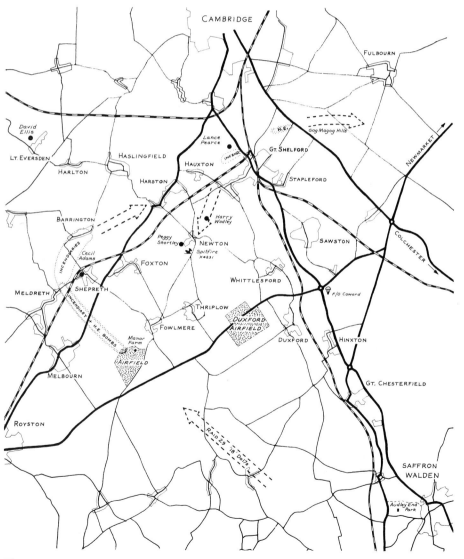

The Duxford Raid 0830–0835.

David Ellis, then a school boy, remembered the event well; it was his sixteenth birthday. The family had just finished breakfast when the sound of explosions was heard, together with the noise of many aircraft. He dashed out to the driveway of the farm house in Little Eversden and, looking up, high and away southeast towards Fowlmere, he could see the faint specks of perhaps a dozen or so aircraft, heading northwards and getting nearer. The sound of machine-gun fire could be heard clearly, and very soon it was joined by an ominous whine. Thinking it was a falling bomb, observation was curtailed and the family dived for a ditch, but no explosion followed. On reflection, he thought that it could have been the sound of empty cartridge cases falling because he heard later that some were supposed to have been found elsewhere in the village.

He need not have worried because the bombers did not venture quite as far north as Little Eversden. As David Ellis was diving for cover the formation was already turning away from its north-westerly heading, towards the north-east, as it passed between the villages of Shepreth and Barrington and on towards Great Shelford, just south of Cambridge. Bombs continued to fall as the formation swung round. Incendiary and high-explosive bombs were both recorded later as having fallen on the parishes of Shepreth, Barrington, Haslingfield, Harston, Hauxton, Newton and Great Shelford.

Another sixteen-year-old alerted by the noise and of equal inquisitiveness, Lance Pearce, then lived at Stonehill Road on the Cambridge side of Great Shelford. Being on slightly higher ground it gave a good view over the flat Cambridgeshire countryside, further west. Hearing the sound of gun-fire he dashed outside to the end of the road and saw, away to the south-west, the bursts of anti-aircraft fire coming from Duxford, but he noted that the aerial bursts were nowhere near the aircraft. He could hear machine-gun fire, but could see no fighters. He watched as the formation (which he estimated to be of perhaps twenty or so bombers, flying in vics of three, line astern) appeared to follow the railway line from the direction of Shepreth towards Great Shelford. They passed just to the south of his vantage point and as they did so some incendiary bombs fell in the field just by the end of the road. When they started to burn, he ran, together with some other people, round the field looking at them, while a War Reserve Policeman tried in vain to stop them.

The formation continued north-east over Great Shelford. Having passed, Lance Pearce watched as it then turned towards a more easterly direction. After the aircraft had gone, he cycled the mile or so across to the other side of Great Shelford, where a line of high-explosive bombs had fallen at Shelford Bottom, situated right on the Cambridge Borough boundary. Most had landed in a ploughed field, between Granham's Road and Hinton Way, but one had made a crater in the road of Hinton Way, just before the junction with the main Cambridge to Colchester road, by the Gog Magog hills.

PC 17, John Barker, was despatched from Cambridge with two Special Constables to take necessary action as incident officer. On arrival, he noted that the craters were quite small; no more than eight or ten feet across. The crater in Hinton Way was causing a traffic hold-up, but within an hour, workmen had filled it in and the traffic was free to flow again.

At that time John Barker had just volunteered for aircrew duties. Later and from his experience in the RAF he presumed that the bombs were probably the fragmentation type and had been jettisoned no doubt.

During the summer of 1940, numerous Army units were camped in the parklands and grounds of various Halls in that part of East Anglia. Of that particular raid the following was recorded in the 6th Battalion Royal Sussex Regiment's war diary:

> *0828 — 15 German aeroplanes flew high over Fowlmere and dropped 126 HE and Incendiary bombs of which 7 fell in the airfield. Total damage slight. Total casualties 2 rabbits.*

In Shepreth, troops from a column of Bren Gun carriers had stopped for breakfast by the village memorial. Cecil Adams, then working as a carpenter in the village, later remembered some of the soldiers stripping off for a wash at the water pump in the yard where he worked, but the sounds of anti-aircraft gun-fire and approaching aircraft brought a rapid halt to their activities and, with some haste, they were soon on the move again. It was later when he returned home that he discovered how lucky he was to still have a house; it was only just around the corner from where the Meldreth-Shepreth road had been blocked by the last high-explosive bomb dropped from the line that had begun at Fowlmere.

In the village of Newton, just south west of Great Shelford and only a couple of miles north of Duxford, the Hall and its surrounding grounds had been commandeered by the Army. The whole area, including the village itself, was 'choc-a-bloc' with tanks, armoured vehicles and lorries from units of the 6th Armoured Division, all parked under the shelter of the trees. The soldiers were all under canvas.

It was a day to remember for Peggy Wadley: her wedding day. At the time, she was living with her parents in a house which was near to the Hall. She was just getting up,

> *. . . when the siren went and, it seemed, a very short time after that all hell was let loose. The rest of the family dashed for the air-raid shelter, sited on the Hall's lawn, shouting for me to hurry up. I had hastily dressed and dashed into the kitchen when a series of thuds shook the house and the glass tumblers on a shelf of my mother's kitchen dresser literally tumbled and smashed on the floor. When I attempted to run across to the air-raid shelter I was stopped by some soldiers who ordered me to take cover as there was a tremendous amount of flak from the anti-aircraft guns at Duxford at that moment.*

The raid in the morning was only the start of a traumatic day for the bride-to-be. Her fiance, who was travelling from Northern Ireland, had failed to appear the previous day. As the Saturday wore on and there had been no word from him, Peggy, fearing he had been killed in an air-raid, was being consoled by her mother while her father was became more and more convinced that she had been jilted! Preparations continued, regardless.

Half an hour before the service was due, the bridegroom arrived, and described an eventful and frustrating journey that had spanned three days. During that early part of the war, every time the siren went everything stopped.

The increasingly anxious bridegroom had spent a great deal of time both in air-raid shelters and in a blacked out stationary train. In the end he had abandoned the train and, at no small expense, hired a taxi for the final twenty miles to Newton, which had included a diversion into Cambridge to renew items stolen from his kit bag on the train the previous night — not least of which was a replacement present for his bride. As a final touch to the day, the siren sounded during the wedding service, but on that occasion the vicar just carried on.

August being a busy month in the rural calendar, her younger brother Harry had been up early to help with the harvest, carting wheat in from the fields. The younger boys were employed working the horses as 'leaders', taking the empty carts out to the fields and leading the full ones, laden with sheaves, back into the stacking yard where the wheat was ready for threshing. Harry had been working in the fields of New House Farm, just to the north-east of the village. It was his last load before breakfast and he was about half way down from the top of the field when the anti-aircraft guns opened up and the sky filled up with black puffs of smoke. He could see men down at the stacking yard, pointing skyward. Looking back up the hill, he could see a formation of bombers, with their fighter escort behind, approaching from the direction of Great Shelford and heading south-west towards Newton. The noise of the anti-aircraft guns was deafening he recalled.

> *The horse was terrified and decided to take off for the farm. My efforts to stop her were in vain and she galloped to the farm with me hanging on to the back ladder of the cart. When I arrived at the farm, minus half the load, the bombers were past the farm* [continuing towards the south-west] *and a dogfight was in full progress overhead between the enemy's fighters and ours.*

He had watched the fighters peel off southward from the bomber formation just before. At the same time he had seen fighters taking off, from the Duxford area, flying low and heading east. These were probably the twelve Hurricanes of No 310 (Czech) Squadron which took off between 0825 and 0830 hr. They were too late to get involved in the local action and, despite being airborne for almost an hour, they did not make contact with the enemy.

Harry Wadley watched as one fighter came in low from the south, streaming smoke as it glided towards the village of Newton. Once obscured by the skyline, it did not reappear.

The anti-aircraft guns were those of No 243 (2nd Norfolk) Heavy Anti-Aircraft Battery, Royal Artillery, which had three-inch guns at Duxford's B site, Thriplow, just west of the airfield. Surviving records from various levels of the Anti-Aircraft Command structure give slightly differing accounts of the results of that engagement. The Brigade's report to Division reads:

> *. . . raid 29 entered the area south of Duxford at 0828 hrs. Formation of 18 bombers identified as Dorniers escorted by fighters. Engaged by Duxford B site 0831 hrs. Height 14,500 ft with 5 rounds. Shells seen to burst in and around the formation. Enemy aircraft broke formation and dropped bombs as follows* [. . . Meldreth-Shepreth-Barrington . . .]. *No damage or casualties reported. Enemy aircraft turned north east and left area . . .*

The War Diary for the 78th Heavy Anti Aircraft Regiment, which covered No 243 Battery, recorded that Duxford B

> . . . *opened fire at enemy formation which turned without dropping bombs. Claimed to have hit one plane, height 15,000 ft. No wreckage within reasonable distance but may have come down outside area.*

No 243 Battery's War Diary records the time as 0820 hr and repeats the claim of one Dornier 17 brought down and a further one damaged, but adds that confirmation of the claims had not been received. No record has been found to substantiate their claim, and it is probably significant that records from the higher levels of command did not mention it. Harry Wadley's 'smoking fighter' does come to mind though.

Witnesses on the ground have identified two different directions for the approach of the enemy formation: one heading north-west past Duxford and through Fowlmere to Meldreth, then turning north-east towards Great Shelford; and the other at about the same time coming from Great Shelford, towards the south-west and Fowlmere.

From the evidence, it is most unlikely that they were both the same formation; which could account for Lance Pearce having noted that the anti-aircraft fire was nowhere near the formation he was watching, whereas the Battery reported that their fire burst in and around the formation. No 19 Squadron's subsequent account, although not altogether clear, together with Sgt Jennings' description of the piles of ash, also adds weight to the theory that more than one enemy formation was in the area at that time. The most likely explanation could be that II/KG2 had divided into two sub-formations, although the presence of an as yet-unidentified formation cannot be ruled out.[1]

When Sgt Jennings 'peeled off' at 15,000 ft, the remaining ten Spitfires of No 19 Squadron were still climbing towards their patrol line of Duxford-Debden. The two Flights had not long joined up before a formation of enemy aircraft was sighted ahead and slightly off to port: Dorniers in vic formation, line astern, stepped upwards, accompanied by Me 110s,[2] both heading in a north-westerly direction towards Cambridge. Although the Spitfires had not reached their designated patrol height of 20,000 ft, they found themselves with a slight height advantage over the bombers however, the escorting fighters were still some two to three thousand feet above. Flt Lt Clouston ordered 'A' Flight to climb up and worry the fighters while he manoeuvred the six aircraft of 'B' Flight to attack the bombers.

'B' Flight were in two vics of three aircraft with Blue Section leading Green. Turning slightly to starboard both sections' aircraft slid into line astern behind their respective Section Leaders. Then as the range rapidly closed each section opened to echelon port as they turned round to port to line up behind the leading two sections of bombers in a standard 'Fighter Command No 1 Attack' configuration. Blue Leader, Flt Lt Clouston, opened fire but, after only fifteen rounds, his starboard cannon jammed. Blue 2, Plt Off Burgoyne, fired ten rounds from port and seventeen from starboard before both cannons suffered stoppages. No result from the attack was observed. The outcome of Plt Off Aeberhardt's attack was not known.

Flt Lt Wilfred Clouston, who led No 19 Squadron during the early morning engagement on 31 August 1940. *(Imperial War Museum)*

Nineteen-year-old Plt Off Raymond Aeberhardt died when his Spitfire crashed on landing at Fowlmere after the early morning action over the Essex/Cambridgeshire border. *(via After the Battle)*

Fg Off James Coward baled out of his Spitfire badly wounded. *(Air Commodore Coward)*

Sqn Ldr David Cox. A Sergeant Pilot with No 19 Squadron on 31 August 19 — claimed one Me 110 as probably destroyed during the melee over the north Thames Estuary. *(RAF Museum)*

Spitfire pilots at Fowlmere. One of a series of official photographs taken at Fowlmere in the latter part of September 1940 (believed to be 21 September). On the Spitfire's wing are, left to right: No 19 Squadron members Sqn Ldr Brian 'Sandy' Lane (by then Commanding Officer of No 19 Squadron); 'Flash'; Flt Sgt George Unwin; 'Rangi'; Fg Off Frank Brinsden. Standing, left to right: Sgt Bernard Jennings (No 19 Squadron); Flt Lt Colin Macfie; Sqn Ldr Howard 'Billy' Burton; Plt Off Phil Leckrone (all from No 616 Squadron). Based at Kirton-in-Lindsay, No 616 Squadron flew to Fowlmere, on a daily basis, between 19 and 28 September for operations at Wing strength.
(Imperial War Museum)

While Blue Section attacked the leading vic, Green Section were poised behind the second group of Dorniers, however, the Me 110s were now very close. Fg Off James Coward, leading as Green 1, aimed for the right-hand aircraft of the three:

> *When almost right astern I was closing to open fire when I felt a bang on the shin of my left leg. I opened fire but the cannons jammed after a round or two. My Spitfire failed to respond to the controls and bunted down into a steep dive leaving me no choice but to bale out.*

Plt Off Arthur Vokes, Green 2, followed in against the leading bomber of the Kette but was obliged to take violent evasive action to avoid an attack by an Me 110. Sgt Cox, the last of the three,[3] found himself in a vulnerable position:

> *. . . with an Me 110 firing at me from a distance too close for comfort. I did a sharp left hand climbing turn into the enemy aircraft and went promptly into a spin. When I recovered I was on my own with no aircraft in sight.*

The attack had been thwarted by the intervention of the escorting Me 110s and the experimental and still very unreliable armament of two 20mm cannon in the Mark I Spitfire's wings, instead of the usual eight Browning .303 machine guns.

'A' Flight, on climbing to engage the escort while 'B' Flight took on the bombers, had lost sight of both the enemy and 'B' Flight. They were then vectored towards Debden, where another enemy formation had been reported.

Fg Off Coward thought he had been the unfortunate victim of anti-aircraft gun fire and it was not until a reunion, many years after the war, that he learned about the Me 110s coming up from astern. As his section had turned in to attack

Sgt Bernard Jennings taking off from Fowlmere, 21 September 1940, in Spitfire X4474 — one of the machine-gun armed replacements for the cannon-armed variant which proved so troublesome during the August engagements. Spitfire QV-I that Sgt Jennings flew on 31 August 1940 was R6917. *(Imperial War Museum)*

the bombers, he had thought that the German fighters were too high to interfere with the attack. Either as a result of anti-aircraft fire or a cannon shell, his aircraft had become unresponsive to the controls. He had a severe wound to his left leg and was soaked in petrol, but fortunately the aircraft had not caught fire. He baled out, but in the process became caught by his parachute on the top of the cockpit.

My arms were blown back along the fuselage and my gloves blew off. My left foot was twisting about at the end of my leg when, suddenly, I blew free. I realized I was losing blood fast and tried to delay opening my parachute but my foot, twisting about in the free fall was too painful, and I pulled my 'chute. When it opened, I was swinging in a big figure of eight and could see my blood, which seemed bright red, pulsing out and I realised that I would have to stem it quickly, if I was to survive. My First Aid outfit was in my uniform breast pocket and as the parachute straps were taut over my flying overalls, and my hands frozen, I couldn't get at it. I therefore took the R/T cord, attached to my helmet, and lashed a tourniquet around my thigh and tightened it until I managed to reduce the bleeding to a trickle, held my leg up as high as possible and continued to float down. When I had time to look around, I could see Duxford clearly and Fowlmere beyond. Two of our Spitfires circled round me on their way back to Fowlmere and the pilots gave me a wave. When I was right over Duxford, at what I judged to be about 8,000 ft, I started to drift back eastwards, towards Whittlesford. I then spent some time pulling down on the parachute cords until I was facing the direction of drift and finally came down in a stubble field, a couple of miles from Duxford by the roundabout where the London-Cambridge road crossed the Newmarket-Royston road. I was busy pulling the parachute up to try to keep my leg off the dirt when a young lad of fifteen or so came dashing up, pointing a pitchfork at me, obviously thinking I was a German. It made me damn cross and I told him in no uncertain terms to get some help. He dropped the pitchfork and did a commendably fast sprint to the gate. The first car he flagged down contained an Army Medical Officer from a local anti-aircraft unit who then despatched his driver to get some medical supplies. When the driver returned, he reported that he had brought everything except the morphia, because the orderly corporal had gone on leave the night before and was believed to have taken the key of the poisons cupboard with him! Surprisingly, except for the few moments when I was trapped on the fuselage of the aircraft, the initial freefall and when I hit the ground, the leg didn't give me a great deal of pain, nor did I seem to suffer from shock. More painful but less visibly dramatic were the petrol burns under my arms and crotch that developed during the long parachute descent.

After half an hour, an RAF ambulance arrived and took Fg Off Coward to Addenbrooke's Hospital in Cambridge, where his left leg was amputated below the knee. A couple of days later, he was transferred to the RAF Hospital at Ely where he remained for the next three weeks. Pending the arrival of a proper artificial limb, his fitter on the Squadron, Cpl Parren, knocked up a temporary one by lining a riding boot with an aluminium sleeve.

Fg Off Coward's operational flying with No 19 Squadron had been brief. It was his second time with the Squadron, having been with them before the war and at the start of the 'phoney war' but, in November 1939, he was posted to help form No 266 Squadron, as a Flight Commander. At the end of June 1940 he returned to No 19 Squadron but almost immediately had a spell in hospital for a routine operation. After a period of convalescence, he returned to operational flying on 29 August — completing four sorties during the 29th and 30th, all without contact with enemy aircraft. Saturday, 31 August was only his third day back on operational flying and only his second opportunity to fire his guns in anger — the first time being with No 266 Squadron, whilst covering the British Expeditionary Force's withdrawal from Dunkirk.

From Ely he received a posting to the Prime Minister's Staff, based at Chequers and Chartwell, where he remained for the next year. Although his flying career had been brought to an abrupt halt, it proved to be only temporary. After a brief period on Winston Churchill's staff, he eventually returned to flying duties in January 1942 but with a 'home service only' restriction. Later, his injuries proved no barrier to a successful career in the post-war RAF and he eventually rose to the rank of Air Commodore, retiring in 1969.

Fg Off Coward's Spitfire ended up in what was known locally as the Violet Plantation,on the west side of the Newton-Fowlmere road, a few hundred yards south of the village church where Peggy Wadley was married. His was the aircraft her brother had seen, gliding in towards Newton. For of the wedding, her brother had been allowed the afternoon off work, and it was not until after the wedding festivities were over that he was able to go and see the crashed plane. Most of it, he remembered, was lodged in some trees not far in from the road, with the tail section raised up into the air. A day or two later the wreckage of X4231 was removed.

The identity of the Me 110s that had intervened so successfully that day is not absolutely clear but Oberleutnant Hans Barschel of the Staff Flight from III/ZG26 claimed a Spitfire north-east of Duxford at 0835 hr that day and Oberleutnant Sophus Baagoe of 8 Staffel ZG26 claimed a Spitfire south-east of Duxford at 0837 hr. Whether or not either of these victims was Fg Off Coward's Spitfire remains uncertain, not least in view of the No 243 Battery's claim and Fg Off Coward's belief that anti-aircraft guns had been responsible for his misfortune!

Twenty minutes before No 19 Squadron's encounter over South Cambridge-shire, the nine Hurricanes of No 111 Squadron had left Castle Camps, with instructions to patrol Debden at 15,000 ft and so protect it from Raid 29 which was approaching from the south-east. Interception had not been made and Raid 29 had passed, unmolested, west of Debden and had continued on to the Fowlmere area.

No 111 Squadron eventually found an enemy formation over the village of Hildersham, eight miles north of Debden, at about 0830 hr. Flt Lt Herbert Giddings, leading the Squadron as Red 1, manoeuvred the Hurricanes in for an astern attack on what he estimated to be a formation of thirty Dornier 17s.

On the approach Red 2, Fg Off Bowring was left slightly behind his leader and his place for the attack was taken by Blue 2, Sgt Wallace. Flt Lt Giddings led his section in, each Hurricane lining up behind each one of the three Dorniers in the last Kette of the formation. Flt Lt Giddings attacked the centre Dornier, opening fire from 300 yd and breaking off at 80 yd, when all his ammunition was finished. Flames appeared from the Dornier's port engine and he could see pieces breaking off. To his left, Plt Off Ritchie fired a thirteen-second burst at the left-hand Dornier, closing in to about 100 yd, before breaking away and seeing large pieces of wreckage falling from his target. To the right, Sgt Wallace gave a more economic five-second burst, as he closed from 300 to 150 yd. He reported later that the return fire ceased and '. . . as some Me 110s were closing in on our tail, I broke away, leaving the bomber apparently out of control'. Pieces were seen to break off all three Dorniers as the attacks were pressed home and all of them jettisoned their bombs onto the open fields below.

While Flt Lt Giddings' section attacked the Dorniers, the two sections remaining provided protective cover against the Me 110 threat. Fg Off Bowring, on seeing the Me 110s close in on Red section ahead, turned and delivered a head-on attack which caused the enemy aircraft to break off its attack. He thought that the aircraft appeared to be damaged and claimed it as such. Flt Lt Giddings claimed his Dornier as 'destroyed', and Plt Off Ritchie and Sgt Wallace both claimed 'probables'. As was so often usual after an initial attack, the Hurricanes became dispersed, then each sought its own quarry (provided that there was one to be found, of course!).

A number of the Squadron's Hurricanes headed towards the south-east and the coast, in search of raiders returning home. Fg Off Ben Bowring had maintained contact and chased a group of enemy aircraft out to Felixstowe, where he managed to attack an Me 110 that had broken away from the main body. He

Flt Lt Herbert Giddings led No 111 Squadron against a formation of Dornier 17s over north Essex, claiming one as destroyed.
(Treble-One (Fighter) Squadron Assocation)

Sgt John 'Bobby' Craig of No 111 Squadron — baled out over the Essex/Hertfordshire border.
(Treble-One (Fighter) Squadron Association)

gave it an eight-second burst from abeam, then saw it wobble and dive for the coast, smoke pouring from both motors. He followed, but ran out of ammunition and finally landed at nearby Martlesham Heath. His Hurricane showed the evidence of the fight, bullet holes dotted the fuselage, propeller, oil tank cover, gunbay and port aileron. He claimed the Me 110 as a 'probable', in due payment for the damage.

The exploits of Sgt John Craig are not recorded in the Squadron's surviving records, beyond the fact that he had to bale out, and he was not credited with any claims that morning. After the Squadron's initial attack, the particular engagement he got involved in moved, well away from the main theatre of activity, towards south-west Essex. As well as damage to his aircraft, enemy fire had also caused Sgt Craig to suffer a leg wound. He eventually baled out, close to the Essex-Hertfordshire border, his parachute bringing him down just inside Essex, in the village of Harlow, and he landed, quite fortuitously, by the village First Aid Post. From there an ARP ambulance took him to St Margaret's Hospital, in nearby Epping, where shrapnel was removed from his leg wound. Sgt Craig's unmanned aircraft finally crashed some distance away, over the border, in Hertfordshire.

Given the time and location of No 111 Squadron's initial attack on the bombers it was probable that the enemy formation was the same one that had left its mark earlier on the landscape between Fowlmere, Shepreth and Great Shelford.[4] II/ KG2, whose target had been Duxford, had only one Dornier written off — U5+CN, which crash-landed in France. One of its crew members received a bullet wound but, other than that, there were no reported casualties in the Gruppe. No other aircraft damage was recorded. It was, more than likely, Flt Lt Giddings' actions that had inflicted the damage on U5+CN; and, from the damage described by the other members of Red Section, the two other Dorniers of the last Kette must have had particularly lucky escapes.

Chapter Twelve
Debden

As Raid 29 passed to the west of Debden on its way north west towards Duxford, so a further formation was crossing the Essex coast set on a similar course. Few references to it can be found today and that might also have been the case at the time if the Operations Room plot had started to lose the overall picture, but that is conjecture. What is known, is that at 0835 the Sector Operations Room at Debden warned the anti-aircraft defences in its sector of Raid 37, located between Chelmsford and Colchester: 20 aircraft at 20,000 feet heading north west. Debden again looked like the target.

All three of Debden's resident squadrons were clear of the airfield: No 111 Squadron was engaging the Dornier formation, further north; No 601 Squadron, having just taken off, was desperately trying to gain altitude for that all-important advantage of height, before making contact with the enemy; and No 257 Squadron, from Martlesham Heath, was also climbing, and heading west to protect its parent base.

Assistance was also at hand from No 12 Group whose Duxford sector lay immediately to the north. The Group's Nos 19 and 310 Squadrons had been scrambled from Fowlmere and Duxford, respectively. No 19 Squadron's 'A' Flight was on its way, but No 310 had only just taken off. Nos 310 and 601 Squadrons were fortunate in that Raid 29 had by-passed Debden and missed Duxford; both could have been caught so easily while taking off. One can only speculate as to why take-off was left so late, especially in the case of No 601 Squadron, when it had become a very strong possibility quite early on that Debden was to be a target.

Raid 37 was, in fact, Major Fuchs' Dorniers of III/KG2, accompanied by an escort Gruppe of Me 110s together with Oberleutnant Gerhard Schöpfel's III/G26 which was providing top cover.[1] All were destined for Debden. The impression of some degree of confusion is given by the somewhat ambiguous record of events in the surviving intelligence reports of the anti-aircraft defences. Which particular hostile formation passed where and when is far from clear. The A.A. Divisional report, which essentially repeats the local A.A. Brigade report, contains a number of changes in detail; some are obviously typing errors but others remain open to speculation.

The Operations Record Book for RAF Debden provides a lengthy account, but the narrative is fragmented and not in chronological sequence. It does, however, attempt to portray a clearer picture of how the prelude to the attack was perceived:

The Roos

To
Saffron
Walden

Abbots Manor

To
Thaxted &
Colchester

Elder St.

Freemans Farm

Rowney Wood

German reconnaissance aerial photograph of RAF Debden, taken on the morning of Friday, 30 August 1940. Bomb craters from the previous Monday's raid can be seen cutting across the landing ground. Twenty-four hours after the photograph was taken another, almost parallel line, ran from Elder Street to Abbots. *(US National Archives)*

. . . the second formation [Raid 37] *came up the same course* [from the south]. *They were 30 Dornier 17s in layers of three vics in line astern. Three aircraft per vic, the layers being stepped up in echelon to 16,000 feet and with 20 Me 110s escorting to port and the same number to starboard 500 feet above. Before reaching Debden they changed course to east and then to north west and approached Debden out of the sun. Bombing commenced at 0839 from 15,000 feet . . .*

The picture is easy to visualise; however, the final manoeuvres remained improbable. The course alterations are quite bold for such a large formation, so close to its target, and seemingly unnecessary because a straight course (north-west from where they had been last reported only twenty miles away, between Chelmsford and Colchester) would have resulted in a direct approach out of the sun. It appears more likely that what initially could have been a confused or uncertain picture suddenly became very clear, when the Dorniers were sighted from the ground at Debden. The 'route' described in the Operations Record Book could have been a means of linking the operations plot with what actually happened overhead.

Effectively, the airfield at Debden formed a triangular parcel of land between two roads — the main Saffron Walden to Colchester road (along which Janet Farnham had made her way to Colchester), running north-west/south-east forming a northern border to the airfield; and its southern boundary was marked by the east-west minor road between Elder Street and the village of Debden. Opposite the Elder Street end, near where the two roads converged, were the airfield buildings, lined to the west by three large 'C Type' hangars. Fanning out further to the west beyond them was the landing ground, ringed by a narrow perimeter track, which provided an 'all-weather' link between the two dispersal points (on the western and northern edges of the airfield) and the main building complex.

Just outside the camp, on the other side of the road at Elder Street, was a line of small cottages and, at intervals along the road to the west, three farms — Braggs, Freemans and Ricketts.

Mrs Ruth Hare lived with her husband at Freeman's Farm, which was situated almost directly opposite the camp's main gate. Just five years earlier the view from their farmhouse had been open fields but that had changed to a line of three large hangars. Ruth Hare could not remember exactly what drew her attention to the impending danger but she suddenly stopped her daily chores around the house and ushered her husband and his elderly parents, together with the maid, outside to the safety of the farm's dugout, behind the house. She remembered opening all the windows of the house as a precaution against blast damage. Having got the others safely into the dugout, Mr and Mrs Hare, together with a visiting nephew and a dog, ran a further two hundred yards to the safety of a ditch by the edge of Rowney Wood. (There had not been enough room for them in their shelter because, although large enough for half a dozen or so people, it had already been filled by airmen from across the road.

When the warning had gone some of the airmen had sought shelter outside the camp — no doubt the damage that had been done five days earlier, when the Dorniers of KG2 had made a similar visit, had been fresh in their minds. On that occasion, three members of No 257 Squadron ground staff had been killed when their shelter had been hit. LAC Tom Cullen, also of No 257 Squadron, had stayed to the last minute to watch the bombs fall during the first raid, as it was a new experience to him, and likewise to most others on the camp. The second time there was no hesitation and he dived for cover into the nearest shelter by his squadron's hangar. To the Hares, of more concern than having their own shelter occupied was the airmen crossing over from the camp and leaving the farm gate open thereby allowing the farm animals to wander off. No sooner than the Hares had reached the safety of the ditch, the bombing started. Ruth Hare remembered that the ground vibrated when high-explosive bombs went off and some incendiaries fell close by.

The bombs had actually started to fall a little further east, in Rowney Wood, a large tree plantation some 300 yd south of Elder Street. In Elder Street two cottages at the eastern end of a small terraced row were set on fire by incendiaries and destroyed; as was another cottage between Bragg's and Freeman's farms. The bombing line continued diagonally through the airfield buildings from south-east to north-west, the bombs adding to the damage inflicted along a similar path the previous Monday. The sick quarters and a barrack block received direct hits and were badly damaged. The Sergeants' Mess, NAAFI, cookhouse, three wooden huts, a hangar and a lock-up garage were also damaged. Beyond the hangars the line of destruction continued on to the northern side of the landing ground, almost paralleling the Saffron Walden road and ending at Abbots Manor (a group of farm buildings that protruded into the landing ground on the north side of the airfield). A quantity of livestock perished at the Manor, at which point the bombing petered out.

Plt Off Chas Frizell was eighteen years old and No 257 Squadron's youngest pilot. He had just landed at Debden, with another pilot, on a routine flight to exchange aircraft. They parked their aircraft by the Squadron's maintenance

Plt Off Chas Frizell — at 18 years old in the summer of 1940, was No 257 Squadron's youngest pilot. On the morning of 31 August he had landed at Debden just before the bombing commenced. *(C. Frizell)*

Bomb damage at RAF Debden. Cpl H. G. Hewett, an armourer with No 257 Squadron, on part of the perimeter track which was damaged by 50kg HE bombs during the late-August raids. This photograph was believed to have been taken on the northern part of the landing field. *(H. G. Hewett)*

hangar and were walking towards it when the bombing commenced. They dived for cover into an air-raid shelter situated beside the hangar. To be bombed or strafed on the ground were experiences with which Plt Off Frizell was to become familiar with on a number of later occasions during the war and were the ones that he considered induced the most fear and gave such a feeling of helplessness.

The damage caused to the airfield was heavy, but the human cost was remarkably light. The occupants of the two cottages destroyed in Elder Street had survived and on the camp casualties were listed as two dead (one civilian and one RAF) and twelve RAF personnel wounded. Ambulance services were drawn from nearby Thaxted and Stansted, and, because the Station's sick quarters were out of action, the hospital at Saffron Walden was kept busy. It was estimated later that about 100 high-explosive and incendiary bombs had been dropped. Despite the damage, the operations side of the station functioned throughout, including the lighting and communications for the so-vital Operations Room.

John Wiseman farmed the land that covered the two-mile gap between the airfield's perimeter and Saffron Walden. That morning, he was having breakfast at 'The Roos' with some Army officers who had been billeted on him, following their evacuation from France a few weeks earlier. On their arrival, the officer in charge had insisted that some form of air-raid shelter had to be constructed. John Wiseman agreed, with some reluctance, to have a slit trench dug across his tennis court which was beside the house.

The trench was utilised that Saturday morning when the siren at Saffron Walden sounded its warning of trouble. Breakfast was curtailed and the assembled group made their way to the slit trench. To many local people who had experienced the previous Monday's raid, the novelty of trying to watch the impending events had worn off and more immediate steps were taken to seek shelter. On the Monday afternoon the bombing had extended almost to The Roos. The final incendiaries had set alight a field of standing barley, a few hundred yards from the house, consuming some three to four acres of the crop.

On that particular Saturday morning, it seemed that no sooner had the siren sounded than bombs began to burst in the direction of the airfield. From his vantage point in the slit trench, John Wiseman could see the raiders, approaching from the south-east and flying very high as they passed Abbots, then continued just to the north of The Roos, on course for Saffron Walden which was a mile-and-a-half to the north-west. As they passed, he could see fighters weaving in and out of the formation.

The raiders must have continued on their way to and reached Saffron Walden because a few bombs fell in the town, and in Audley Park which was immediately to the west. (No doubt they were 'hang-ups' which were jettisoned.) A string of bombs fell in the fields behind the Friends School to the south of the town, and one bomb did not explode. Another unexploded bomb landed on the Maltings Field situated off Station Road, and a few incendiaries came down in the cemetery.

In all, some thirteen high-explosive and seventy-two incendiary bombs were reported to have fallen within the parish boundary of Saffron Walden. A number of them fell close to the town, on the eastern end of Audley Park, where an

Army unit was camped. Two soldiers were wounded, but it could have been worse. Fortunately the bulk of the men were engaged on an early morning exercise leaving the encampment virtually empty.

When the bombers delivered their loads over the airfield, the anti-aircraft defences did not respond. According to the Station's Operations Record Book that was 'because of the height of the raiders', although no mention was made to that effect in the Anti-Aircraft Defence's report. Unlike Duxford's Heavy Anti-Aircraft Batteries, Debden's defences consisted of only four Bofors guns and an assortment of machine guns: more appropriate for defending against low-level attack and dive-bombing. Defence against higher flying raids required fighter aircraft.

Hurricanes of Nos 601 and 257 Squadrons were on their way to Debden but were too late to intercept the raid before the bombing commenced. The Spitfires of No 19 Squadron were already at altitude, and the four aircraft of 'A' Flight were close to Debden, having lost their Me 110 quarries during the earlier engagement near Duxford. Their controller had subsequently directed them towards Debden and they arrived there in time to see the large formation of enemy bombers and fighters below them, and bombs bursting on the airfield.

Red Leader, Fg Off Brinsden, ordered the attack. As he was about to attack, his aircraft was hit from below and his controls went dead. A bullet also pierced his petrol tank and his aircraft started to go down. Red 3, Sgt Roden, was prevented from making a successful attack and was forced to take evasive action. Yellow 1 and 2, Sub-Lt Blake and Sgt Potter respectively, were prevented from delivering their attacks also and became involved with single-engined fighters. Initially, Sub-Lt Blake thought that he was being attacked by Hurricanes but, later, considered them to be the mysterious 'He 113s'.[2]

The single-engined fighters were probably Me 109s, although it would perhaps be surprising for members of such an experienced fighter squadron to mis-identify such aircraft. However, Me 109s were hardly expected to be that far from home, and at what was considered to be almost the limit of their operating range. It was significant, however, that Major Adolf Galland (leading the Me 109s of JG26) recorded his 25th victory at 0842 hr that morning, 20km south-east of Cambridge.

The encounter had not been a successful one for No 19 Squadron. Sgt Jennings, after solving his oxygen problem, had flown to Debden. Finding no sign of the enemy over Debden, he headed off towards the mouth of the River Thames. Having made no contact again, he eventually returned to Fowlmere. After he had landed the Squadron's other aircraft began to arrive, a couple doing a circuit around Fg Off Coward who was descending over Duxford. Some of the aircraft were battle-scarred. Sub-Lt Blake's aircraft had had one of its control wires cut, but he managed to bring it in for a safe landing.

Plt Off Aeberhardt was not so fortunate. Sgt Jennings watched from the ground as the young pilot put his Spitfire's flaps down on his final turn at low altitude. Only one came down. The aircraft rolled over, hit the ground the right way up, on the other side of a three roll barbed wire fence, and burst into flames. By the time the fire tender reached the wreckage, it was too late. The message was brought home, all too vividly, to those who witnessed the tragic event: following combat, allow plenty of height and check all controls, including undercarriage and flaps. What had gone wrong on that occasion would never be known.

Fg Off Brinsden, after his brief engagement over Debden and with the greatest difficulty, baled out of his aircraft over the Essex-Hertfordshire border, a considerable way west of Debden. He parachuted to safety and came down on the outskirts of the village of Brent Pelham.

Puttocks End Farm was situated a mile to the west of the village, on the Anstey road. Ernest Fox had just left his parents' farmhouse and had reached the end of the drive by the road, when a Spitfire swooped down low from the direction of Anstey and heading towards Brent Pelham.

> It was going like the dickens and, of course, I didn't take that much notice because I thought the pilot was still in it, but he wasn't. As I followed the aircraft's line of flight eastward, I could see a parachute descending above Brent Pelham. He eventually came down by Beeches Manor, to the east of the village on the way to Starlings Green.

The aircraft continued to glide and crashed on the boundary of the farm, about half way to the village. The Spitfire hit a ditch between two fields. It was still recognizable as an aircraft, but well beyond any sense of repair. Then Ernest Fox's attention was drawn to the sound of aerial combat high above but he could see nothing in the sky.

Altogether, No 19 Squadron had lost three aircraft, and had one damaged. One pilot was dead and another badly injured. The strength of the enemy fighter force had proved overwhelming and, once again, they had been let down by their aircrafts' experimental armament. The German fighters had successfully defended their bombers and had prevented some of the Spitfire piltos from even being able to bring their sights to bear on the bombers.

After passing over Saffron Walden, the Dorniers of III/KG2 turned for home. The RAF Debden Operations Record Book described later how, after the bombing

> . . . the enemy aircraft then circled the aerodrome, anti-clockwise, singly, in line astern and were attacked and broken up by fighter aircraft.

Such a course of action for the Dorniers would appear rather pointless and it is probably a confusion, with the sighting of a group of what were assessed to be Me 109s, circling just to the west of Debden at about 20,000 ft. That was a more plausible explanation, as No 19 Squadron's 'A Flight' found out.

Chapter Thirteen
Homeward I

A little after 0840 hr there were several formations of enemy bombers over north-west Essex, all racing south-east towards the coast. During the ensuing fifteen minutes, air battles raged over a twenty-mile wide swathe of Essex countryside as RAF fighters made contact with the returning raiders moving towards the Thames Estuary. Along what could be considered as a rather indistinct northern flank, No 111 Squadron had already made its mark and, after the initial attack, individual actions continued across north Essex and towards Felixstowe, Harwich and Clacton.

Bombs, jettisoned after the unsuccessful attack on Duxford, had been spread over a wide area of South Cambridgeshire and North Essex and probably caused the damage which occurred further south-east at Colchester. At about 0845 hr a string of ten 50kg high-explosive bombs and various incendiaries were reported to have fallen on East Colchester. There were two clusters, dropped in a general line, north-west/south-east.

A cluster of four high-explosive bombs fell to the east of Colchester Castle, causing damage to many houses in Roman Road, Land Lane and East Hill. Three cottages in Land Lane were destroyed totally, and a four-inch gas main was severed in Roman Road, cutting off the supply to sixty houses. There was one casualty, a woman who was injured by a falling ceiling. She was taken to hospital, where she died later.[1]

A second cluster of six high-explosive bombs fell further south-east, near the new sewage works at the Hythe. A large, thirty-two-inch water main was fractured and the sewage works were flooded as a result. In between where the two clusters fell, incendiaries were dropped on Barrack Street, Brook Street, the Paxman Engineering Works, and near the rectory at Greenstead.

On the southern flank of the battle, between Bishop's Stortford, Chelmsford and the River Crouch, No 56 Squadron was about to enter the fray. Of the two fighter squadrons based at North Weald, No 151 (temporarily operating from Stapleford Tawney) had concluded its first action of the day (over east Kent) already, and was on its way back to base to re-arm and re-fuel. No 56 Squadron, although still based at North Weald, had been sent (on most days in August) forward, at first light, to operate out of Rochford near Southend, returning to North Weald in the evening. (A situation which had become commonplace for many of Fighter Command's squadrons at that time.)

During the final week of August, the Luftwaffe's offensive had been switched to Fighter Command's airfields further inland (which also happened to be the more vital controlling Sector Stations). No 56 Squadron, which had been in action regularly since the beginning of the Luftwaffe's onslaught, found itself being committed more and more. It had had success in the air, but its losses were mounting steadily.

On Friday 30 August it was scrambled five times to intercept hostile raids, and on two occasions it had been engaged in combat. The final flights of the day were made as dusk approached after which the pilots were relieved to learn that they were to be 'released' until lunchtime the following day.

Fg Off Innes Westmacott (an experienced pilot but a relative newcomer to the Squadron, having only been posted there at the beginning of the month) had added a further forty hours' flying time already to his logbook since joining. On his seventh and final landing that Friday evening the runway lights were switched on. Making his final approach, with the cockpit hood open, he pushed up his goggles for a better view. On lowering the undercarriage, a tremendous draught blew through the cockpit, blowing the goggles off his forehead and smashing them against the armour plating behind his head. He intended to obtain a new pair, at his leisure the next morning. But that was not to be.

The following morning he was enjoying a hot bath in the Officers' Mess and thinking about breakfast when the tannoy called No 56 Squadron to immediate readiness. He leapt out of the bath, dressed quickly and dashed out of the Mess. His aircraft was on the opposite side of the airfield and, together with other pilots, he had just managed to reach the dispersal point when the order to take off came through.

Eight Hurricanes[2] took off from North Weald and were led by 'A' Flight Commander, Flt Lt Percy Weaver. Plt Off Maurice Mounsdon, also of 'A' Flight, recalled that he heard the controller on the radio, as soon as they were in the air, instructing them to climb to 15,000 ft and patrol Chelmsford. It was a day he was to have good cause to remember. The Hurricanes headed initially north then turned towards the east. Just before reaching Chelmsford, they spotted ahead and slightly above, a formation of fifteen to twenty Dorniers, in vics of three in line astern, making off towards the south-east. Behind was a fighter escort. The eight Hurricanes went straight in to attack both the escort and bombers.

Plt Off Mounsdon attacked the Me 110s behind the bombers, approaching on their starboard quarter,

> *I got a good burst at an Me 110 and then had to break away, as I was being hit by enemy fire. I passed over and through the end of their formation and turned to make another approach, but never completed it. Quickly looking around to see if there was any opposition I glanced over my left shoulder to see an Me 109 with yellow spinner as he opened fire close behind and beneath me. He couldn't miss. Shrapnel hit my left leg, then the instrument panel shattered and glycol and petrol spilled everywhere. Then up it all went. Suddenly I was sitting in a blow lamp. I undid the Sutton harness, put the aircraft into a roll to starboard, stood up and pushed myself over the side.*

There had been no need to open the hood, it was already locked open in case such a rapid exit had to be made: A failure of the sliding mechanism at such a vital moment would have been catastrophic.

Plt Off Mounsdon's radio lead was still connected and, as he disappeared out of the cockpit, the lead was torn from its socket and his flying helmet was wrenched from his head.

> *Falling, I could see my trousers were nearly all burned away but the remaining cloth and my tunic edges were still soaked in petrol and burning. I knew I had plenty of height and so didn't deploy the parachute straight away in case it caught fire too. The flames soon went out and, when down to about 10,000 or 12,000 feet, I pulled the rip chord to commence a more sedate descent.*

'B' Flight's Green Section tackled the Dorniers. Flt Sgt Taffy Higginson led the section in towards the bombers' starboard quarter. He opened fire at 400 yd on the leading section of bombers, closing in until he was almost on top of them. His Combat Report for that action continues:

> *I saw no visible effect and carried on between the first and second section of bombers. Then I turned and the enemy fighters were just opposite me. I opened fire on an Me 109 and he climbed steeply, emitting white smoke. I broke away, downwards and saw an aircraft going straight down, emitting white smoke, and I saw it crash and burst into flames in a field, west of the road and railway between Chelmsford and Colchester.*

Flt Sgt Higginson had recorded his eleventh victory but the crashed aircraft had not been his victim, that belonged to his companion Fg Off Westmacott.

Fg Off Westmacott was on the extreme right of the Section as it approached the bombers. The Dorniers were still slightly above and he picked the outside one of a vic of three.

> *I just pulled up under his belly and shot at him. I know I hit him because I saw my tracer striking him and I saw the flashes of the 'de Wilde' incendiaries as they hit, but he flew happily onward. I broke away to starboard to come in for a second attack. I had a quick look behind and saw a number of 110s belting in from behind on my starboard quarter. I thought I would have time for another attack and turned back in for the Dornier. I think fatigue had affected my judgement, for the enemy arrived much sooner than I thought fair. I was just pulling up to open fire when, with a tremendous crash, my instrument panel disappeared in fragments, followed immediately by a searing blast of flame as my reserve tank, holding 28 gallons of petrol, went up in my face. My instantaneous reaction was 'This is it!', followed by the thought that I really ought to try and get out. I don't know if I made the aircraft do it but it had pulled clear of the bomber. I undid my straps, and by that time the aircraft was climbing again. The hood was already open in case of just such an event, so I pushed the stick forward and, under the negative 'g', out I came.*

Fg Off Westmacott found that his clothes were on fire as he tumbled earthward. Conscious that the flames could set his parachute alight, he let himself fall until everything felt cold, then he pulled the rip chord. The absence of his goggles was then painfully felt. The whole of the upper part of his face was burned and his eyelids were stuck together.

Not relishing the thought of hitting the ground without seeing it coming, I started to pull my gloves off with the idea of trying to get my eyes open but, at that moment, I heard the unmistakable sound of an Me 109, apparently coming towards me. I had never before felt so frightened and helpless. Then I heard the noise of a Hurricane in a dive, followed by a burst of fire and the sound of the 109 died away. I later learned that one of our pilots, Sgt Robinson, had intervened to divert the 109 from any evil intent.

Half an hour earlier in a different engagement further south over Kent, Sqn Ldr Harold Starr, the new Commanding Officer of No 253 Squadron, had also been forced to bale out. His parachute returned his lifeless body to earth; apparently he had been the victim of a similar type of attack.

Whether or not a pilot, having baled out of his aircraft, was a justifiable target was debatable. Was he to be considered as a helpless non-combatant or a likely adversary, in the future? A pilot, having baled out over his own territory, could have returned to fight at a later date, unless he was badly hurt. However, if he baled out over enemy territory, he was unlikely to pose any further threat.

Invariably, RAF personnel were fighting over their own territory at that time. The final decision to attack a pilot who had baled out rested with the individual in the air. Killing the enemy was a remote and detached business for the fighter pilot. The objective, as was stated often by fighter pilots, was to shoot down an enemy aircraft and the pilot inside was considered not the target. But how much could the reality and emotional impact be changed by, for example, a pilot watching a friend disappear earthward in a ball of fire? It was not a gentlemanly game, but a deadly serious struggle between life and death.

The experiences that day of one Me 109 pilot demonstrate the consequences of escape. Leutnant Heinz Ebeling was Staffel Kaptain of 9/JG26. In the Chelmsford area Leutnant Ebeling had just added one more Hurricane to his tally (probably that of Plt Off Mounsdon because the attack from below and behind agrees, and Leutnant Ebeling recalled that smoke came from the aircraft and that the pilot baled out).

It was only after disengaging from the fight that he realised his own aircraft had been hit in the radiator (probably the 'white smoke' seen by Flt Sgt Higginson). He managed to gain some height before the engine seized and he then began to glide down over Kent. Clearing Dover and well out over the Channel, he finally baled out at about six or seven hundred feet. (Although there is conclusive proof, the evidence seems to indicate that it was his aircraft that became Flt Sgt Higginson's eleventh victory claim.)

Heinz Ebeling (far left), with other members of III/JG26, after his rescue from the Channel on 31 August 1940. Left to right: Lt Ebeling (Staffelkapitän 9/JG26); Oblt Schöpfel (Gruppen Kommandeur III/JG26); Lt Haibock (Adjutant III/JG26); Lt Naumann (9/JG26). *(H. Ebeling)*

He was in the water an hour before he was picked up by a Dornier 18 sea rescue aircraft and returned safely to base. Having only sustained a slight cut to the head, he was fit enough to be airborne again that same evening. At six o'clock, over mid Kent, he added two more Hurricanes to his score.

In all, II and III/JG26 claimed at least five RAF fighters over south-east Essex on the morning of 31 August, and the Me 110s of III/ZG26 claimed a further ten. No 56 Squadron only had sustained losses there, but not that many! Together with Plt Off Mounsdon's and Fg Off Westmacott's aircraft, two others had been hit. Sgt 'Kim' Whitehead was shot down by an unseen aircraft, but parachuted to safety, uninjured. Flt Lt Percy Weaver fell victim to another attack as the running battle moved towards the coast. He went down with his aircraft into the River Blackwater. He was an experienced pilot and a well-liked member of the Squadron. The compiler of the Squadron Operations Record Book recorded sadly, 'He had been given the DFC this very day and was a great loss to the Squadron.'

Without loss, the Dorniers continued to head south-east over the flat Dengie peninsula, and out over the Thames Estuary. During the conflict, any bombs remaining had been jettisoned. Incendiaries were reported later to have been spread across the countryside from Stansted, passing just north of Chelmsford, through to Burnham-on-Crouch. Most fell between Chelmsford and the coast and nearly all fell harmlessly in open countryside. There were no casualties, and negligible damage, with reports such as 'minor damage 100 yd east of Rosendale Farm at Latchingdon', and 'damage to telephone wires in Spital Road Maldon'. The local fire brigade turned out for the latter which had formed part of a concentration of incendiaries to the south of the town. The searchlight post off Fambridge Road received the greatest density — twelve — but all were dealt with effectively. The only high-explosive bombs reported were a couple on farmland at the mouth of the River Crouch.

On the ground, the aerial activity could be clearly heard as it passed by. To those who watched the activity, the aircraft were high enough only to be seen as tiny specks, but it was not high enough to produce the distinctive sky-writing of vapour trails. When the noise faded, things returned to normal; except in a few places where the results of the combat were about to become vivid and memorable. Four of No 56 Squadron's aircraft were heading earthward and three parachutes hung in the clear, blue sky. The memories of that particular aerial drama were subsequently to be imprinted firmly on the minds of some of the Essex villagers.

In the village of High Easter, some seven miles north-west of Chelmsford, the air-raid warning had been sounded, but for most people life continued very much as normal until the sound of approaching aircraft was heard. Derek Bircher (then a fifteen-year-old living at the village Post Office) noticed that the noise of the aerial battle seemed to be louder than usual and went outside, into the garden, to see what was going on.

Looking up, he saw the tiny dots that were many aircraft moving around the sky. Then, high up towards the west, he saw a ball of smoke pass from one dot to another. For a moment nothing seemed to happen, then suddenly flame and smoke began to trail out from the second dot. The smoking aircraft began to dive and a small object appeared to drop from it; some seconds later, it blossomed into a parachute. (Plt Off Mounsdon, whose aircraft that was, had pulled the parachute release, when the fire in his clothes had gone out.)

Derek Bircher's attention switched to the aircraft, then much lower and descending to the north-west of the village; smoke was streaming from it but, as it got lower, the smoke disappeared. It came round, in a wide circle, to the north of the village. Momentarily, he lost sight of it as it disappeared behind the trees at the bottom of his garden. It re-appeared, continued its clockwise circuit over the village, then veered away to the north again. As it passed, almost overhead, Derek Bircher noticed a blackened mess under its body. Completing one full circuit, it disappeared behind the trees again, low down and did not re-appear.

When it was out of sight, a burst of machine-gun fire was heard and bullets struck the roofs of some council houses (Bellhouse Villas) on the Dunmow road, just outside the village. Whether or not the bullets were fired from the doomed or another aircraft was never known. The Hurricane was pointing in the same direction from which the bullets came, and was within range, but it is hard to imagine how the guns could have fired without a pilot.

One mile due north of the village Jack Warder, Len Joyce and Fred Altridge had been working in a field. When the noise of the battle drew closer they thought it wise to take cover in a nearby ditch. From there they heard a thump on the ground, followed by a noise that sounded like tin cans being dragged across the field. When all had gone quiet, they raised their heads to see an aircraft lying in the field. It appeared to have made a good wheels-up landing. The three men rushed over to it and were surprised to find no pilot in the cockpit.

When the aircraft had gone behind the trees for the second time, Derek Bircher's attention returned to the parachute, then getting lower and approaching the village from the west. The parachute passed over the church at one end of the street and it became obvious that it would continue over the top of the village and come down somewhere on the outskirts, to the east.

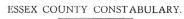

ESSEX COUNTY CONSTABULARY.

Telephone No. 3686/7.

DIVISIONAL HEAD QUARTERS,
Chelmsford,
Essex.

In reply please quote
Ref. No. P.LFB/62/40.   21st September, 1940.

'Dear Sir,

        I beg to forward herewith for your disposal, a flying helmet.

        This article was found by a Mr Leonard George Hartrupt, of "Lyndhurst", Ford End, Chelmsford, during the evening of Tuesday, the 17th instant, in a field at Good Easter, Essex.

        It is believed to be the property of a British Pilot who had recourse to vacate his machine by parachute some two weeks previously.

        I will be obliged if you will kindly acknowledge the receipt of this helmet, at your convenience, on the form below.

                        Yours faithfully,

                        [signature]

The Commanding Officer,
ROYAL AIR FORCE,
NORTH WEALD, Essex.   Superintendent.

Flying helmet worn by Plt Off Maurice Mounsdon when he baled out over High Easter on 31 August 1940. The radio lead shows clear evidence of having been wrenched from its socket as Plt Off Mounsdon rapidly vacated his burning machine without disconnecting it. The helmet was found in a field in the adjacent parish of Good Easter and was eventually returned to North Weald with the accompanying letter. (M. H. Mounsdon)

The head ARP warden for the village, Charles Wright, was following the course of the parachute in his car; but he was not the only one. Some of the older men in the village were following the parachute's descent also — they were armed with hay forks and the like.

At that time in 1940 there appeared to be an almost instinctive belief that a shot-down aircraft must be German, and frequently a premature cheer would go up only to be followed by the sight of an RAF pilot coming to earth. It also led to many RAF pilots finding themselves more concerned about their safety as they approached the ground than they had at altitude engaging the enemy. Charles Wright sought the help of another warden, Len Hill[3] and together they headed east out of the village.

About a quarter of a mile outside the village the parachute brought Plt Off Mounsdon to earth in a stubble field, known locally as 'Bones'. By the time the wardens got to him he had freed himself from his parachute but was obviously in a very bad way. That he had managed to unclip the harness amazed them because his hands were so badly burned. He was blackened and a large part of his trousers had been burned away. Having not been at 'readiness' before take-off, he was dressed in the standard uniform of tunic and slacks. In the rapid scramble there had been no time to don flying suit and boots, which would have provided the all-important protection. He had been without gloves also.

Charles Wright brought his car across the stubble field and Plt Off Mounsdon was helped inside for the short drive to Len Hill's house which was in the village. The village nurse arrived and offered her assistance. Martin Hill, then coming up to nine years old, later remembered clearly the pilot's blackened appearance and that he was ushered away from the scene as it was considered to be not suitable for young eyes.

The burns obviously required more attention than the nurse could offer, so the patient was taken by car to the local doctor in nearby Dunmow. From there, he was quickly passed on to the hospital at Black Notley, where he spent the next eleven weeks. Eventually, he was moved to the Service hospital at RAF Halton. His protracted period of hospitalization was to last, on and off, for almost two years.

He became one of Archibald McIndoe's 'guinea pigs' at East Grinstead's Queen Victoria Hospital and there met up again with another No 56 Squadron pilot who was in a similar condition: Plt Off Geoffrey Page, who had suffered a similar fate earlier in the August battles when he had baled out of his aircraft also after the gravity fuel tank had been hit. They had both joined No 56 Squadron together under somewhat unusual circumstances three months earlier and two weeks late!

They were both at the Flying Practice Unit at Meir near Stoke-on-Trent, having just left Flying Training School and were awaiting their squadron postings. The postings came by telephone to an adjutant who could not have heard the instructions clearly and consequently they were both despatched to No 66 Squadron which was operating Spitfires out of Old Catton and Coltishall, near Norwich. There, they settled in and had almost become operational on the Spitfire when the RAF Military Police arrived to arrest them for desertion! The mix-up was soon sorted out and, although their new Commanding Officer wanted to keep them — quite naturally as he had trained them so far — they had

Above left: North Weald, August 1940. Flt Sgt 'Taffy' Higginson (No 56 Sqn) at rest between sorties. *(Wg Cdr F. W. Higginson)*

Above right: Flt Lt Percy Weaver — No 56 Squadron's 'A' Flight Commander, who was shot down over the Essex coast whilst leading the Squadron against a formation of Dornier bombers. *(via After the Battle)*

Right: Plt Off Maurice Mounsdon (No 56 Sqn) with the aircraft he was to abandon in flames high over the Essex countryside on 31 August 1940. *(M. H. Mounsdon)*

Below left: Innes Westmacott (No 56 Sqn). Later, in 1942, when a Squadron Leader. *(I. B. Westmacott)*

Below right: Pilots of No 56 Squadron early in 1941. Sgt Peter Robinson far left, Innes Westmacott is fifth from left and 'Taffy' Higginson is far right. *(via I. B. Westmacott)*

to pack for North Weald and start again with No 56 Squadron on Hurricanes.[4]

Geoffrey Page returned eventually to operational flying but Maurice Mounsdon was not passed fit to fly again until 1942 and then in a limited flying category only. His parachute to safety was long remembered by the villagers of High Easter, not least in their prayers, as Martin Hill remembered so clearly from his time pumping the church organ. Each Sunday morning the Reverend Vincent would pray for 'the men of our village away at war and for Plt Off Mounsdon'.

Ten miles further south-east, between Chelmsford and Maldon, Fg Off Innes Westmacott's empty aircraft was hurtling earthward. In the parish of Boreham, on the outskirts of Chelmsford, the large country house of New Hall had been converted temporarily from a nunnery to a geriatric hospital. The hospital's previous location was close to RAF Hornchurch, so a more rural setting had been sought for the duration of the war. Wilf Chatley's mother was on the staff, so he too was accommodated temporarily in the large house.

He had just left New Hall and was making his way down the long driveway to meet up with a school friend (who lived a mile away at the White Hart public house, on the other side of the main Colchester to London railway line) when the sound of aircraft high above drew his attention.

> Then, ahead of me, cartridge cases began bouncing off the roadway, and high up towards the Danbury direction I noticed smoke coming from one aircraft as it headed away towards the coast. As the rain of cartridge cases ceased, I left the driveway and headed off across the fields as a short cut. I then noticed one particular aircraft was smoking fiercly. Thick, black, oily smoke was coming out of it as it spiralled round in wide circles. Crossing into the next field I noticed the plane was much lower than before and now appeared to be coming towards me. I paused for a bit then ran back, as I had a feeling it was going to hit me. I took cover by a ditch as the plane sliced into the top end of the field. I ran over and reached it in only a few minutes. There was no fire but it was black and oily and had pancaked in by a hedge. The canopy was open and as the engine had buried itself in a bit, I was able to look in and see inside the empty cockpit. Along the fuselage there were tears and rips and jagged holes in the aluminium at the tail. While I was still looking around some soldiers arrived from the nearby anti-aircraft site and it was then I noticed the parachute in the sky, high up over the Danbury direction.

Just like Plt Off Mounsdon's aircraft, what suddenly had became an inferno at 15,000 ft had apparently extinguished itself by the time it had reached the ground.

While descending but still at a great height, Fg Off Westmacott had managed to get his eyes open. The sound of aircraft had faded and he was assessing his situation as he drifted slowly down. His trousers had been reduced to a pair of singed blue shorts and his legs looked and felt most unpleasant. In the rush to get airborne, he had also been dressed in the standard uniform of jacket, trousers and shoes. The lower parts of his legs did not have the extra protection of flying boots, but he had been wearing gloves, which saved his hands, no doubt.

On surveying the landscape beneath him, he found the familiar landmarks of a countryside he knew well, as he had been brought up in this part of Essex. Away to the east, at the head of the Blackwater Estuary, was Heybridge where he had been born and his grandparents had the family business of Bentalls Iron Works. He could see their house, by the church at Wickham Bishops, away to the north-west of Heybridge. Further west was the thickly wooded area of Danbury and Little Baddow and it was in that direction that his parachute appeared to be taking him. As he descended, he could see the Blackwater Estuary recede until it merged with the horizon, and it began to look even more likely that he was destined to land in the wooded area by Danbury. The thought of crashing through the trees added to his discomfort.

Many local people watched as the parachute gently brought its load lower, unaware of their visitor's local connection. The early bus from Maldon to Chelmsford had been held up by the air battle overhead. A couple of miles out from Danbury it had been stopped by soldiers who were billeted at a large house called 'Potash' — later Potash Farm — just off the main road. The passengers were ushered out and directed to a ditch by the side of the road as the sky rained down cartridge cases.

Mrs Bew, one of the passengers on her way to work in Chelmsford, later remembered the clatter on the top of the bus roof as she sheltered in the ditch. When all was quiet again the passengers reappeared and it was then that they saw the parachute, coming down in the direction of Little Baddow and Danbury.

Both villages lay in the heavily wooded area on what forms a low but distinctive ridge in otherwise flat, open countryside. Danbury, the more southerly of the two was a more compact village, whereas the dwellings in Little Baddow were more dispersed amongst the woodland. The falling cartridge cases in Little Baddow told of what was happening high above.

Norah Shipman, who had been milking in her cowshed at Aldermanburgh Farm, in the centre of Little Baddow, stayed put until the rattle on the roof ceased. Then she peered out of a window to see a parachute floating down. She went outside and could see it, getting lower and headed for the edge of Blake's Wood, just to the south of Colam Lane which linked Little Baddow with the village of Boreham, a couple of miles north-west. Just as the landing place looked certain, she thought a gust of wind must have caught it because the parachute picked up and headed further into the wood.

Stan Brazier thought it was going to come down on top of him, until it suddenly veered away across Colam Lane, towards the northern edge of Blake's Wood. He had stopped his gardening work (at a house later called 'Ollands') and was chatting to the owner while the aerial combat took place overhead. When the parachute appeared suddenly quite low and headed for them both, Stan Brazier did not hesitate. His first instinct was to get a gun as he thought it could have been a German. As it veered away towards Blake's Wood he dashed down to the lane, and then back towards the village, in the direction where the parachute had been carried.

Others were of a similar mind. Half a mile away to the west, Ron Joslin and his father, had seen the parachute coming down and were running across the fields already armed with pitchforks, but when it became obvious that it would land further away, they gave up the chase. Others were closer at hand and help was not long in coming, when Fg Off Westmacott touched the ground finally.

Luck was with him in those final few moments when he came low over the lane, towards the edge of the wood. There was no doubt in his mind that he was going to have a most uncomfortable landing, however a small clearing appeared, only a few yards across, and he went straight into it, missing the trees completely.

> *Once on the ground, I was too shocked to stand and couldn't undo my harness, so I waited until I heard the Home Guard crashing through the woods. Knowing that they tended to be somewhat trigger happy, I called out to them before they could see me, and the shouted answer, 'All right, mate. We're coming.' was the most comforting sound I had heard for some time!*

He was taken to a small cottage in the wood to await the arrival of some transport. The cottage was surrounded closely by trees and the lane to it was so narrow that it proved to be impassable for the ambulance. Indeed, it was with only the greatest of difficulty that a police car managed to negotiate the route. Stan Brazier arrived as Fg Off Westmacott was being helped out to the car. He later remembered thinking what an awful state Fg Off Westmacott was in — his face burned, clothes all torn and his legs in a dreadful condition.

The car took Fg Off Westmacott the few miles to the hospital in Chelmsford, where visitors started to arrive even before the doctors had finished tidying him up. (The local police had telephoned his relatives and the news had spread rapidly.) The hospital was delighted to see him. He thought that that was partly because he was a local boy, but also because they had been waiting for a burns case on which to try out various concoctions they had thought up and which they were convinced were better than those recommended officially. He thought that there must have been something in that because he made a remarkably quick recovery, had very few scars and in just over a couple of months he was able to rejoin his squadron.

It had been an expensive encounter for No 56 Squadron. Heavily outnumbered, they had lost four aircraft in less than half an hour. One pilot, the Commander of 'A' Flight, was dead and two pilots were wounded severely. One Me 109 was claimed but the bomber formation had remained intact. Three more times that day the remaining aircraft of No 56 Squadron were scrambled to meet incoming raids. The following day they were relieved by No 249 Squadron and sent to Boscombe Down to reform. It was there that Innes Westmacott rejoined them in November. Maurice Mounsdon did not, for him many months of hospitalization lay ahead.

Chapter Fourteen
Homeward II

As the eleven Hurricanes of No 601 Squadron raced to gain height over Debden they could see the explosions on the airfield beneath. They were flying at 7,000 ft and still climbing flat out to meet their objective of patrolling base at 15,000 ft, but they had been ordered off far too late to prevent III/KG2's attack. The Dorniers were a further 8,000 ft above and the damage was being done already. Ten minutes earlier and the Hurricanes would have been where the bombs were now falling.

While Fg Off Brinsden was leading the four Spitfires of No 19 Squadron's 'A' Flight against the Dorniers, No 601 Squadron continued to climb. Fg Off Jerzy Jankiewicz, a Polish pilot with the Squadron, spotted a group of Me 109s, circling about 5,000 ft above. He left his formation to observe them and simultaneously one dived down and opened fire, head-on. As the 109 banked away Fg Off Jankiewicz delivered a beam attack, applying full deflection to his aim. A few seconds later, he saw black smoke coming from the 109's starboard side. It dived and Jankiewicz followed, the chase continuing at low level, east, towards the coast.

Six miles from Debden, soldiers manning a searchlight post saw the pair hurtle low overhead,[1] smoke pouring from the tail of the 109. They had a go at the 109 also, with rifles and a light machine-gun, but it sped on, pursued by the Hurricane.

Seven miles further east, over Sible Hedingham, the chase caused people to dive for cover when machine-gun bullets hit buildings in the village. The local paper, *The Halstead Gazette & Times*, used the incident to drive home the point about taking cover, reporting how the Hurricane, hot on the tail of the Messerschmitt, released several short bursts of machine-gun fire which broke several tiles on bungalow roofs. It emphasised how one bullet had passed through the scullery window of one bungalow, through an open doorway to the next room, where it penetrated a bureau wherein it was found subsequently.

Fg Off Jankiewicz was unable to close on his quarry and when south of Colchester and with the Me 109 about a mile ahead, he broke off and turned back for Debden. He claimed one Me 109 as damaged. Despite the trail of smoke, in all probability the Me 109 made it home because the Luftwaffe recorded only one 109 loss during this raid, that belonging to Leutnant Ebeling.[2]

Having left the Debden area and headed towards the east, Plt Off Tommy Grier encountered a group of Me 110s together with single-engined fighters to the west of Colchester, which he described as Me 109s and He 113s. He was alone and attacked one Me 110 which he later reported as going down, burning badly. He claimed one Me 110 destroyed, but he almost did not survive to register the claim. As he was breaking away from that successful encounter one of the 'He 113s' he had identified, fired at him from close behind and it took some violent manoeuvring before he was able to throw it off. His aircraft had been hit several times, the radio was useless and the hydraulics did not work, so he headed back for Debden.

On his approach, the engine started to leak glycol coolant and, because he could not get the undercarriage down (even with the emergency release), he decided to do a wheels-up landing. It was successful and he was able to walk away from his aircraft with only a slight shrapnel scratch, caused by enemy fire. He had been fortunate.

Of No 601 Squadron's 'A' Flight, Plt Off Humphrey Gilbert claimed an Me 110 as well. As the fight had moved east towards the coast, he became involved in a dogfight, to the north of the Thames Estuary.

> *I waited high up in the sun for a single enemy aircraft but three 110s presented good targets so I proceeded to attack these. I singled out one of them and, after a running fight, it crashed into the sea about twelve miles out, having crossed a convoy at about 1000 ft.*

14 Staffel of (Z)LG1 lost two Me 110s to the waters of the Thames Estuary that morning, and the Me 110 Plt Off Gilbert saw go down was almost certainly one of them.[3] 14/(Z)LG1's escort duties had been uneventful on the outward trip and it was not until they were on the homeward leg that the opposition troubled them.[4] The Me 110s of V/(Z)LG1 flew behind and to the right of the bomber formation, the two Schwarms (of four aircraft each) that made up No 14 Staffel bringing up the rear. Leutnant Karl-Joachim Eichhorn, flying 'L1+4K', was the 'Schwarmfuhrer' of the second and last Schwarm in the formation.

The attack was a complete surprise. It came from behind, but the first Leutnant Eichhorn knew of it was when bullets crashed into his cockpit and over

Fg Off Jerzy Jankiewicz — a Polish pilot with No 601 Squadron. He damaged an Me 109 during a chase across the north Essex countryside. *(Polish Inst. and Sikorski Museum)*

Plt Off Tommy Grier, No 601 Squadron. *(Imperial War Museum)*

Plt Off Humphrey Gilbert, No 601 Squadron. *(via C. H. Goss)*

the whole aircraft. Miraculously, he was not hit, but the starboard engine caught fire immediately. Leutnant Eichhorn put the aircraft into a steep dive to escape and only levelled out when just above sea level; having crossed the coast to the Estuary by then. He had shaken off his attacker but his radio operator, Unteroffizier Gröwe, had been killed and the aircraft was flying only twenty feet above the sea and on one engine.

Ten minutes later the other engine began to lose power. He had no choice but to ditch. Rapidly. he prepared, threw back the damaged cockpit canopy and checked his inflatable dinghy. Close to the North Kent coast, off Margate, the aircraft touched water. As soon as all was still he scrambled out, just in time as the aircraft went down like a stone. But his troubles were not over completely as he then found great difficulty in climbing into the dinghy — being weighed down by his water-logged, sheepskin flying boots. After many attempts, he made it and lay back to await his fate.

From the shore at Margate, the aircraft had been seen to enter the sea some three miles out, towards the east-north-east, off Foreness Point. At five minutes past nine the Margate lifeboat, the 'J.B. Proudfoot', was launched and headed for the scene. A fishing vessel arrived first and, spotting Lieutnant Eichhorn's rubber dinghy, took him on board. Just afterwards, the lifeboat arrived. On learning that there was a second crew member unaccounted for, the cox'n continued to search the area in the lifeboat, while the fishing vessel headed for the shore. The lifeboat crew found no further sign of life, only a parachute floating on the water.

Leutnant Eichhorn was taken to hospital where he met up with another member of his Schwarm, Obergefreiter Karl Döpfer, the radio operator and rear gunner of Me 110 'L1+AK' which had suffered a similar fate in the sudden attack: A Hurricane had came out of the sun and scored hits on the cockpit cabin; the port engine had caught fire and the starboard engine had stopped. His pilot, Feldwebel Gottlob Fritz, had dived the Me 110 to sea level and likewise had been

A snap-shot taken during an interlude in the fighting. The aircraft is Me 110 L1+AK of 14/(Z)LG1, flown by Feldwebel Gottlob Fritz and Obergefreiter Karl Döpfer, on 31 August 1940 and which crashed into the inner Thames Estuary. *(via C. G. Goss)*

Leutnant Karl-Joachim Eichhorn, of 14/(Z)LG1, having a head wound bandaged after being rescued from the sea off Margate. *(via B. L. Davis)*

forced to ditch in the Thames Estuary, but closer in, between the Isle of Sheppey and Foulness. All three began what was to be five long years in captivity.

While the residents of Sible Hedingham had been subjected to the low flying activities of Hurricane chasing Me 109, another drama was being played out over the villages of Great and Little Yeldham, immediately to the north. The whole North Essex area between Haverhill and Halstead had experienced aerial engagements, as the retiring raiders moved further south-east. Hurricanes of No 1 Squadron, having been thwarted in their initial attack over the Chelmsford area, had moved further north and were in contact again with the enemy formations.[5]

As it was a fine morning Fred Sale, a signalman at Great Yeldam railway station, was standing on the veranda of the signal box watching the goods wagons being loaded with hut sections, manufactured by a local company, for searchlight units. There was a red alert on but, as elsewhere in the rural areas, there was only a limited response to it.

The rumble of engines high up to the north-west warned of the approaching aircraft. Soon after, the sound of machine-gun fire could be heard also and cartridge cases began to rain down on the goods yard. Work on the loading stopped as the men took cover in a low-lying bridle-way, nearby. After the formation had passed over, Fred Sale went across to the loading point and, looking up to the south-east, where the formation of aircraft was heading away from him, he saw what he thought was a lone aircraft, climbing up through the formation then come back down through it again. As it did so, he saw a puff of smoke, then more smoke and then a parachute. He later remembered thinking at the time how brave the pilot was.

Sgt Henry Merchant of No 1 Squadron had become involved in a dogfight with some Me 110s. He had scored several hits on the forward fuselage of one and had damaged the starboard engine of another, seeing pieces of cowling fall off and a large quantity of black smoke appear. His Combat Report continued:

The Me 110 executed a slow roll to the right, on to its back and then went into a vertical dive, smoke and flame pouring from the starboard engine. As I turned away from this attack another Me 110 fired at me from about 400 yds from quarter astern and hit my reserve petrol tank low down.

(The location tallies with the claim made by Feldwebel Kaufman, of 7/ZG26, except that his claim was for a Spitfire.)

Flames immediately filled the cockpit and Sgt Merchant jumped clear. It was the first time he had been forced to take to his parachute, and only became apprehensive when, on nearing the ground, he saw men running towards him and pointing rifles at him. The Local Defence Volunteers were on the alert.

Despite the fuel tank having erupted in front of him, he had survived the experience, having only sustained limited burns to his hands and face; his clothing and goggles had protected him well. He was taken to the Halstead Cottage Hospital where the burns were attended to. Dr Gemmell, who treated him, later remembered Sgt Merchant's comment of being more afraid of the Home Guard reception party than he had been of the Germans! Sgt Merchant also confided to the doctor that he could not recall getting out of the aircraft, just suddenly finding himself descending slowly on the end of his parachute.

Local people working in the fields by Great and Little Yeldham had seen the incident, which was to cause more concern to some than others. Maxse Gardiner in Little Yeldham, who had been unloading harvest wagons in a dutch barn, took shelter there as cartridge cases rattled on the roof. When all had gone quiet, he looked out to see a parachute descending, away to the south towards the Hedinghams. But of more direct interest was the aircraft which was streaming smoke and gliding down towards the north-west in the direction of his family's farm at Ovington. He stopped work and hurried over to the farm which was a couple of miles away. There, he saw that an aircraft had crashed, a few hundred yards from the farm buildings, into a field, a total wreck.

In the general meleé that followed the initial encounter, several other claims were made by pilots of No 1 Squadron. Plt Off Dibnah reported that he had seen black smoke streaming from the starboard engine of an Me 110 that he had fired

Sgt Arthur Clowes of No 1 Squadron with the Hurricane (P3395) which he flew on 31 August 1940. This photograph was taken at RAF Wittering in October 1940 and shows the aircraft as 'B' which is believed to have been its identity also on 31 August. (Changing aircraft's individual letters was not unknown.) *(Imperial War Museum)*

at from long range (although it was conceivable that it also could have been the one fired at by Sgt Merchant). Plt Off 'Jack' Mann having seen black smoke coming from the port engine of another aircraft, claimed one Me 110 damaged. Together with other Hurricanes, Plt Off Peter Boot, having lost contact during the initial engagement, chased the aircraft to the coast and later became involved in a dogfight over the Thames Estuary, to the south of Colchester.

Sgt Arthur Clowes claimed one Me 110 'probably destroyed', having seen its starboard motor stop and the aircraft dive down to ground level, and two Dorniers probably destroyed. He was the only one of the Squadron to claim to have damaged any of the Dornier bombers, which he described as having been in two formations of fifteen, each in five vics of three. The large numbers of escorting fighters were proving effective as No 1 Squadron again found their attacks on the bombers hampered by them. Sgt Clowes got in finally from below and climbed up for a frontal beam attack and gave a two seconds burst of fire.

> *I half-rolled down and climbed up again for a* [second] *attack and saw only thirteen left. One was spinning down and the other was leaving the formation in a steep turn to the left.*

There, Sgt Clowes left them because he found himself being attacked by the Me 110s.

The Dorniers were, in all probability, those of III/KG2.[6] Walter Schlüter's aircraft, on the right flank of the second vic of three in III/KG2's formation, had come under attack from a Hurricane from his starboard side and ahead. As the Hurricane opened fire, the Dornier's pilot put U5+BD into a dive and Walter Schlüter opened fire on the Hurricane as it broke away. The dive exposed the Gruppe Commander's aircraft (U5+AD) to the Hurricane's fire. It was hit and Major Adolf Fuchs, the Gruppen Kommandeur, was wounded. Both aircraft made it safely back to France.

Sgt Merchant's aircraft was the only loss suffered by No 1 Squadron. Having been in the air for just over an hour, some of the Squadron's aircraft began to break off and turn back for Northolt to refuel and re-arm. Others who left later stopped off at Hornchurch on the way back.

So far, five squadrons had engaged the retiring raiders, and initial, co-ordinated attacks had fragmented, leaving individuals then pursuing their quarries or searching for them in the direction of the Thames Estuary. Of those squadrons who had been committed, No 257 Squadron had yet to make contact.

Chapter Fifteen
At the Coast

No 257 was a new squadron, formed[1] at Hendon on 17 May 1940, a week after the start of the German offensive in the West. The Squadron had become operational on 1 July and moved to nearby Northolt three days later. During the early activity along the Channel coast, in late July and early August, the pilots had invariably found themselves flying to Tangmere or Hawkinge, operating from there during the day and returning to Northolt in the evening.

The majority of the Squadron's pilots were drawn from the RAF Volunteer Reserve, No 257 being their first squadron posting. They were inexperienced and until joining the Squadron some had never flown a high-performance monoplane like the Hurricane. The Squadron had little combat experience and up to early August they had been involved with nothing more than single enemy aircraft at any one time.

Their first encounter with a sizeable opposition came on 8 August, over the Channel coast, just off the Isle of Wight. Of the eleven pilots who took part, three did not return and were never seen again. Two enemy aircraft were claimed 'destroyed' and two 'damaged', but the victories were overshadowed by their losses. These were felt more keenly because they had included two of the most senior pilots; one of which was the Flight Commander of 'B' Flight, who had been leading the Squadron at the time.

Four days later, in another large engagement, in the Portsmouth area, two more aircraft were lost for no definite claims of enemy aircraft destroyed. From the two aircraft, one pilot survived, but his injuries kept him from operational flying for the ensuing three months. The other was killed. He had been with the Squadron for a month only and the engagement had been his first.

Three days afterwards, on 15 August, the Squadron moved from Northolt to Debden and began to operate either directly from there, or from Martlesham Heath which was near to the coast and Ipswich. The arrangement again involved setting off early in the morning and not returning to base until evening. On 19 August the move to Martlesham Heath became permanent for the aircraft and pilots, the Squadron's maintenance and administrative sections remained at Debden. At Martlesham Heath daily aircraft checks and preparations were carried out by the ground crews of No 17 Squadron, whose Hurricanes had been moved to Tangmere on the south coast in the latest shuffle of No 11 Group's fighter squadrons. Routine aircraft maintenance was still done by No 257 Squadron ground staff, the aircraft having to be ferried back to Debden for that purpose.

From Martlesham Heath the Squadron found itself engaged mainly on convoy patrols over the East Anglian coast and Thames Estuary but, as the Luftwaffe's offensive intensified and moved further inland, scrambles became more frequent. During the final week of August the Squadron was sending up aircraft three or four times a day, but actual combat with the enemy remained limited.

When it did occur, the losses mounted. Of the twenty-two pilots who were with the Squadron at the beginning of August, fourteen only were still flying as the month closed. There were no replacements in August, and with the increasing flying commitments, the pressure mounted.

Six new pilots did arrive on 1 September but, within a week, four more of the original Squadron members had been shot down. Three were killed — two were both the Flight Commanders — and the fourth was severely burned. The Squadron's Intelligence Officer, Fg Off Geoffrey Myers, summed up the situation in his personal diary.

> We've all been through hell since the Squadron was formed a few weeks ago. We've all grown old. We've changed. It's grim.

It was not until mid-September and the arrival of more experienced replacement pilots, drawn from other operational Squadrons (including the charismatic Flt Lt Bob Stanford Tuck), that the Squadron's fortunes took a turn for the better.

On 31 August, with Fighter Command as a whole under increasing pressure, No 257 Squadron found itself heading for another large scale encounter. As the raids had developed over Essex, Sector Operations at Debden had scrambled the Squadron at 0825 hr, to patrol their own airfield (Martlesham Heath) at 10,000 ft, at the same time as No 601 Squadron had been scrambled to patrol Debden.

By 0830 hr, No 257 Squadron had nine aircraft airborne, led by 'A' Flight's Commander, Flt Lt Hugh Beresford. Shortly after, a new instruction — to patrol Debden at 15,000 ft — was received. The aircraft headed west still climbing, but, like No 601 Squadron, they were in no position to save Debden from the bombs of III/KG2.

While the bombs were falling on the airfield at Debden, the Sector Operations Room heard No 257's 'Tally-ho!'. To the west of Colchester and at 14,000 ft, they had seen, ahead and a couple of thousand feet higher, two large formations of, what they later reported to be, Ju 88s, followed by various formations of Me 110s.[2] All were heading south-east towards the coast.

Flt Lt Beresford put the Squadron into line-astern, crossed behind the enemy formation, then turned to port to parallel their course. The bombers were then three-to-five miles ahead and just off to port. It was soon apparent that the bombers would not be caught, so as they crossed the coast at the mouth of the River Colne, the Hurricanes turned their attention to the Me 110 escort. With individual aircraft from Nos 1, 19 and 111 Squadrons all converging on the same location, the scene was set for a major confrontation.

Flt Lt Beresford (Red 1) led the six aircraft of Red and Yellow Sections against one formation of Me 110s which had started to form a defensive circle. He opened fire, almost head-on, at an Me 110 which he then saw break up and go down, but his own aircraft had also suffered damage. Red 3, Plt Off Gundry followed his leader into the head-on attack and fired at one Me 110, closing from 400 to 200 yd, but with no conclusive result. Breaking away, he engaged another but then found himself well behind the rest of the enemy aircraft which were moving further out over the Estuary.

Red 2, Plt Off Alan Henderson, had fallen behind the others of his section during the turn and change in Squadron formation. Following the other two into the head on attack, he suddenly found two Me 110s coming directly at him, in line-astern. Realizing that he would present an easy target if he broke away, he flew straight at them and started firing. His Combat Report of the engagement continued:

> . . . *Both enemy planes broke away at point blank range, passing straight through my sights. The first enemy aircraft must have shot at mine before the break-away, as my instruments were shattered. A second or two later, as the second Me 110 appeared, there was a great explosion in my aircraft as my petrol tank was hit, presumably by cannon. The cockpit immediately became a mass of flames and I baled out . . . .*

Drifting down in his parachute he saw that he was not alone. Two other white canopies had blossomed not far away — the crew of Me 110 '3U+HS' from III/ZG26, had also had to make a hurried exit.

The Me 110s of III/ZG26 were having an eventful time of it on their escort duty. The eight aircraft of 8 Staffel, led by Oberleutnant Conny Meyer, had been reduced to five even before contact had been made with the RAF fighters. Three aircraft of the second Schwarm had had to turn back, leaving Oberleutnant Eric von Bergen, flying Me 110 '3U+HS', as the only one of his Schwarm to give protection to the rear of the unit. Soon after the turn for home, he had spotted four RAF fighters, approaching from out of the sun. He managed to warn the others in his unit, which were able to take evasive action and the fighters failed in their attack.

Reforming, he took up last position at the back again. Nearing the coast, he saw four other fighters [of No 257 Squadron] about to mount an attack, this time from below. He warned the others but they did not react, so he turned towards the Hurricanes and attacked. He fired at the last Hurricane and saw it go down but any thought of victory was short-lived when a burst from the first Hurricane found its target. The oxygen bottles in the rear of his aircraft exploded and the fuselage broke. He gave the order to his radio operator, Unteroffizier Hans Becker, to bale out then followed immediately.

The aircraft Oberleutnant von Bergen had seen go down (from what he assumed to be the result of his fire) was almost certainly that of Plt Off Henderson because he had seen the pilot bale out of the stricken Hurricane. They were destined for a closer meeting later. There were multiple claims for Oberleutnant von Bergen's aircraft by pilots of No 257 Squadron. His own description of the damage caused to his fuselage was quite distinctive and the combat reports of the three Section Leaders of No 257 Squadron each describe similar damage to aircraft they attacked, but III/ZG26 only recorded one aircraft as having failed to return that morning.

Red 1, Flt Lt Beresford, in his head-on attack, saw the Me 110 'break up and go down'. Yellow 1, Plt Off Cochrane, countersigned his Flight Commander's report to witness that he had seen 'the aircraft which Flight Lieutenant Beresford attacked, break up'. In his own combat report, however, Plt Off Cochrane gives a clear description also of what must have been 3U+HS going down. He had climbed up into the sun and

> *Seeing an opportunity I did a diving astern attack. Then at about 300 yds I opened fire with one burst of about 6-8 secs. Seeing no result I closed into 200-100 yd with another long burst. Smoke appeared from fuselage, then I saw two objects bale out of e/a and parachutes open. I did not wait to see the Me 110 go down as there were too many others around.*

Green 1, Fg Off Lance Mitchell, with his section in line-astern, described how he attacked the tail end of a group of Me 110s which had started to form a defensive circle.

> *. . . Green 3 [Plt Off Carl Capon] guarded my rear. I opened fire from 250 yds deflection shot with short bursts at first until E/A more or less straightened out. Then I gave a 4 secs burst. As I was doing my attack Green 3 informed me that the leading E/A were closing in on our rear. By this time I had shot down the end Me 110. I saw the tail unit crumple up and fall away and bits fly off the aircraft which went down in a spiral dive . . . .*

All three had claimed an Me 110 as 'destroyed'.

Plt Off Peter Boot. of No 1 Squadron, having broken off from his earlier engagement, had latched on to the Hurricanes of No 257 Squadron, as he saw them chasing the enemy formations out over the coast.

> *. . . With them I attacked a defensive circle of Me 110s and severely damaged one. I expended all my ammunition and a piece fell from off the tail plane. My main tanks ran out.* [He had been airborne for over an hour.] *I saw an Me 110 hit ground with tail shot away, but am uncertain if it were mine.*

He claimed a more cautious 'Me110 damaged'.

Plt Off Boot was one of a number of pilots from other squadrons who had made their way to the coast, in search of the retiring raiders and then joined No 257's dogfight, which had developed over the River Colne and then moved south-east, past Clacton and further out into the Thames Estuary.

Two of No 111 Squadron's Hurricanes also became involved. Plt Off Atkinson had joined in with No 257 Squadron as its aircraft formed up in line-astern for a head-on attack on a circle of Me 110s. He saw his fire enter the fuselage of an Me 110, which he thought must have caused considerable damage but saw no sign of it before he broke away. He claimed an Me 110 as damaged.

Sgt Wallace, after an earlier encounter with a Dornier formation further inland, had also arrived in time to witness No 257's head-on attack, and saw Plt Off

Henderson's Hurricane go down in flames. As the fight drifted out to sea, he climbed up-sun, above a defensive ring of Me 110s, then dived into the centre of the circle, attacking three Me 110s in quick succession, at close range, head-on. He saw his tracer hit an Me 110 causing thick, black smoke to pour from it.

> . . . *The rest of the Hurricanes had disengaged by this time and the bandits made east in a very broken formation. As my petrol was very low, I could not wait to see the Me 110 fall into the sea so I turned home.*

He added one Me 110 'destroyed' and one 'damaged' to his earlier claim of one Dornier 'probable'. However, later evidence suggests that all of the enemy aircraft subsequently made it home, albeit with varying degrees of damage.

No 19 Squadron's, Sgt Jennings, having rectified his oxygen problem, had made for the Thames Estuary after finding nothing in the Debden area, but he was too far south and missed the large dogfight taking place further north. Sgt Cox, whose attack, as part of No 19 Squadron's 'B' Flight, on the Dorniers near Duxford had been thwarted, had found himself alone in the sky. Learning, on the radio, that the enemy formations were to the south-east, he had climbed and headed in that direction.

Over the coast, he saw '50 Me 110s, milling around', and a large formation of enemy bombers further south. He saw four Hurricanes attack the Me 110s and joined in. Getting behind an Me 110, he gave a burst of fire for three seconds and saw it turn slightly to port and dive vertically down, its port engine belching thick black smoke.

He could not wait to see the result of the attack as he came under attack from other aircraft. Being out of ammunition he dived away, as fast as possible, through some small clouds and headed back home. At Fowlmere, he came straight in to land, coming in over the burning wreckage of Plt Off Aeberhardt's aircraft. Sgt Cox claimed one Me 110 'probably destroyed', but that was small compensation for No 19 Squadron's loss of three Spitfires.

After No 257 Squadron's initial head-on attack, the fighting fragmented into a series of skirmishes at section or individual level. As the fight moved further out to sea, the Hurricanes disengaged when they had exhausted their ammunition or fuel ran low. For others, like Flt Lt Beresford, battle damage would have been of concern also. During the initial attack, his aircraft had received hits in the oil tank, engine and starboard gun bay.

Other 257 Squadron aircraft remained in a position to maintain the chase further out to sea and attempted to pick off stragglers. Yellow 2, Plt Off David Hunt, after following his Section Leader, Plt Off Cochrane, into the initial encounter with the Me 110s, had followed them out to sea, along with two or three others. He managed to catch the Me 110s and, after letting off all his remaining ammunition in a long burst at the nearest one, saw white smoke issue from its starboard engine and a black square object fly off and go straight past his aircraft. Out of ammunition, he turned and headed back to base, where he claimed 'one Me 110 damaged'. The only damage to his own aircraft was a single shot in the port wing.

Red 2, Plt Off Gundry, continued the chase down as far as Deal, on the Kent coast, before realising there was no further chance of catching them. He turned and headed back across the Thames Estuary. After crossing the Essex coast, he saw a large formation of, what he estimated to be, 120 enemy aircraft,[3] stepped up from 12,000 ft to 25,000 ft, going south-east over the Chelmsford area.

Alone, he positioned himself for an attack on the Me 110 escort. Approaching from behind, he was spotted and two sections of five Me 110s turned back towards him. In the engagement that followed, he received some hits in the cockpit and with the odds heavily stacked against him he did not linger too long and eventually made a bolt for it by doing quick diving turns heading towards Clacton. The enemy formation re-grouped and continued on its way.

By 0900 hr the northern part of the Thames Estuary was clear of aircraft. All that remained were three parachutes drifting down and the marks where aircraft had fallen, but that was not many. Despite the numbers involved in that particular engagement over the coast and the claims made, actual casualties proved to be light on both side. Two Hurricanes from No 257 Squadron had failed to return: Plt Off Alan Henderson was coming down by parachute over the entrance to the River Colne, and Plt Off Gerard Maffett was missing.

No bombers had been attacked and for the escorting Me 110s of III/ZG26, the Luftwaffe's records list Oberleutnant von Bergen's aircraft only as lost that morning. Two other Me 110s from ZG26 crash-landed back in France, as a result of fighter damage: U8+JH from the Geschwader Staff Flight at Wizernes, and 3U+CD from III Gruppe Staff Flight at Arques. The radio operator of the latter aircraft had been wounded but he was III/ZG26's only recorded casualty, the fates of Oberleutnant von Bergen and Unteroffizier Becker were both unknown.

If there was uncertainty about the losses reported by those involved in the air, it was also not much clearer on the ground. The officers at the newly formed Naval Base at Brightlingsea, *HMS Nemo*, watched the events overhead, some with the aid of telescopes, according to Plt Off Henderson, who was later to find himself as a guest at the establishment. Later, in his combat report of the incident he described how the officers of the base watching his particular combat noted

> *. . . that it took place at some distance behind the main engagement, that there were only three aircraft in it,* [this following from his head-on encounter with two Me 110s] *and that all of them crashed. They confirm that one of the Me 110s, probably the first, crashed quite near the shore, and I understand that it is being salvaged. They say that the other e/a appeared to be crashing when the pilots baled out. The aircraft waffled out to sea. My aircraft crashed in the creek of the Colne and, I was informed, bounced into the water, a total wreck.*

Royal Engineers, at a searchlight battery to the north-east of Brightlingsea, recorded a time of 0847 hr for what later proved to be Plt Off Henderson's aircraft falling into the River Colne. The 9th Battalion Cameronians, defending the coastal strip between Brightlingsea and Clacton, recorded a time of 0845 hr for the same location, but noted that, immediately afterwards, another aircraft crashed into the sea further south, less than a mile from their 'C' Company's position. Both units saw the three parachutes descending.

However, uncertainty remained within the ARP for some time, as revealed by the surviving, hand-written Message Forms, which were used by telephonists when relaying incident reports along the chain of command. An hour and three-quarters after the incident, the Divisional Control at Colchester was relaying to Essex County Control that military authorities had reported

> . . . *one enemy bomber crashed on East Mersea beach near gun position. One enemy bomber crashed in mouth of River Colne. 3 enemy airmen picked up by patrol boat. Full details . . . not yet to hand.*

Three-quarters of an hour later that report was followed by another of a British aircraft having crashed in the River Colne at approximately 0900 hr and with no occupant being discovered, but that a wounded British airman, who was not connected with it, had landed at Brightlingsea. A further three-quarters of an hour later the last report was corrected to the effect that the British airman was connected with the crashed aircraft, and added that two German airmen had also landed at Brightlingsea, but there was no clarification as to the final number of crashed aircraft.

The second aircraft that was seen to go into the sea by members of the Cameronians, would have been Oberleutnant von Bergen's Me 110. It came down in the water off Mersea Island, just west of the River Colne. One DB601 engine was found subsequently on land, complete with a red propeller spinner (the colour to be expected on an 8 Staffel aircraft). Despite the individual RAF pilots' claims, the hard evidence on the ground appeared to agree with the losses reported in the Luftwaffe's records.

The soldiers watched a motor boat head out from Brightlingsea in the direction of the parachutes which were about to come down in the sea. Oberleutnant von Bergen, although sour at his bad luck, raised a smile when the occupant of a small boat approaching him pointed a rifle in his direction and called, "Hands up!" He was hauled aboard and then transferred to another boat, which had already picked up Unteroffizier Becker. The boats then went in search of the third parachute.

Jo Culling — who was part of the First Aid party that met the crew of Me 110 (3U+HS) from ZG26, when they were landed ashore at Brightlingsea.

Oberleutnant Eric von Bergen, pilot of Me 110 '3U+HS' of III/ZG26. *(via C. H. Goss)*

Plt Off Henderson had dislocated his shoulder during the escape from his blazing aircraft and, being burned on the hands and face, he was in some discomfort. Oberleutnant von Bergen later recalled that when they found Plt Off Henderson his wounds prevented him from getting into the boat by himself. As the boat only had a crew of two, Oberleutnant von Bergen and Unteroffizier Becker tried to help the RAF pilot, but he declined the offer and waited until a second boat arrived and he was taken ashore.

At Brightlingsea, a reception party had gathered at the waterfront. Earlier, Jo Culling, on hearing the air raid siren, had mustered at her post at the church hall. By day, she was a teacher at the local school, but out of school hours she was on call as part of the ARP's No 1 First Aid Party in Brightlingsea. As the boats were on their way back in, a first aid party was summoned to meet them. Jo Culling and her driver took their ambulance (a converted laundry van) down to the water's edge to await the boats' arrival.

The small boat carrying the two German aircrew came in first. Unteroffizier Becker was transferred to a stretcher and carried to the ambulance. Jo Culling later remembered that his face was puffed up to such an extent that he could hardly see. She was given to understand that he had got caught up with the straps of his parachute as it deployed, so causing a nasty friction burn across his face. He was badly shaken and she remembered having thought how young he looked.

Oberleutnant von Bergen had escaped injury but, still annoyed at his bad luck, resisted Jo Culling's attempts to usher him into the ambulance. In the end, it took some soldiers to persuade him to do otherwise. Jo Culling climbed in after him and the ambulance set off on its short journey across town to the Naval Sick Bay at 'Ashmore', a converted house in Church Road.

There, Unteroffizier Becker was left to have his injuries attended to. Oberleutnant von Bergen was taken the few hundred yards to the local police station. After treatment, Unteroffizier Becker joined him and they both spent the night in the cells, registered in the Police Log as prisoners, numbers 1 and 2 for the year 1940. The next morning, they were handed over to a military escort for onward transmission to an interrogation centre and then to a Prisoner of War camp.

Plt Off Henderson was also taken to the Naval Sick Bay, where he became a permanent resident while his dislocated shoulder and burns were treated. He was there some days and when able to get up and about, enjoyed the hospitality of the Captain and Officers of *HMS Nemo*. He was later transferred to an RAF convalescent home in Torquay and did not return to his squadron until November, but not to operational flying. In January 1941, after a brief spell on the staff of No 5 Flying Training School at Tern Hill, he was sent to Canada for flying training duties.

While Plt Off Henderson was being brought ashore, reports were coming in of another Hurricane which had come down at Walton-on-the-Naze, eleven miles to the east. Plt Off Gerard Maffett had been found dead beside his aircraft

While Flt Lt Beresford had led Red and Yellow Sections in their head-on attack, Green Section, bringing up the rear, had engaged a line of about ten Me 110s behind and above the others. Green 2 (Plt Off Maffett) had fallen behind his leader, and Green 3 (Plt Off Capon) had slotted in to guard Fg Off Mitchell's rear as the Section Leader went in against the tail end of the line, which had already started to curve round to form a defensive circle. What happened to Plt Off Maffett then was not recorded in contemporary records and was probably only ever known by himself and his attacker. However, some aspects of the engagement were seen from the ground.

To the north of Walton-on-the-Naze a gang of men were working on the sea wall that surrounds the Naze peninsula. Away to the west, in the direction of Hamford Water marshes, they could see a dogfight taking place at great height. The noise of machine-gun fire was quite clear.

Cyril Studd later recalled having seen the aircraft going round and round,

> . . . then one broke away from the fight and came gliding out as if he were heading towards Harwich way. We thought he was short of fuel or ammunition. There was one big cloud and he went under it and as he came out the other side another plane seemed to come out of the cloud and dived down on him and fired. It was only a short burst and the plane started to come down, while the other continued out to sea.

RAF personnel at the Chain Home Low Radar Station, half a mile away, on the higher ground at the Naze, saw the aircraft go into a dive and then pull out at about 5,000 ft, but then to go completely out of control and when it was at approximatley 400 ft they saw the pilot bale out.

The workmen on the sea wall had watched as the aircraft descended, expecting to see the pilot come out at any moment, but nothing happened. 'There was no fire or smoke, it just came spiraling down', Cyril Studd later recalled. It was not until the aircraft was near to the ground that the aircraft just flipped over and the pilot came out, according to Alec Cross, then a fifteen year old working on the sea wall.

Stan Martin, a farm worker, had watched the drama unfold from his vantage point of Walton Hall Farm, where he had been working. He also had been waiting for the parachute to appear. When, at last, the pilot appeared, he could see that it was far too low — the parachute tried to open, but it was too late. He joined the others, who had seen the crash, as they made their way down to the marsh at the far end of the Tamarisk sea wall.

The aircraft lay with its nose buried deep in the mud, its wings stretched out and its tail pointing out to sea. But there was no fire. Plt Off Maffett lay on the sand, less than a hundred yards away, his parachute beside him.

At the Police Station in Walton, news of the crash sent PC Watson and Special Constable Bocking to investigate. They cycled up to Walton Hall Farm, where they left their bicycles and continued, on foot, down the rough track to the edge of the fields. Threading their way through the defensive minefield strip, they reached the Tamarisk Wall. By the time they arrived, Plt Off Maffett's body had been carried to the landward side of the sea wall on a make-shift stretcher. The two policemen took over and carried it back up to the farm, where an ambulance was waiting. There, they parted company with Plt Off Maffett's body, for dealing with RAF aircrew was a military affair — enemy aircrew casualties only were a police responsibility.

By this time, the Dorniers of III/KG2 were back on the ground at Cambrai.

PC Watson.

Special Constable Bocking.

PC Watson and Special Constable Bocking were despatched from the Police Station at Walton to investigate the crashed aircraft at the Naze.

Walter Schlüter completed his log, recording a flying time of two hours thirty minutes and a landing at Cambrai at 0935 hr. U5+BD had made it safely back, despite the encounter with the Hurricane — as had the Gruppen Kommandeur's aircraft, U5+AD.

III/KG2 had suffered only light casualties with only two aircrew wounded, but one was the Gruppen Kommandeur, Major Fuchs. His was the only aircraft to have received sufficient damage to make it worthy of a mention in the Luftwaffe's Quartermaster General's Returns.

II/KG2 had been almost as fortunate — one aircraft was a write-off, one person only was wounded, and there were no fatalities. The Quartermaster General's Records list no aircraft as having fallen on enemy soil for both Gruppen of KG2.

Of the escorting fighters, one Me 109 from III/JG26 had been lost, but its pilot had been rescued from the Channel. From V/(Z)LG1 and III/ZG26, three Me 110s had been lost over England; one crew member was dead and five had been captured. Two other aircraft from III/ZG26 had crash-landed in France but the crews were safe, although one pilot had been wounded. With hindsight, it could be said that for the damage inflicted, the price had not been too heavy.

On the other side of the Channel, the cost to the RAF had been higher, despite the claims. In something like half an hour eleven fighters had been lost. Three pilots were dead and five were injured to such an extent that they would not be able to fly for some time. Four of them had suffered burns when their Hurricanes' fuselage fuel tanks, containing twenty-eight gallons of high octane fuel and barely three feet in front of the pilots' laps, had been hit. In a tragic sort of irony it could be said that these injuries were a means of survival: so many of the pilots who continued operational flying, after that morning, did not survive the war.

Of the eleven pilots of No 19 Squadron who flew that morning, six only survived the war; of No 601 Squadron — only two of the eleven; and of No 257 Squadron only two of the nine survived — one was Plt Off Alan Henderson, who was a casualty on 31 August; and the other was Plt Off David Hunt who, only four days later, suffered a similar fate when his fuselage fuel tank went up in flames.

He also was destined to follow Plt Off Maurice Mounsdon and many other aircrew, to the East Grinstead hospital for plastic surgery treatment in the skilled hands of Archibald McIndoe, a pioneer in that field of medicine. The patients often thought of themselves as guinea pigs and as their number increased and the long sequence of treatment dragged on, so came into being that rather exclusive club that all aircrew hoped they would never join: The Guinea Pig Club.

On Saturday 31 August, while the day was still young and the Dorniers of KG2 were returning home over the North Sea, Me 109s of I/JG53 busied themselves shooting down the Barrage Balloon defences at Dover. A little later, there were signs that more formations were assembling in the Pas de Calais and just before 1000 hr the first formation of the next raid came over the Channel, via Folkstone.

North of the Thames, nine Hurricanes of No 601 Squadron had taken off at 0940 hr and at 0958 hr eight Hurricanes of No 151 Squadron were scrambled from Stapleford. Forty minutes later aircraft from No 56 Squadron took to the air again, followed by the Spitfires of No 19 Squadron, and so it continued.

In all, four major raids occurred that day and Fighter Command lost a total of thirty-nine aircraft and had fourteen of its pilots killed. It was to be Fighter Command's highest daily loss of that summer's conflict, which was to become known as the Battle of Britain.

Peter Townsend, then a Squadron Leader in command of No 85 Squadron, was to write later, '30 August saw the beginning of the fiercest 48 hours of fighting of the whole battle . . . . 31 August was the blackest day of all.' (*Duel of Eagles*). He became a casualty also on 31 August when, later that day, his aircraft was hit by cannon-fire and he was forced to bale out, with a piece of cannon shell embedded in his foot.

Of the nine pilots of No 257 Squadron who took part in the action of 31 August 1940, only two survived the war: Alan Henderson and David Hunt (right).

Chapter Sixteen
Speculation

The final moments of Plt Off Maffett's flight that day have been described by a small number of eye witnesses, but what still remains unanswered is: Why was he apparently alone? and: Why did he leave it so late to bale out? Plt Off Maffett only would have known the answers. However, some conclusions can be drawn and speculation attempted, based on the sequence of events seen and related subsequently by eye witnesses, and evidence obtained from the surviving wreckage.

During its excavation, it became apparent that the aircraft had been on fire at some time. Early speculation was that the irregular pattern of fire-damage pointed to a fire after the crash. This was borne out subsequently by eye witness accounts of there having been no smoke-trail or fire as the aircraft came down. Likewise, nobody recalled having seen a fire immediately after the aircraft crashed and so it must have been localised and at depth.

Of the actual battle damage, there is some evidence on the surviving wreckage, but its interpretation must be treated with a degree of caution. Two points are relevant: First, not all the aircraft's structure has survived and so damage to other parts remains unknown. Second, the places where shrapnel and bullet holes are found are on parts which had lain buried close to the marsh's surface and it is conceivable that later tampering could have caused the damage.

During the latter part of the war the Tamarisk wall became part of a small-arms firing range and it is quite possible that the occasional pot shot was aimed at the remaining wreckage — not that much of it would have been visible above the ground by then.

Stan Martin later related how the remains were gradually reduced in size by soldiers who hacked off sections and took them back to their camp. For what purpose is not known — to become souvenirs was a possibility but more likely, in view of the wartime shortages, would have been to use them as source material for some other purpose.

Today, the surviving section of the port wing shows the most evidence of the 'battle' damage. Two clear strikes, from what was probably 20 mm cannon-fire, can be seen in the rear spar, one in the steel centre section, the other at the start of the aluminium outer wing, by the gun-bay. The line of fire appears to have come from the starboard quarter and would therefore have passed through the wood and fabric rear fuselage first. The surviving structure of the gun-bay also shows hits, whether by bullets or shrapnel from strikes elsewhere is not clear.

The gun-bay access doors and adjacent torsion box structure from the upper surface of the outer wing, are peppered with the marks of fragments penetrating from underneath and it could be construed that the cause was exploding ammunition but the large number of rounds recovered intact makes that theory unlikely.

The starboard wing, of which little now remains, shows clear strikes from ahead on the front spar by the gun-bay. That was the lone spar that could be seen protruding from the marsh in the 1960s, but being the most exposed piece it might have been a more obvious target for practice shooting. It is not exhibited with the rest of the aircraft's remains as most of it was removed from the marsh some time before the main excavation.

There are a couple of nicks in the undercarriage fairing, and what appear to be the spatter marks of shrapnel (from within) on the port wing root fairing panel by the rear spar; but there are no marks to be seen on the surviving panels of the forward fuselage and engine cowling. Then there are the holes in the back of the pilot's seat, punched through from the rear but earlier discounted as original damage because the armour plating immediately behind it had been recovered intact with the wreckage, or had it?

Two important finds came to light some ten years after the excavation as the process of coastal erosion steadily lowered the general foreshore level. One was a flat piece of armour plating, badly rusted, but with one sizeable hole in it, showing a slight flair around its jagged edges. It proved to be the centre section of the three pieces that made up the armour protection behind the pilot's seat and had obviously broken free from the remainder of the framework. The piece recovered still connected to the wreckage, when examined more closely, was found to be the lower portion. Being attached to the framework along one edge, it had swung round, giving the impression that it was the middle piece. At the time, there had been no reason to doubt its location and the correctness of its shape had not been checked. Although not easy to physically replace the newly discovered piece into its correct position on the airframe, because of distortion to that particular part of the fuselage structure, the hole appears to line up with the damage in the rear of the seat.

The other item to come to light at about the same time was one of the aircraft's Browning machine-guns. The barrel was slightly bent, but otherwise it was remarkably well-preserved. Part way in the chamber was found an unfired round — a warning to all who may meet such items and be tempted to treat them lightly. It seemed as though the gun had jammed on firing. Could that have been the cause for the Hurricane having to break away from the fight, seen by the gang of workmen on the sea wall?

As Cyril Studd later found out, it was not through lack of ammunition, as had been thought at first, because there was plenty left in the gun-bays. So much so that he was able to retrieve three boxes of ammunition to supplement his Home Guard allowance: the advantage being that they were not accountable rounds! There was certainly no need to doubt the presence of large amounts of ammunition as at least a hundred intact rounds, linked together, were found during the main excavation. When the control column was inspected, the gun firing button was found to be switched to 'fire' rather than 'safe'. Although that was no indication that Plt Off Maffett had used his guns, it showed that he was certainly prepared to do so at the time his aircraft was shot down.

The sequence of events leading up to the crash could have been as follows: During the initial attack on the Me 110s, Plt Off Maffett's aircraft was reported to have fallen behind the other two of his Section. He was probably singled out for attack and received damage in one or both of his gun-bays, making his guns inoperable. He disengaged and started to head back for Martlesham Heath (which would agree with the direction observed by Cyril Studd). It was unlikely that the aircraft was short of fuel as it had only been airborne for less than half an hour.

Alone, the Hurricane was attacked again with a short burst of cannon-fire from behind. One shell hit the armour plating behind the seat, forcing shrapnel through the thin aluminium seat and severely wounding Plt Off Maffett in the back. The aircraft went into a dive as he lost control. Unconscious, he only came to when the aircraft was very low and, having managed to undo his straps, he baled out as the aircraft flipped over onto its back, but at a height of about 400 ft only there was no time for the parachute to have any effect.

However, this is speculation and should not be interpreted as fact. What actually happened will never be known for sure.

In combat, a fighter pilot's job is a solitary one. He is alone in his cockpit with his emotions as he approaches the opposition. There is no one to witnesses the heroic struggle or lack of it just before death strikes. No record for citations for bravery or cautions for lack of commitment.

Those who paid the ultimate price in such circumstances were unable to give an account of their final deeds. It is left to later accounts, such as this, to try and piece together surviving information to tell an individual's story, but it can never be the whole story. What deeds had Flt Lt Weaver performed before being lost to the depths of the River Blackwater? Sgts Craig and Whitehead both baled out but no record has been found to describe what they went through or what happened to them. Neither survived the war and so their stories are lost with them. Either they did not make out Combat Reports or, like others, the reports have not survived the passage of time. Flt Lt Weaver was denied the opportunity to complete a report. His name is mentioned only briefly here because he did not survive to tell his tale and nobody else knows or will ever know.

The same could have been said of Plt Off Maffett until over thirty years after the event. For some the evidence still remains — their aircraft were never recovered during the war — so there is still a chance to find out something if the wreckage is located. Some people say that such things should be left unknown, some that they should not. Understandably it can become an emotive topic.

Appendix A
Explanatory Notes

Messerschmitt 109. Throughout the text the term 'Me 109' is used to denote this aircraft, in preference to 'Bf 109'. This makes for continuity with quotes from contemporary records.

Home Guard. In mid 1940 the name of the Local Defence Volunteers (LDV) was changed to the now more familiar title of Home Guard. Both terms appear in the text but they refer to the same organisation.

ARP. Air Raid Precautions — Part of the Civil Defence organisation established pre-war in response to the anticipated threat and effects of enemy bombing. Civilians were recruited for Warden duties, First Aid Parties, Rescue Parties etc.

RDF. Radio Direction Finding — The now more familiar term 'Radar' has been used instead of its 1940 equivalent 'RDF'. This early warning network covered the approaches to the East and South coasts and was made up of two chains, designated CH (Chain Home) and CHL (Chain Home Low); the latter having a reduced detecting range but better coverage at low level.

Readiness. Part of a sequence of terms indicating the state of availability of an RAF Fighter Squadron:

      Released — not required for operations, pilots able to leave the airfield.
      Available — pilots required to be on the airfield and to be within range of the tannoy system or telephone.
      Readiness — pilots at their flight dispersal — Mae West lifejackets on or to hand, parachute on aircraft wing ready for immediate clip on and flying helmet in the cockpit already plugged in.
      Standby — pilots, sitting in their cockpits, fully prepared for take-off.
      Scramble — immediate take off.

Approximate equivalent RAF & Luftwaffe ranks:

Aircraftsman 2	*Flieger*
Aircraftsman 1	*Gefreiter*
Corporal	*Obergefreiter*
Sergeant	*Unteroffizier*
Flight Sergeant	*Feldwebel*
Warrant Officer	*Oberfeldwebel*
Pilot Officer	*Leutnant*
Flying Officer	*Oberleutnant*
Flight Lieutenant	*Hauptmann*

| Squadron Leader | *Major* |
| Wing Commander | *Oberstleutnant* |

RAF Fighter Command and Luftwaffe organisation

Fighter Command's basic operating unit was the Squadron which would be expected, when called upon, to be able to put a force of twelve aircraft into the air. More aircraft and pilots were on the Squadron strength to allow for aircraft maintenance, pilots' leave etc. In command was a Squadron Leader. Administratively and operationally the Squadron aircraft and personnel were divided into two Flights, 'A' and 'B', each under the command of a Flight Commander, usually of Flight Lieutenant rank. When airborne, the Squadron of twelve aircraft would be led either by the Squadron Leader, taking the formation slot of one of the Flight Commanders, or by one of the two Flight Commanders. Flights were further subdivided into two Sections of three aircraft, each with a colour designator. Red and Yellow Sections formed 'A' Flight, and Blue and Green Sections 'B' Flight. Within each Section aircraft were known by numbers 1, 2 and 3; thus Green 1 was the leader of Green Section in 'B' Flight. By the summer of 1940 rank had often been overtaken by combat experience when it came to allocating Section Leaders, so a Flight Sergeant with combat experience in the Battle for France might have found himself as a Section Leader, with his numbers two and three being of commissioned rank and with just as much flying experience but less, if any, combat experience.

The colour/number identity was used for formation flying organisation and radio communications between aircraft, and it also followed through into report writing. Individual aircraft were visibly identified by a three letter combination painted either side of the fuselage roundel. A two letter code to one side identified the Squadron and a single letter on the other, the individual aircraft within the Squadron. Which set went which side of the roundel varied considerably between individual Squadrons. Generally, the individual identity letters of 'A' Flight aircraft were between A and K, leaving L to Z for 'B' Flight aircraft.

Strategically the airspace over Britain was divided into Sectors, with one main airfield, or 'Sector Station', being the co-ordinating and controlling centre for each Sector. Sectors were identified by a letter but also became known by the name of their Sector Station. The main airfields within each Sector maintained a strength of three Fighter Squadrons. As the summer fighting intensified, a policy of greater dispersal meant that many Squadrons found themselves operating out of adjacent satellite airfields, often with only grass landing grounds and little, if anything, in the way of domestic and maintenance facilities.

In the air each Squadron acted as an independent unit, being controlled by the Operations Room at the Sector Station. By late August attempts were being made in some quarters to group three Squadrons for combined interceptions at 'wing' strength. It was a concept which, within the operational scenario of the time, was to become a topic of considerable controversy.

Sectors were geographically and operationally combined into 'Groups', with four Groups covering the United Kingdom, numbered sequentially from south-west England through to Scotland: 10, 11, 12 and 13. No 11 Group covered the Sectors 'A' to 'F' in south-east England and bore the brunt of the Luftwaffe's offensive in 1940.

Numerically the Luftwaffe's equivalent to the Squadron was the *Staffel*, of approximately twelve aircraft of the same type. However, unlike the RAF's embryo Wing, the Luftwaffe equivalent of three *Staffel*, the *Gruppe*, formed a much more cohesive unit, linked both administratively and operationally. In general, three *Gruppen* then formed a *Geschwader*, although some contained more. A *Geschwader* was the Luftwaffe's basic tactical unit and a prefix to the title designated its operational role: *Kampfgeschwader* (KG) — bombers; *Jagdgeschwader* (JG) — fighters (single-engined Me 109s in 1940); *Stukageschwader* (StG) — divebombers; *Zerstörergeschwader* (ZG) — twin-engined (Me 110) 'destroyer' fighters; *Lehrgeschwader* (LG) — by designation these were Operations Training Units but they had an operational role and contained some experienced aircrew. Individual *Gruppen* within the *Geschwader* had different roles and aircraft types.

A number of different types of *Geschwader* (and sometimes incorporating other individual *Gruppen*) were combined into *Fliegercorps*, which in turn were grouped into *Luftflotten*, or 'Air Fleets'. In 1940 *Luftflotten* 2 and 3 covered the Channel coast of Northern France and the Low Countries: *Luftflotte* 3 to the west and *Luftflotte* 2 to the east including Belgium and the Netherlands. The dividing line between the two was projected northwards into Britain with each having its own operational sphere of influence.

Staffeln within a *Kampfgeschwader* were further sub-divided, for formation flying into units of three aircraft in arrowhead formation — a *Kette*. Each *Gruppe* had a Staff Flight, or *Stabskette*, as did the *Geschwader* as a whole.

Staffeln within a *Geschwader* were uniquely numbered: 1, 2, 3 *Staffeln* formed I *Gruppe*; 4, 5, 6 *Staffeln* formed II *Gruppe*; and 7, 8, 9 *Staffeln* formed III *Gruppe*. Thus 7/KG2 was the 7th *Staffel*, which belonged to III *Gruppe*, in *Kampfgeschwader* 2. A colour code incorporated into the unit markings helped to identify individual *Staffeln* within each *Gruppe*: White — the first *Staffel* in each *Gruppe* (1, 4, 7, etc. *Staffeln*); Red — the second *Staffel* in each *Gruppe* (2, 5, 8, etc. *Staffeln*); Yellow — the third *Staffel* in each *Gruppe* (3, 6, 9, etc. *Staffeln*). *Gruppe* and *Geschwader* Staff Flights used Green and Blue.

The markings on each bomber consisted of four characters, two either side of the national black cross symbol. The two to the left of the national marking used a number and letter combination to identify the *Kampfgeschwader* (U5 for KG2). The two to the right designated the individual aircraft and the *Staffel* it came from. The individual aircraft letter was either painted in, or outlined in, the *Staffel* colour.

In the air *Staffeln* of Me 110 aircraft (either from a ZG or LG) were sub divided into groups of four aircraft (a *Schwarm*), with a *Schwarm Führer* in command of each sub unit. The markings of these twin engined *Zerstörer* aircraft followed the same pattern as for the bombers described above. The *Stukageschwader* aircraft also followed this same basic pattern.

Staffeln within a *Jagdgeschwader* similarly were sub divided into the flying unit of the *Schwarm*, and then also into pairs, or *Rotte*, each containing a leader (*Rottenführer*) and a wingman (*Rottenflieger*). This arrangement was in contrast to Fighter Command's more rigid close formation flying in Sections of three, combined with set piece attack formations. The Luftwaffe's approach provided greater flexibility of operation, and later was also adopted by Fighter Command. Markings for *Jagdgeschwader* aircraft differed from other Luftwaffe units in not using the four character combination. Individual aircraft within a *Staffel* bore numbers sequentially from 1, painted in the *Staffel* colour. The *Gruppe* was identified by a symbol on the opposite side of the national marking, in the form of a horizontal or vertical bar, a wavy line, or a blank space. Staff aircraft and unit leaders used a combination of chevron and bar symbols in place of the individual aircraft number. The particular *Geschwader* could only really be identified by a small motif painted on the fuselage sides, which either denoted the *Geschwader* as a whole, or was unique to one of the *Staffeln* or *Gruppen* within it.

Appendix B
Notes

Chapter Ten (Build up)

1 The time II/KG2 took off from Arras is not known, but it is a reasonable assumption that they took off before III/KG2 as their target of Duxford lay nine miles beyond III/KG2's (Debden) and the bombing in the Duxford area is recorded as having occurred some ten minutes before that at Debden.

2 Documentary evidence exists to show that both V/(Z)LG1 and III/ZG26 acted as escort for the early morning bombing raids north of the Thames Estuary on 31 August 1940. Other Me 110 units may have been present but no evidence has been found to substantiate this or to give a clue as to their identity. It has not been possible to state categorically which of the two identified Me 110 units flew with which bomber formation. However, all the circumstantial evidence points to V/(Z)LG1 being with III/KG2 against Debden and III/ZG26 being with II/KG2 against Duxford. (See also 10.4.)

3 The strength of the Me 109 force is not certain. Aircraft taking part have been identified as having come primarily from III/JG26, but a claims list for II/JG26 indicates that they were also involved.

4 Evidence for the exact routes used by II and III/KG2 is very sparse and information provided by a small number of former Luftwaffe aircrew (primarily from the escort aircraft) is often conflicting. Overall, the dog-legged sea route via the southern North Sea and Thames Estuary is considered most likely, not least in view of the, albeit limited, evidence of the Sector Operations Room plot and the coastal reports. Further support is added by the lack of any indication from similar sources that the more direct path, over North-East Kent and South Essex, was used.

5 The report of the second formation of aircraft heading 'south-west', stands alone. No other evidence has been found to support suggestions of enemy aircraft movement to the south and west of Chelmsford at this time. That is not to say that such a route was not used, but no other evidence for it has been found and it leaves doubt as to whether or not 'south' in the report really should have been 'north'.

6 The numerical strength of aircraft formations described in Combat Reports frequently do not specify whether they refer to the bombers alone or include the escorting fighters as well. Therefore it is often not possible to use these valuable source documents to help plot the movement of bomber formations of known size. In this particular case, the implication is that the bombers' numbered about 100. Such a figure appears excessive when considering all the other evidence that has been found.

7 Raid 29A was almost certainly a formation of Dorniers from II/KG2.

8 The county of Essex is well served with a comprehensive set of wartime ARP records, which include detailed daily incident reports. For 31 August 1940 there is no record of bombs falling at or near Harlow.

Chapter Eleven (Duxford)

1 Reports of the numbers of enemy bombers over the South Cambridgeshire area, both from eye witnesses and contemorary documents, range from between twelve and eighteen. This is far short of the full 'Gruppe' strength which, subject to aircraft availability, would have been nearer 30+ aircraft. No German source has been found to indicate the strength of II/KG2 during this particular raid.

2 The first enemy formation No 19 Squadron met, heading north-west towards Cambridge, was almost certainly Dorniers from II/KG2, supported by Me 110s from III/ZG26.

3 There is conflicting evidence as to who was Blue 3 and who was Green 3 (Sgt Cox or Plt Off Aeberhardt). Sgt Cox's Combat Report indicates that he was Blue 3, but one part of the Squadron's Operations Record Book lists him in Green Section. At the time of writing Wg Cdr Cox is certain that he was in Fg Off Coward's Section and therefore was Green 3. He considers the error to be in the Combat Report.

4 At the time of interception recorded in No 111 Squadron's Combat Reports, III/KG2's Dorniers were still south-east of and approaching Debden, which was their target. One inconsistency is that No 111 Squadron reported that the formation they were attacking was 30 strong. For II/KG2 this is an unlikely figure in view of 11.1 above.

Chapter Twelve (Debden)

1 The Me 110s over Debden were most likely those of V/(Z)LG1. See 10.2 above. That the Me 109s were from III/JG26 is based primarily on the location of two of their 'victory' claims. One was from Maj Adolf Galland, then Geschwader Kommodore of JG26, who recalls that the morning mission was 'an enlarged escort activity for a group of KG2 attacking Debden'. He made his twenty-fifth victory claim on that mission, some 20 km south-east of Cambridge; which would make it close to Debden.

2 Reported sightings of the mysterious 'He 113' were positive results for the German propaganda effort. A pre-war single-engined Heinkel competitor to the Me 109 was not selected for full-scale production like its rival, but later its existence was used to promote the emergence of a new high performance German fighter, the so-called He 113.

Chapter Thirteen (Homeward I)

1 Believed to have been Colchester's first civilian fatality of the war.

2 The number of aircraft No 56 Squadron managed to get airborne is not certain. The Squadron's Operations Record Book 'daily summary' page does not give

a figure. The Squadron divided the recording of individual flights between the two Flights. 'A' Flight's listing for August 1940 is complete and records five aircraft airborne for that scramble. 'B' Flight's records contain no entry for 31 August 1940. However 'B' Flight must have managed to get at least three aircraft airborne, as one pilot completed a Combat Report and two others were shot down. The Operations Record Book for RAF North Weald gives a figure of thirteen, but with five aircraft only listed from 'A' Flight that would have left eight for 'B' Flight — most unlikely at that time in view of the Squadron's heavy losses in August.

3 Len Hill was not a member of the local ARP organisation at High Easter. He was an ARP Warden in London where he worked, returning to High Easter at the weekends.

4 By the end of May 1940 the pilots of No 56 Squadron had just moved north to RAF Digby for a few days rest. It was while they were there that Plt Offs Mounsdon and Page caught up with them before the Squadron flew back to North Weald on 6 June to continue operations.

Chapter Fourteen (Homeward II)

1 In the narrative it has been assumed that the low-level chase of an Me 109 by a Hurricane, seen just east of Debden and also over Sible Hedingham, was the same pair, and that the Hurricane was piloted by Fg Off Jankiewicz. His is one of three No 601 Squadron Combat Reports covering that particular scramble that still exist today, describing a chase eastwards towards Colchester which would have taken him over such areas. Other Combat Reports may not have survived the passage of time or were never submitted. The Squadron's 'Daily Summary' of this early morning encounter adds no further details of other combats that would indicate other pilots were involved in such an encounter. (It concentrates more on the lunch time engagement which had more significant results for the Squadron.) It is therefore a reasonable assumption, but only an assumption, that the chase incidents are linked.

2 The Luftwaffe Quartermaster General's return of aircraft losses and damage provides a valuable record against which to measure the validity of claims made by the British defences. It is not a fool-proof document though, and instances have been reported of definite losses not being recorded and others under dates later than when they occurred. However this is believed only to be a small percentage and on the whole the record is a reliable one.

3 The other likely claims for the attack on Leutnant Eichhorn's Schwarm include Plt Off Gundry of No 257 Squadron (note 15.3), Sgt Clowes of No 1 Squadron (page 137) or even Sgt Merchant of No 1 Squadron (page 136), but Plt Off Gilbert is the only one of the four to record seeing an Me 110 go into the sea.

4 The quiet outward trip, with fighter attacks only on the way home is a common experience recalled by Schlüter of III/KG2 and Eichhorn and Döpfer of 14/(Z)LG1. This helps to add weight to the latter being the former's escort. (See also 10.2.)

5 This is an assumption based on No 1 Squadron's Combat Reports. They include the description of an early attack on large formations inbound over Chelmsford but then the narratives continue through to activities that must

have occurred at a much later time but without a break in the description to indicate as much. The North Essex (Great Yeldham) connection is based primarily on the recorded loss of Sgt Merchant's machine. However his Combat Report account starts over Chelmsford at 0810 and then describes what reads as a continuous engagement through to his crash over half an hour later at Ovington. This is most unlikely and more probable is that there were two engagements separated by a time gap which has been omitted in the written reports: the first over Chelmsford and the second over North Essex.

6 The identity of the Dorniers Sgt Clowes attacked must remain speculation in view of the uncertainty of the location of his attack and the 'time problem' described in 14.5 above. His attack is consistent with Schlüter's recollections and so remains a strong possibility, but the situation is not helped by there being few details to pin down the exact track III/KG2 used on their homeward leg.

Chapter Fifteen (At the Coast)

1 No 257 Squadron was originally formed at Dundee in August 1918 and disbanded in June 1919, and so strictly speaking the Squadron was 'reforming'.

2 Besides No 1 Squadron's reports there are no other references to Ju 88s at that time of day. It is suspected that the enemy bombers seen by No 257 Squadron were in fact Dornier 17s of II/KG2 together with the Me 110s of III/ZG26. However the existence of another 'unrecorded' unit cannot be ruled out, especially as two independent Squadrons reported having sighted Ju 88s and in view of the lack of clarity of unit tracks over South Cambridgeshire and North-west Essex it must remain a possiblity.

3 It is likely that the enemy aircraft Plt Off Gundry met going south-east past what he described as Chelmsford, were the Dorniers of III/KG2, together with their escort from V/(Z)LG1. There is no hard evidence to reinforce this opinion but the timing and approximate location would be correct, although somewhat out of his way on a direct flight from Deal back to Martlesham Heath. It is stretching a point to suggest that it was Plt Off Gundry who delivered the attack on Leutnant Eichhorn's Schwarm of Me 110s, although the scenario makes it entirely possible. Aircraft of No 601 Squadron were almost certainly in the vicinity at the same time and Plt Off Gilbert is the other most likely contender for this particular attack. (See page 133.)

Appendix C
The Pilot

Gerard Hamilton Maffett, second son of Lt Col and Mrs R.E. Maffett, was born in Murree, India on 11 June 1916. He was educated in England at the Imperial Service College, Windsor and after leaving in 1934 he joined the circulation staff of the *Daily Mail* newspaper in London. His elder brother had previously joined his father's Regiment for a career in the Army but at about the same time as Gerard joined the *Mail*, his brother was seconded to the RAF for Army co-operation duties; a move that was later to become a permanent Service transfer. It was probably this link with the RAF which awakened Gerard's interest in the possibilities of flying. In the spring of 1938 he enlisted in the Royal Air Force Volunteer Reserve, becoming a Sergeant Pilot on 1 May 1938. During the next year and a half, before the outbreak of war, he trained with the Reserves at White Waltham airfield near Maidenhead, learning to fly on Tiger Moths.

The day before war was declared he reported to No 1 Training Camp, London as part of the general mobilisation of the Reserves. There, he spent two months

Pilot Officer Gerard Maffett.

before being posted to No 1 Initial Training Wing at Cambridge, where basic military training was completed and preliminary instruction was given in such subjects as the theory of flight, navigation, radio procedures, etc. Six weeks later, at the end of December 1939, he moved to RAF Grantham in Lincolnshire to join No 12 Flying Training School to put the theory into practice, using military procedures on military aircraft. He completed his training on 22 June 1940 and on 9 June, just before leaving, he was granted a commission in the rank of Pilot Officer RAFVR.

At this point in the training sequence, selections were made as to whether or not pilots would be better suited to flying single- or multi-engined aircraft. Plt Off Maffett was selected for the former and was transferred to No 2 School of Army Co-operation at Andover as a 'supernumery pending posting', but it was short-lived. After only a week at Andover he was on his way to No 5 OTU, based at Aston Down, for two weeks operational training, prior to joining the newly formed No 257 (Fighter) Squadron which was equipped with Hurricanes.

It was at about that time he met up with Alan Henderson, another Pilot Officer in the Volunteer Reserve, also destined for No 257 Squadron. Plt Off Henderson had also found himself at Andover after Flying Training and a spell at the RAF College at Cranwell, but with the fall of France his course had been cut short and he was packed off to the OTU at Aston Down. On 7 July 1940 they both joined their first operational squadron. Their stay was to be short, and fate was to ensure that they left operational flying together as well — in the same aerial engagement. A third new squadron member, Plt Off Chomley, also joined the same day. His stay was even shorter, as he was shot down and killed five weeks later, during his first engagement with enemy fighters.

In the couple of years since joining the Volunteer Reserve Plt Off Maffett had accumulated just over 140 hours solo flying in his log book, but in the eight weeks he was to be with No 257 Squadron that figure was to increase by half as much again.

No 257 Squadron had become operational only a few days before the three pilots joined and it was just establishing itself at its new base, Northolt, west of London, having moved there a couple of days earlier after its formation at Hendon. While Plt Off Henderson joined 'A' Flight, Plt Off Maffett became part of 'B' Flight. He spent the first few days acclimatising to the Hurricane and the Squadron's operational role. Day one included circuits and landings, followed on successive days by radio procedure, practice air firings, oxygen climbs up to 25,000 ft and formation flying. On the sixth day, and after only ten hours flying on the Hurricane type, he fell foul of what was not an infrequent mishap to pilots at that time who had been so used to aircraft with fixed undercarriages. Coming in to land, he failed to select 'undercarriage down' and made a belly landing. He was not hurt and the 'early version' canvas-winged Hurricane although damaged, was repairable.

The following few days included combined aircraft practice at formation flying and attack practices using standard Fighter Command set procedures. Twelve days after joining the Squadron, and with less than fifteen hours experience on the Hurricane, Plt Off Maffett was involved in his first operational flight — on 19 July when nine Hurricanes were scrambled, but no contact was made with enemy aircraft. The next day he was involved in a second scramble, being one of a section of three, but again there was no contact. The next week was quiet operationally, for Plt Off Maffett and the Squadron generally, but the activities of non-operational flying went on.

Towards the end of July the Squadron found itself being sent forward on a daily basis to operate from airfields nearer the south coast. Plt Off Maffett was with them at Hawkinge on 28 and 31 July, but despite one scramble he was still yet to come face to face with the enemy as the month drew to a close.

August saw the Squadron's operational flying increase a-pace. On 1 and 3 August Plt Off Maffett was with the Squadron again at Hawkinge but it was five more days before he was eventually to encounter enemy aircraft. It was to be a memorable initiation. On 8 August the Squadron flew to Tangmere and from there was scrambled to render assistance to a convoy under aerial attack off the Isle of Wight. It was the first time No 257 Squadron had contacted enemy aircraft in large numbers and the air fighting that ensued was costly. Three aircraft were lost together with their pilots. After the survivors returned to Tangmere, Plt Off Maffett was one of a section of three which refuelled and took off again to search the sea for signs of their missing comrades, but nothing was found. It was a severe blow to the Squadron and, unfortunately, a taste of things to come.

A few days later, on 12 August during the Squadron's next encounter with the enemy, two more aircraft were lost and another pilot killed. On 13 August the Squadron was in action again against a formation of Ju 88 bombers and this time suffered no casualties. Plt Off Maffett was not with them on either of these occasions and it was some ten days after his first combat before he encountered enemy aircraft again. In the meanwhile routine flying continued. On 11 August he flew with the Squadron to North Weald for the day but they were not ordered off whilst there. On 12 and 14 August, although airborne, it was non-operational flying involving sector reconnaissance, formation flying practice and dogfight practice.

On 15 August the Squadron moved to RAF Debden, the flying then concentrated mainly over the East Coast and Thames Estuary. From then on, right through to the end of the month, Plt Off Maffett was in the air every day, except for one day of non-operational flying, two or three times a day, either on convoy patrols or scrambles.

According to the Squadron's Operations Record Book he first teamed up with Hurricane P3175 on 18 August. However, it is more likely to have been on 17 August as on that date he is recorded as having flown R4094 (obviously a mistake as that was one of the aircraft lost during the 8 August encounter off the Isle of Wight). R4094 had been aircraft 'S' and P3175 was effectively the replacement aircraft taking on the letter 'S'. From 17 August P3175 'S' became Plt Off Maffett's regular machine.

On 18 August he piloted P3175 as one of twelve Squadron aircraft which left Debden in the early morning to operate out of Martlesham Heath. There, he took part in one uneventful convoy patrol during the middle of the day, but otherwise things were quiet — until it came to the return flight to Debden.

At just after five o'clock in the afternoon the Squadron took off with orders to return to their parent base, but no sooner had they got airborne they were vectored south to patrol Canterbury. After following a number of vectors, which almost took them back to their starting point, they were finally sent south again to the Thames Estuary. Over the northern part of the Estuary, Sqn Ldr Harkness spotted a mixed formation of fifty bombers, heading north-west. He turned the Squadron onto a westerly course to head them off. The bombers also turned to a more westerly heading. A second Hurricane squadron then appeared, approaching head-on to the bombers which turned to port and reversed course. No 257 Squadron engaged the bombers from the beam. Plt Off Maffett was flying No 2 to the Squadron Leader. Later, in a letter to his parents, he described the encounter:

> *You remember the other day when the Hun sent over about 60 aircraft heading towards London via the Thames Estuary: well it was 257 (F) Squadron who headed them off: when they were turning round in formation other fighters joined in and we had quite a good scrap while it lasted. I got in about three attacks — the first at the leading bombers: we were also in formation. The next was alone and I was lucky enough to have a crack at the leader of a sub formation of five Heinkel 111s. I think it was probably rather unpleasant for them as I found them above me and I fired from a position where they could not fire at me. I think the leader was damaged. The third and last attack was on the middle of the main formation and I picked out a Dornier 215. I attacked him from above and dived down on him. The intelligence people have given me the aircraft as shot down as there was quite a glow in the fuselage as I dived away. I suggested that the glow may have been the sun but they think he was destroyed. The amazing part of the whole show was that my aircraft was not even scratched let alone hit — the Hurricane certainly is a grand aircraft.*

It was the most successful encounter to date for the Squadron. Although later reckoning casts doubt on the reported aircraft types, claims at the time were:— one He 111 destroyed, one Ju 87 probably destroyed and two Dornier bombers 'damaged' (one by Plt Off Maffett). Only one Hurricane was lost but its pilot, Sgt Girdwood, parachuted to safety. His aircraft had been hit by one of the Me 110 fighter escort after he had broken off from the attack which had led to the He 111 claim.

The day after their success over the Thames Estuary the Squadron's aircraft and pilots moved to Martlesham Heath permanently, rather than flying back and forth from Debden each day. Plt Off Maffett took part in nine sorties from Martlesham Heath during the ensuing three days, either on convoy patrols or scrambles, but no contact was made on each occasion. On 23 August, while on convoy patrol as part of Blue Section, a lone Dornier '215' was intercepted, but the result of the Section's attack was inconclusive. On the morning of 26 August, also as part of Blue Section on convoy patrol, another lone enemy aircraft was intercepted. Plt Off Maffett made three attacks on it, but having seen no conclusive result again, made no claim.

During the next four days the pattern of convoy patrols, interspersed with scrambles continued. Plt Off Maffett made eleven operational sorties during the period, all in P3175, but made no further contact with enemy aircraft until the fateful scramble on the last day of the month. It was his fifth time in combat, but only the third which involved enemy fighters and multiple aircraft.

The incident in which Plt Off Maffett was killed was reported in *The Times* of 2 September 1940. The same edition also carried his obituary. He was buried on Wednesday 4 September at Bray in Berkshire. On the first anniversary of his death his former colleagues at the *Daily Mail* penned the following lines, in memoriam:

> Plt Off Gerard Maffett
> Killed in action 31st August 1940
>
> This day, a year ago, in gallant fight,
> His plane sped down to earth, in rapid flight;
> He died in deadly struggle with his foe,
> Defending London from dark death and woe.
> One of the Few, to whom we owe so much,
> Who blazed a trail, with an immortal touch.
> So young to die! — Yet deathless in his youth,
> He journeys on, to wider realms of Truth.

Appendix D
The Hurricane

Hurricane Mk 1 P3175 built by Gloster Aircraft Company Limited under contract No 962371/38

29 June 1940   Taken on charge by No 10 Maintenance Unit

9 August 1940   Issued to No 257 Squadron

Flight Details[‡]

Date (August)	Place	Time	Pilot	Remarks
† 12	Northolt	1020–1050	Sgt Hulbert	Recce of Northolt Sector
		1350–1420	F/O Mitchell	To Tangmere
		1600–1640	„	Convoy patrol and combat
		2000–2025	„	Return to Northolt
† 13	Northolt	0620–0735	F/O Mitchell	Scramble — engaged enemy aircraft south of Tangmere, F/O Mitchell claimed a Ju88 as probably destroyed
		1625–1755	„	Convoy patrol from Tangmere and interception
		1905–1935	„	Return to Northolt
† 14	Northolt	1155–1340	F/O Mitchell	To North Weald
		1725–1750	„	Return to Northolt
† 15	Northolt	0630–0700	F/O Mitchell	To North Weald
		1000–1140	„	Convoy patrol and return to Northolt
		1700–1720	„	Movement of Squadron to Debden
† 16	Debden			No flights
† 17	Debden	1030–1130	P/O Maffett	Sector recce
		1430–1530	„	Sector recce
18	Debden	1210–1335	P/O Maffett	Convoy patrol
		1700–1800	„	Scramble and combat, P/O Maffett claimed one Do 17 damaged

19	Debden	1000–1030	P/O Maffett	To Martlesham Heath
		1050–1110	„	From Martlesham Heath
		1245–1310	„	To Martlesham Heath
	Martlesham	1500–1605	„	Convoy patrol
		1915–1955	„	Patrol, scramble
20	Martlesham	0920–1030	P/O Maffett	Scramble
		1500–1550	„	Scramble
		1825–1915	„	Scramble
21	Martlesham	0920–1040	P/O Maffett	Scramble
		1430–1530	„	Scramble
22	Martlesham	1010–1040	Sgt Robinson	To Debden. Exchange of machines. Sgt Robinson returned with P3620
23	(Debden)			No flights. [Under maintenance?]
24	(Debden)			No flights. [Under maintenance?]
25	(Debden)	1400–1420	P/O Gundry	Exchange of machines. P3175 returned to Martlesham
26	Martlesham	0900–1030	P/O Maffett	Convoy patrol
		1300–1445	„	Convoy patrol
		1955–2015	„	Scramble
27	Martlesham	0810–0940	P/O Maffett	Convoy patrol
		1115–1205	„	Convoy patrol
28	Martlesham	0910–0955	P/O Maffett	Scramble
		1330–1410	„	Scramble
		1540–1550	„	R/T test
		1600–1610	„	R/T test
29	Martlesham	0630–0730	P/O Maffett	Convoy patrol
		1017–1136	„	Convoy patrol
		1450–1540	„	Convoy patrol
		1810–1905	„	Scramble
30	Martlesham	0930–1040	P/O Maffett	Convoy patrol
		1110–1235	„	Convoy patrol
		1615–1735	„	Scramble
		* 1700–1820	„	To Debden
		* 1930–1955	„	To Debden
31	Martlesham	0825–	P/O Maffett	Scramble — crashed

Notes: ‡ Based on details contained in 257 Squadron's Operations Record Book.
† The aircraft flown on these days is mistakenly recorded in the Squadron's Operations Record Book as R4094, which was shot down and lost on 8 August 1940. P3175 took over its marking of aircraft 'S' and hence the error.
* An undated page in the Squadron's Operations Record Book lists these times in the sequence for 30 August. Almost certainly the page is out of sequence but the true date to which it refers is not clear.

Appendix E
RAF Participants During 'The Raid'

Code Letters		Serial Number	Flight Position	Pilot	Remarks
No 1 Squadron — Northolt — Hurricanes					
JX		P2751	B1	S/Ldr D.A. Pemberton	
		V7376	(B)	P/O C. N. Birch	
	Y	P3396	(B)	P/O N. P. W. Hancock	
		P3042	(R1)	F/O P. G. H. Matthews	
		V7375	R2	Sgt H. J. Merchant	Baled out, injured
		P2548	R3	P/O R. H. Dibnah	
	(B)	P3395	Y1	Sgt A. V. Clowes	
		V7258	Y2	P/O P. V. Boot	
		V7302	Y3	P/O H. J. Mann	
No 151 Squadron — North Weald/Stapleford Tawney — Hurricanes					
DZ	C	V7630		F/Lt R. L. Smith	
		P3813	Y	F/Lt K. H. Blair	
		V7384		P/O I. S. Smith	
		P2826		P/O J. L. W. Ellacombe	
		P3312		Sgt P. R. C. McIntosh	
		P3739		P/O F. Surma	
		(P6537)		P/O W. B. Patullo	
		P3301		P/O F. Czajkowski	
No 56 Squadron — North Weald — Hurricanes					
US		V7378		F/Lt P. S. Weaver	Killed
		P3384		P/O B. J. Wicks	
	C	R4197	R3	P/O M. H. Mounsdon	Baled out, badly injured
		V7432		P/O P. D. M. Down	
		P2863		Sgt P. E. M. Robinson	
		V6625	G1	F/Sgt F. W. Higginson	
		V6628	(G)	Sgt C. Whitehead	Baled out
	O	V7341	(G)	F/O I. B. Westmacott	Baled out, badly injured
No 111 Squadron — Debden/Castle Camps — Hurricanes					
JU			R1	F/Lt H. S. Giddings	
			R2	F/O B. H. Bowring	
			R3	P/O J. R. Ritchie	
		P2888	(Y)	Sgt J. T. Craig	Baled out, injured
			(Y)	Sgt F. H. Silk	
	(D)	P3961	(Y)	Sgt V. H. Ekins	
		V6562	(B1)	Sgt R. J. W. Brown	

	V6539	B2	Sgt T. J. Wallace
	V7400	B3	P/O R. E. Atkinson

No 601 Squadron — Debden — Hurricanes

UF	V7238		F/Lt P. B. Robinson	
	R4214	R2	F/O J. S. Jankiewicz	
	R4218		P/O H. C. Mayers	
	L1894		F/O J. Topolnicki	
	P3382		F/O C. R. Davis	
	P8818		F/Lt W. H. Rhodes-Moorehouse	
	P3735		Sgt R. N. Taylor	
	P3949	B2	P/O H. T. Gilbert	
	P3383		P/O M. D. Doulton	
	P3230		F/O C. J. Riddle	
	P5208	G2	P/O T. Grier	Crash-landed at Debden

No 257 Squadron — Debden/Martlesham Heath — Hurricanes

DT	B	P3705	R1	F/Lt H. R. A. Beresford	
	E	V6601	R2	P/O J. A. M. Henderson	Baled out, injured
	A	P3704	R3	P/O K. G. Gundry	
	F	P3709	Y1	P/O A. L. Cochrane	
	G	P3775	Y2	P/O D. W. Hunt	
	(H)	P3776	Y3	Sgt R. H. B. Fraser	
	Y	L1706	G1	F/O L. R. G. Mitchell	
	S	P3175	G2	P/O G. H. Maffett	Killed
	N	P3620	G3	P/O C. F. A. Capon	

No 19 Squadron — Duxford/Fowlmere — Spitfires

QV		R6888	B1	F/Lt W. G. Clouston	
		R6890	B2	P/O E. Burgoyne	
		R6912	(B3)	P/O R. A. C. Aeberhardt	Killed on landing
		X4231	G1	F/O J. B. Coward	Baled out, badly injured
		R6882	G2	P/O A. F. Vokes	
		R6924	(G3)	Sgt D. G. S. R. Cox	
		R6958	R1	F/O F. N. Brinsden	Baled out
	I	R6917	R2	Sgt B. T. Jennings	
		R6833	R3	Sgt H. A. C. Roden	
		R6809	Y1	S/Lt A. G. Blake R.N.	
		R6923	Y2	Sgt J. A. Potter	

These details are based primarily on the contents of the Squadrons' official records, but are supplemented by other sources, such as individual pilots' Log Books etc. Items enclosed by brackets indicate that some uncertainty may exist.

Appendix F
The Scammell Pioneer 6x4 SV2S
Heavy Breakdown Vehicle

At the time of the Hurricane recovery operation in 1973 the significance of the vehicle used to haul it from its muddy resting place was not appreciated. However it was not long afterwards that the vehicle itself was rescued from dereliction to become a museum piece in its own right.

Nearly 1500 of these vehicles were manufactured for the Armed Services between 1939 and 1946, with the vast majority going to the Army but a few were destined for RAF service. Vehicle number 05 AH 78 was built in 1945 and left the Scammell works on 26 June that year as part of a batch of six bound for the RAF. Its Service history is not known, but it was with the RAF for seventeen years before being put up for disposal. In March 1962 it was bought at a sale of military vehicles in Portsmouth by 'Kennings Car Mart', for use as a breakdown vehicle to operate out of their garage at Marks Tey near Colchester. One of the firm's employees was Percy Wheatley, a Flight Lieutenant in the RAF Volunteer

The Scammell in action hauling the remains of P3175 down the landward side of the sea wall.

Reserve and Commanding Officer of 308 Squadron ATC. He pursuaded the Managing Director of Kennings Car Mart to sanction the use of the Scammell for the Hurricane recovery operation. In charge of the vehicle for that work was the garage foreman, Dick Hipkin.

A few years later Dick Hipkin moved to another garage in the Colchester area where he met Nigel Everett who, from a mechanical point of view, had long admired the unique and long lasting design concept of the Scammell Pioneer — first introduced almost fifty years earlier. Talk strayed to the machine at Kennings, which by then was no longer in use. Nigel Everett bought the derelict vehicle in 1978 and set about the long process of restoration. It was while stripping off the layers of old paint, that the former RAF connection was confirmed. The complete restoration task took some seven years of spare time work but in 1985 the vehicle was back on the road in full working order and returned to its original RAF livery.

The Scammell is now used primarily for displays at vintage vehicle rallies but, to date, it can also be seen around the village of Dedham in Essex, still occasionally carrying out recovery or winching operations.

The Scammell 'Pioneer' 6x4 SV2S Heavy Breakdown Vehicle (05 AH 78) now fully restored and presented as it would have been during its RAF service. (N. G. Everett)

Index